Demons?!

You're kidding ... <u>right?</u>

from Doug Perry

www.FellowshipOfTheMartyrs.com
fotm@fellowshipofthemartyrs.com

Copyright © 2007, 2011 Doug Perry, Fellowship Of The Martyrs

ISBN: 146379874-1
ISBN-13: 978-1463798741

Quotes used with permission from NIV, KJV, ASV, Amplified and BBE.

The Bride gets her jewelry, but it's going to hurt to get it on,
and once you're used to it, you're never going to want to
rip it back off again. Heaven is free. HOLINESS is hard!
If not us, who? If not here, where? If not now, when?

DEDICATION

This book is dedicated to Jesus Christ.
In fact, everything I've written, recorded, sung,
spoken or ever done is dedicated to Jesus Christ.
Not that it was all perfect, but that's not His fault.
If you don't like it, blame me, not Him.

I want to take special note of the people who were so instrumental in
helping grow me. Some were used to encourage me, some were used to
teach me patience, some were used by God to motivate me to find the
demon on them that I might never have seen if they weren't on my last
nerve. Some taught me to endure persecution, even from the closest
friend. Some showed me holiness. Praise God! They were all a blessing in
one way or another and I really do love them all.
(You know which one you were.)

Bob, Nancy, David, Marilyn, Kim, Constance, Stephanie, Ric, Brad, Keith,
Steve, Minnie, Jeannie and Stevie, Andrew, Rachael, Elijah, Bob, Clare,
Gary, Kristi, James, Cindy, Helen, Sherri, Jen, Dennis, Merri, Joseph,
Gary, Cary, Emily, Lili, David, Yolanda, Suzanne, Tabitha, Josh, Austin,
Chris, Candi, Nataliya, Helen, Ron, Rusty, Josh, Barry, Barron, Glynda,
Steve, Bianca, June, Andrew, John, Lisa, Diane, Larry, Dewey, Jason,
Sarah, Dave, Doug, Michael, Nichole, Dorothy, Tyler, Ky, Kathy, Lizzie,
Patrick, Sharon, Stevean, Randy, Bob, Casey, Amy, Cathy, Chuckie,
Roger, Nils, Ryan, Shelly, Kurt, Sharon, John, Mikey, Becky, James,
Jennie, Angela, Gus, Zach, Jason, Jacob, Greg, Tres, Daniel, J.R.,
Tatianna, Patti and Carolyn and HUNDREDS that I pray will not feel left out
but I don't have room to mention.

And a couple million intercessors all over the world pouring their hearts out
and crying rivers on our behalf without whom I'm not sure how we could
have made it this far.
I'm humbled. Please don't stop praying.

I love you all and I'm not going to stop no matter what.

Psalms 18:29-42 (Amplified)

29 For by You I can run through a troop, and by my God I can leap over a wall. 30 As for God, His way is perfect! The word of the Lord is tested and tried; He is a shield to all those who take refuge and put their trust in Him. 31 For who is God except the Lord? Or who is the Rock save our God, 32 The God who girds me with strength and makes my way perfect? 33 He makes my feet like hinds' feet [able to stand firmly or make progress on the dangerous heights of testing and trouble]; He sets me securely upon my high places. 34 He teaches my hands to war, so that my arms can bend a bow of bronze. 35 You have also given me the shield of Your salvation, and Your right hand has held me up; Your gentleness and condescension have made me great. 36 You have given plenty of room for my steps under me, that my feet would not slip. 37 I pursued my enemies and overtook them; neither did I turn again till they were consumed. 38 I smote them so that they were not able to rise; they fell wounded under my feet. 39 For You have girded me with strength for the battle; You have subdued under me and caused to bow down those who rose up against me. 40 You have also made my enemies turn their backs to me, that I might cut off those who hate me. 41 They cried [for help], but there was none to deliver – even unto the Lord, but He answered them not. 42 Then I beat them small as the dust before the wind; I emptied them out as the dirt and mire of the streets.

*"Your growth in Christ is
directly proportional
to your willingness
to RUSH HEADLONG
into the refining fire
and give it a wet, sloppy kiss."*

- Doug Perry

CONTENTS

ACKNOWLEDGMENTS

I want to thank Jesus Christ. Without Him I'm nothing. This is all about Him and not about me. Everything good that I have learned came from Him. Everything false that I have learned came from Man – me included. God used some people to speak His Truth to me and I'm grateful to all of them as well for their obedience. God also used some people to speak lies to me so that I would learn how to tell the difference, and I'm grateful for them as well. I'm also grateful to the folks that were oppressed by demons so that we could learn and practice on them.

If you don't know Jesus, if you're not talking to Him every day and communing with Him and letting Him direct all your paths, then you're missing out on the greatest adventure in history! And you're totally defenseless against the spiritual wickedness in high places that is in charge of this world. And there is no peace and joy and victory without being all the way full of Jesus. We're getting to the end of The Book. Bad stuff is coming and you're going to need all the peace that passes understanding that you can get! You might want to hurry.

If you don't have Him, then you need Him. If you need Him and we can help, please get in touch with us and we'll introduce you to Him. He doesn't just want Sundays and Wednesday nights – if you open your heart to Him, do it in as big a way as possible. Give Him ALL right up front and see what He does with you.

Push ALL your chips out onto the table and bet it ALL on God – every single time. He'll back you up.

FOREWORD

This book is really three books combined. There is the demon listing and categorization, there is the Red Dragon book which was originally released as a stand-alone book, and there is the Jezebel book that has not been released previously, but is also independent of the others and was actually the one written first. Because of the timing of these and the desire not to overly edit them, there will be some repetitive information or stories retold here and there. I'm sure that this is the way the Lord's timing was supposed to work on these three and I've seen much fruit already from the Red Dragon book. Please excuse any repetition or redundancy and give grace now that you understand the process here. Thank you.

Otherwise, please let me encourage you to digest as much of this as you can and know that I'm not asserting this is final or absolute or that I'm right. I was told to write this down, so here it is. Personally, I think it might have been better to keep a lot of this stuff in my head because people will just use it as more ammunition to say I'm totally crazy – but the Lord doesn't seem to mind that little potential pitfall. So here you go. Do with it as you will. I hope it opens eyes and does some serious damage to the forces of evil. I know that this is far from comprehensive, there are folks that have spent their whole lives documenting this stuff and aren't finished yet. This is just my effort to add to the pool of useful intelligence about the enemy.

If you find that you are being totally chewed up by some of these things I describe, get full of Jesus and get them off. If you can't, and we can help, you're welcome to come to Liberty, Missouri or write or email. Whatever the Lord leads and you can get free enough to do before the enemy stops you. Just believe that our God is bigger and that He'll never let it go too far.

Again, I say it repeatedly in the book, but let me affirm again that we MUST keep our eyes on the Cross. The enemy is real and we shouldn't pretend that they are not. Although this whole book is about demons and spiritual warfare, this is a TINY piece of all that I teach and preach and write about. It's just that it's all condensed into one place here. The main thing is that we need to get our cup all cleaned out, inside and out, and walk before God in holiness and obey His voice. Whatever comes against us because we're like Jesus, whether physical or spiritual, is incidental and cannot do any real harm in the big picture. But it will come and you do need to understand it. Mostly I write this stuff so as to help you see that demons are real, they are doing you damage and you need to get them off. Without that, you can't walk in the fullness of all that God has for you.

Other than that, just know that I love you and I desperately want to see you as shiny as you can possibly get. May the Light of Jesus blast out of your every pore unhindered by anything! Amen.

Doug Perry, servant of God
fotm@fellowshipofthemartyrs.com

LET'S PRAY AND GET RIGHT TO IT

Lord Jesus, I pray right now in agreement with those reading this document that you would bind up anything of the enemy that might mess with them or keep them from hearing You clearly. I ask that you would put a shield around them and set angels over them. I ask that whatever parts of this document that are Your words would sink into their heart and mind and accomplish Your purposes. I ask that anything here that isn't pure Truth would fall harmlessly to the ground. I accept responsibility for any damage done by anything here that isn't of You, Father. Please just accomplish Your purposes through this and in this time. In the mighty Name of Jesus Christ our Lord, Amen.

OK, so let's just get right to it.

Are demons real? Is there such a thing?

And if so ...

Can the enemy afflict or oppress or possess Christians?

Aw, c'mon. Are demons really real? I don't think so.

Some people don't think demons are real at all. But that just flies in the face of the specific command of our Lord in the Great Commission in Mark 16:15-18 that we are to go into all the world and cast demons <u>out</u> of people. Jesus spent a pretty fair amount of time dealing with demons and training His followers to handle them. It also flies in the face of the normal daily experience of Christians all over the world that are wrestling with spiritual powers and principalities and wickedness in high places (Eph. 6:12). The New Testament sure spends a lot of time training us up and explaining that our battle is NOT against flesh and blood for it to all be worthless because demons don't really exist! I can assure you that they do and that they're real and that the vast majority of people (even Christians) have stuff messing with them (or rooted in deeply) that needs to be ripped off and crushed.

If I haven't convinced you yet, then put your money where your mouth is and go play with a Ouija board. If demons aren't real then who is it that's talking to all the witches and warlocks loose in our public schools? Who is telling the psychics on TV details about dead people? Yeah, some of that stuff is fake, but some of it is real, too. There IS a war between good and evil and I can't hardly see how you can believe in Jesus and angels, and not think demons and satan are real. And if they're real, they're doing stuff to slow us down, they're not just hanging around Ouija boards in toy stores. Go to any third world country and ask them if they've seen demons and KNOW that they are real! Ask anybody that has smoked crack or meth or shot heroin if they've seen demons and believe they're real. For years I didn't believe they were real and, despite being a Christian, when the Lord gave me the gift of discernment of spirits and dialed it up real high, I realized how much they had been oppressing me for years – including lust and gluttony and sloth and love of money and fear and others. I wasn't free until I learned how to see them for what they are, identify them, get them off and keep them off.

OK, so let's make a list of stuff and see if you think it comes from your own flawed nature or from the enemy. I don't believe demons can possess Christians, but they can sure _oppress_ them. And if you entertain them long enough and give them enough ground and authority, they'll run your life completely, so you might as well be possessed for how it looks from the outside. They surely do hang around and mess with us and try to gain an entry. Else why would the Lord urge us to keep watch over our houses so that the enemy can't return stronger? Some Christians fling open all the doors, throw their arms around them and give them the best seat in the house! Who do you think benefits most from a theology that says demons don't exist?

> **Mark 12:43-45** - _When the unclean spirit is gone out of a man, he walketh through dry places, seeking rest, and findeth none. Then he_

saith, I will return into my house from whence I came out; and when he is come, he findeth it empty, swept, and garnished. Then goeth he, and taketh with himself seven other spirits more wicked than himself, and they enter in and dwell there: and the last state of that man is worse than the first. Even so shall it be also unto this wicked generation.

Get that? You <u>can</u> get free from them and then they <u>can</u> come back if you're not watching. Even if the house is swept clean and in order. Have you ever met a non-Christian whose "house" was swept clean and in order? That really requires the Holy Spirit. Jesus Himself is warning Christians here that they can come back – and they will probably try to come back worse! So is it really possible that a person could find Christ, get saved, get cleaned out, get lazy and they would come back worse? Yes. There's no other way to explain the behavior of some Christians!

Forget your theoretical models and look around! We're riddled with badness! Just look at all the mega-ministry leaders that start out great and end up exposed on the news for having sex with the masseuse or their chauffeur or their secretary or something. The enemy can't mess with somebody that is armored up and full of Jesus, but as soon as you let your guard down – especially if you stop praying – they are going to find the gap in your armor and rush in and try to wreck you, your life, your family and your ministry. That's what they do. They seek to kill, steal and destroy. And not necessarily in that order. And they are kicking our rears in the "church" because we've got gaps in our armor all over the place because we're not fully under Christ's headship and fighting the way He instructed us. (In fact, we're under a Red Dragon curse directly from God. See Appendix B.)

Not sure yet? OK, try this. The Bible says <u>Fear</u> is a spirit and it's not from God.

> **Romans 8:15** - *For you did not receive a spirit that makes you a slave again to fear, but you received the Spirit of sonship. And by him we cry, "Abba, Father."*

> **2 Timothy 1:7** - *For God hath not given us the spirit of fear; but of power, and of love, and of a sound mind.*

So if you have fear, the Word of God says it's a _spirit_ and it's _not_ from God. And since you only have ONE spirit yourself and it's not a spirit of fear, if you DO have a spirit of fear it's from an external source (that's not God).

So if we have people in the church that have any of _these_, it's a _spirit_ and it's _not_ from God.

Anxiety or panic attacks

Phobias of all kinds

Nightmares, night terrors

Suicidal thoughts

Depression, Manic depression ... and others

Know any Christians with any of those? Yep – me, too. That's because we're not breaking the yokes of oppression and freeing the captives – we're just entertaining their brains and feeding their bodies. But that's not the order it's supposed to go in – read Isaiah 58. FIRST you have to break off the oppressions, THEN you can feed and clothe them. What good is a food pantry or a homeless shelter that doesn't address the spiritual afflictions first? What kind of hospital ignores the bleeding, sucking chest wound and only treats the skinned knee? Which is more dangerous in the long term, that they are underfed or that they can't work or relate to people well because of the addiction and fear and confusion and hallucinations and voices in their head? If we really loved them, wouldn't we free them first and THEN feed them? How can they _ask_ to be freed if they have demons controlling them? Maybe we should just free them first and ask them _afterwards_ if it was OK with them. If it wasn't, it's OK, cause the demons will just all come back if they don't keep the doors shut. No harm done.

Clearly the result of all of these afflictions is that they can kill, steal and destroy your life and your quality of life (John 10:10) – and in a Christian, destroy their witness and effectiveness for the Gospel. Since that is the same goal that the demons have, shouldn't it be obvious that fear is a spirit? Who benefits most if a Christian is living in fear? Gotta be the bad guys. Didn't come from God – He wants the exact opposite. He wants peace and rest and joy and power and a sound mind. So it had to come from somewhere, because the Bible says it's a SPIRIT – not a chemical imbalance or a bad habit or a random thought.

Is the Bible the infallible and inerrant or isn't it? Is it reliable and true or isn't it?

IF the Bible is true and we say we're Christians, **THEN** we should not try to explain things away by other means.

IF the Bible says fear is a spirit, **THEN** it must be so.

IF Christians exhibit spirits of fear oppressing them, **THEN** demons really CAN mess with Christians.

IF Christians exhibit spirits of fear oppressing them, **THEN** it's because we allowed them back in.

IF we allowed them in, **THEN** it's probably because we got lazy and didn't guard the doors.

IF we didn't guard the doors, **THEN** it's probably because we're convinced demons aren't real – or can't hurt us.

IF we have authority to kick them out, **THEN** we need to get to doing it as fast as possible!

IF we need to break the yokes of oppression, **THEN** we need to start in the churches.

In the early days of scientific exploration, the dominant method was philosophical and theoretical. Guys with big brains would sit around a table arguing about how many teeth a horse had. All kinds of theories would be advanced about what must surely be the way a horse's teeth would look and work. Eventually some genius just got up from the table and went and found a horse and looked in its mouth! And observational science was born.

In the church, we've kind of been doing the same thing. We build our philosophical structures based on our interpretations of scriptures or the doctrines of our denominations that were handed down to us or our own preconceptions and fleshly opinions (or more likely, what the demons have been whispering to us!). Then we make affirmative statements with absolutely finality. But maybe we should just get up from the table and go look around. What is working and what's not? What is the REAL state of the "church"? Are we winning this war or aren't we?

If we did get up and go look around, we would see that the people of God are shackled and yoked and spiritually oppressed by the forces of darkness. How else can you explain these?

5

I John 4:3	Romans 8:11	Romans 8:15	Mark 9:17-29
Rebellion	Stupor	Bondage	Mental illness
Witchcraft	Sleepiness	Gluttony	Insanity
Unbelief	Stupidity	Obesity	Seizures
Self-exaltation	Laziness	Addiction	Epilepsy
Occult practices	Lethargy	Anorexia	Multiple
Magic	Apnea	Bulemia	personalities
	Sluggishness	Phobias	Hyperactivity
	Confusion	Despair	Self-mutilation
		Fatigue	

Just to list a few!!

So, you say these are just acts of nature or learned behaviors or habits or just generalized sin? Then you must believe that angels aren't real and that God can't heal people and nobody can hear the still, small voice of the Holy Spirit. There is no other alternative! If one side can bless you, the other side can curse you. If one side can whisper to you, they both can. If you can be <u>filled</u> with the Holy Spirit, you can be just as <u>filled</u> with evil. (See Appendix A)

YOU **CANNOT** BELIEVE THERE IS A WAR BETWEEN GOOD AND EVIL AND THEN DENY THAT <u>ONE</u> SIDE HAS ANY INFLUENCE!!

IF there is a war between Good and Evil, **THEN** both sides have weapons.

IF the war between Good and Evil is over, **THEN** you sure better hope and believe that GOOD won.

IF Good won, **THEN** why is it so dark out there!?!?

IF Good won, **THEN** why can't we keep kids in church? Why are we addicted to the world?

IF Good won, **THEN** what's keeping us from preaching the Gospel to all nations already?

IF Good won, **THEN** why do we start a whole new denomination EVERY TWO DAYS?

IF Good won, **THEN** why are Christians sick – mentally and physically and emotionally?

IF Good won, **THEN** why aren't the blessings of Deut. 28 in full effect? (In fact, we're seeing the opposite!)

IF the outcome is certain, but the battle is in our hands, **THEN** we better start shooting at something!!

It just flies in the face of the blatantly obvious observations around us. We are getting creamed by the darkness! Inside and outside the churches, the badness is closing in. How did spiritual evil get such a strong foothold on this country and on our own lives? Probably because we started preaching that demons weren't real and couldn't oppress Christians. That the war was over and we'd already won. Now who has benefited most from that bit of theology? Has it resulted in Christians who are free and living victoriously? Has it resulted in transformations of towns and countries for God? No. It has resulted in week, oblivious, sickly, addicted, angry, divorced, oppressed Christians who are dropping out of church in droves because there is nothing there to really help them!

Now, given the state of things around you, how can it possibly be true that the battle is over? Did Jesus win the victory? YES!!! The outcome is certain. But have we claimed it, embraced it fully and are walking in His power? NO!!!! If we were, the Christians would be FREE! And they're not. They're just not. For Pete's sake, we have people that are more addicted to football or NASCAR than to Jesus! We have witches in our youth groups and nobody even notices. We have satanists sitting on the boards of our churches. We have pedophiles as priests and youth pastors. We have people cursing the pastor and the church in false tongues and nobody notices!

What happened to the Gift of Discernment of Spirits? (I Corin. 12:10) How come nobody asks for that one anymore?! If there is a war and somebody is shooting at you, wouldn't you want to see them so you can fight back? Particularly if you know your weapons are great and you could crush them like a bug and free lots of other people. There is no Goliath of hell that can stand against a fearless David full of Jesus and armed with Wisdom and Discernment of Spirits. People say we should just focus on love and not bring glory to satan by all this talk of demons. What?! Whose idea could that be?! This is a WAR!

The Pentagon is going to have a strategy room where they get together – but they NEVER talk about the enemy for fear of accidentally glorifying them?! NO! They're going to learn where they are and how they act and how to best defeat them. They're going to assess their own strengths, amass forces in the places under attack, improve weapons systems that can counter the weapons of the enemy. They're going to know how the enemy thinks, what they eat, how they smell, when they sleep, where they hide – everything! They're going to track and catalog and investigate and gather intelligence from all available sources – even the enemy's own communication networks. They're not going to worry about someone thinking they're on the wrong team because they know their enemy! They are never going to spend ONE SINGLE SOLITARY SECOND debating about whether by gathering intelligence on how to crush the enemy they might be accidentally worshiping them!! C'mon, that's just dopey. This is a WAR!

In fact, it's a lie from the pit designed to keep us from talking about demons at all. Who benefits most from us avoiding the whole subject? Not Jesus. He didn't avoid it. He wasn't scared of them. He trained up His disciples on how to handle them and then sent them out to crush them. In fact, He COMMANDED us to go crush them in the Great Commission. Folks, it's not the Pick-and-Choose Commission. It's not the If-It-Fits-With-My-Theology Commission. It's the GREAT Commission. Be like Jesus. Go and crush the badness! We're getting creamed out there because of so many people that insist the enemy isn't even real or that it's wrong for us to go after them!

I know, I've heard it before, you're going to say that the Great Commission in Matthew doesn't say anything about casting out demons and that some scholars don't think Mark 16:9-20 was part of the original manuscripts. Well, tough beans! It made it into the King James and you assert that this is the Authorized, inspired, infallible word of God – so you're stuck with it. You can't say the Bible is infallible and then dismiss the parts you are uncomfortable with as not being pure. Either God wanted it in there or He didn't. If it should be taken out, then what else would you like to edit out? Maybe the whole book of Revelation where we CLEARLY see demons coming out of the Abyss and torturing anybody that has taken the mark of the beast (Rev. 9). Surely some of them prayed the salvation prayer at the church summer camp in 8th grade, but have now chickened out and taken the mark. Are they Christians or aren't they? Are they oppressed by demons or aren't they? Are demons real or aren't they? Is the Bible the word of God or isn't it?

If I didn't convince you, you better stop reading now. It's just going to make your head hurt more. I'm warning you, don't say I didn't.

OK!! Fine! You win. I get it. Demons are real. So what do we do about it?!

If you don't have Jesus in your heart, then you are defenseless against the badness. Only the Holy Spirit can defend your "house" well enough to keep the badness out. You can't do it in your own power. You better lay everything down and beg for Jesus to take over right now. And you better mean ALL, not SOME of your life. He's a King, pray with respect. He's not fire insurance, He's Lord. Jesus is the Savior and He died so that His blood could protect you from sin and from the enemy. Tell Jesus you're a sinner, say you're sorry and ask Him to free you of everything messing with you and take over ALL of your life right now. Go ahead, ask Him. He'll do it. He wants you. He's been calling you. How long are you going to put Him off? How long do you want to wait to be free? Believe He is big enough to break all the chains that bind you. In the Name of Jesus and by His redeeming Blood. Amen.

Whether you needed that or not, start praying for the Gift of Discernment of Spirits – and don't stop. Maybe He'll give you a lot or maybe a little, but ALL Christians need as much as they can get. The gifts aren't on/off switches, they are dials. As soon as you get SOME Holy Spirit in you, all your dials move off of zero. How much they move depends on your hunger and the Lord's willingness. But the Holy Spirit in you can recognize all the other spirits around. It's just a matter of you listening really well. He'll teach you how to use it and what to do with it if you'll listen. Some people sense the spirits in a vague way and some people see snarling black things sitting on people and can smell them and feel them in the "spirit". Some people see them with their eyes open in the "natural" and can't shut it off. (That one can put you living under a bridge smoking crack to make it stop if God doesn't help.) Some people don't see anything, they just ask the Lord what's going on and He tells them.

Just ask for whatever He wants to give you and don't hold back or be afraid. He knows what He's doing. But you have to also know that "discernment" means telling the difference, not just seeing the bad guys, but seeing the good guys too – and being able to tell who is on whose team. You'll probably see angels and the good stuff, too, but my experience is that God will probably let you see the bad stuff first to see if you'll trust Him or if you'll chicken out. If you start seeing (or already started seeing) the bad stuff – but panic and ask to shut it off, you might not get to see the really cool stuff. And once you see the angels, or you see yourself the way God sees you, or you see heaven or something – you won't be scared of the bad guys anymore. Speaking from personal experience, I wouldn't trade the good stuff for <u>any</u> amount of demons I have to face!

In the meantime, you have to know how to deal with the stuff in your own head. We all hear things, we just mostly think it's us, but then we look back later and say, "What was I thinking? That was a HORRIBLE idea!" Or sometimes we look back and realize that it was so beautiful and perfect and divinely inspired that it HAD to be God whispering to us.

There are only three choices when you hear something in your head. It's either YOU, the white hats or the black hats. Now, you and the bad guys can sound a lot alike – because neither of you are holy. And when they whisper in your ear they always put an "I" in front of stuff to make you think it's your idea. ("I'm gonna get even with that guy!" "I'm the best singer here." "I could be like God!") But what they are suggesting to you will always be anti-Christ in some way when projected out.

That is, we're to take captive every thought (2 Corin. 10:5), so when something pops into your head, just ask yourself, "Who is glorified most if I follow through with that?" If it's going to glorify you OR the enemy, then rebuke it and crush it in the name of Jesus and refuse it. "If you resist, he will flee." (James 4:7) He who? The enemy? Yep. My own thoughts and wants and selfish desires? Yep. Works the same way (Rom. 8:13). In fact, if you resist the Holy Spirit, he will flee, too. If you harden your heart toward God, you won't be able to hear Him either (Job 9:4, Ps. 95:8, Prov. 28:14, Heb. 3:8, Heb. 4:7). So don't do that.

You need to have an armor-plated, indestructible, unbreakable, impenetrably hard heart – but just to the right stuff. It needs to be tender toward God and His still, small voice and rock hard to everything else – including your own wants and thoughts and pride and self. Only in this way can He direct ALL your paths. (I Corin. 14:20) Toward malice be as innocents (virginal, naive, inexperienced), but toward God be mature and experienced. And regardless of the black hats, there's stuff in YOU that qualifies as "malice."

Why is it important that we be cleansed of all the bad stuff?

> **I Corinthians 10:20-21** – *But I [say], that the things which the Gentiles sacrifice, they sacrifice to devils, and not to God: and I would not that ye should have fellowship with devils. Ye cannot drink the cup of the*

Lord, and the cup of devils: ye cannot be partakers of the Lord's table, and of the table of devils.

You can't play for both teams. You can't play footsies with the badness and walk with God in righteousness and purity. Please pick a side and stick to it. You're just embarrassing all the Christians that are really trying hard – and you're giving Jesus a bad name. There are no lambs or bunnies or piggies at the final judgement – everybody is either a full grown sheep or a full grown goat. (Matthew 25:31-46) He's going to polarize everybody so that nobody can straddle the fence anymore. Time is running out, so pick a team and stick to it.

Ask the Lord to take control of your thoughts and turn your mind into the mind of Christ. Ask Him to let you see through His eyes, so that you see the temptations of the world the way He does. If you burst into tears for the salvation of those poor girls on the "Fantasy Ranch" billboard and repent for your own part in the pain they suffer and for the church not reaching them sooner, it will be real hard to get overheated and lustful about them.

Want more? Why do you need to get all cleaned out? Because you're not useful otherwise. Read this:

2 Timothy 2:20-26 – *20 But in a great house there are not only vessels of gold and silver, but also of wood and earthenware, and some for honorable and noble [use] and some for menial and ignoble [use]. 21 So whoever cleanses himself [from what is ignoble and unclean, who separates himself from contact with contaminating and corrupting influences] will [then himself] be a vessel set apart and useful for honorable and noble purposes, consecrated and profitable to the Master, fit and ready for any good work.*

22 Shun youthful lusts and flee from them, and aim at and pursue righteousness (all that is virtuous and good, right living, conformity to the will of God in thought, word, and deed); [and aim at and pursue] faith, love, [and] peace (harmony and concord with others) in fellowship with all [Christians], who call upon the Lord out of a pure heart.

23 But refuse (shut your mind against, have nothing to do with) trifling (ill-informed, unedifying, stupid) controversies over ignorant questionings, for you know that they foster strife and breed quarrels. 24 And the servant of the Lord must not be quarrelsome (fighting and contending). Instead, he must be kindly to everyone and mild-tempered [preserving the bond of peace]; he must be a skilled and suitable teacher, patient and forbearing and willing to suffer wrong. 25 He must correct his opponents with courtesy and gentleness, in the hope that God may grant that they will repent and come to know the Truth [that they will perceive and recognize and become accurately acquainted with and acknowledge it], 26 And that they may come to their senses [and] escape out of the snare of the devil, having been held captive by him, [henceforth] to do His [God's] will. (Amplified Version)

If you want to be a vessel of gold or silver, then you better get cleansed and separate yourself from contact with contaminating and corrupting influences. Only THEN will you be a vessel set apart and useful for honorable and noble purposes! Only THEN will you be consecrated and profitable to the Master. Only THEN will you be fit and ready for any good work.

You have to aim at and pursue righteousness and faith and love and peace – and be in fellowship with ALL who call upon the Lord out of a pure heart. You do NOT have to be in fellowship with those who do NOT call up on the Lord out of a pure heart – with those folks, you need to pray for them and exhort them (and/or rebuke them). How can you really fellowship and grow with folks that are not seeking the Lord with a pure heart?

You must refuse and shut your mind against useless quarrels over trifling controversies. You must be mild-tempered and patient and forbearing and willing to suffer wrong. (I Corinthians 6:7) You must correct with courtesy and gentleness, in the hope that GOD may pour out on them the GIFT of repentance so that they'll come to know the Truth. So that they may come to their senses and escape out of the snare of the devil, having been held captive by him. (2 Timothy 2:22-26) Hmmm. That sure sounds like they have demons messing with them and need to be free – and the only way to get them free is through gentleness and love and praying that they will repent. You see, the only way they got demons on them in the first place was because they stepped out from under God's umbrella of protection by going their own way. And the only way to get back is to say you're sorry. God will turn you over to your own depraved mind and anything the enemy wants to throw at you if you go your own way and get out from under His cover. (See the Red Dragon portion of this writing.)

Anyway, here's the thing, demons are real, people that hear God really well and have their Discernment dialed up really high can see them and hear them. People who have authority and are walking in holiness before God can rip them off of you and crush them and cast them down. People that are doing deliverance now, need all the ammunition and intelligence about the enemy that they can get. People that have a sensitivity to things of the spirit, but don't understand what they're seeing or what to do about it, need to know that they're not crazy and that they can make a difference in this war if they'll get up to speed and start shooting at the enemy.

The rest of this book is just a documentation of what we have seen and faced as the Lord taught us all about this stuff. It's not the only way that people might see demons, it's just how the Lord showed them to us (or to me). We're not arguing that this is the only way, or even the best way, it's just all the information about the enemy that we have, presented to whoever might benefit from it. It's just a summary of the intelligence we have gathered in our little corner of the world about enemy movements and activities and types.

If you still don't believe in demons, then just consider all of this a science fiction writing that's entirely made up out of my own imagination. Whatever, I don't really care what you think of me. I'm only interested in pleasing my Father and He told me to write this. I guess the proof is in the fruit. If people are getting free and being transformed and hearing God better and walking in holiness and learning how to keep their cup so full of Jesus that nothing else can fit, then maybe we're onto something.

WARNING!
WARNING!
DANGER! DANGER!
Proceed at your own risk!

We will NOT be responsible for ANYTHING that happens from here forward. You have been warned. The enemy DOES NOT want the Body restored.
And God can only use broken and contrite vessels.

We want you to be ABSOLUTELY clear that this is <u>FOR SURE</u>, <u>NO DOUBT ABOUT IT</u> going to hurt <u>A LOT</u>.

You can drive 20 miles an hour and you probably won't get hurt too bad in an accident.
If you drive 200 miles an hour and you make a mistake, it's going to get really ugly.

This IS <u>NOT</u> for sissies!
If you have ANY desire in you to maintain the status quo, STOP NOW! DO NOT GO THIS WAY!!
DO NOT take our advice on this stuff!!
It will totally transform your life and things you love will be ripped from you.

Nothing – <u>NOTHING</u> – you have will be your own any more. So He can rebuild you His way, God will IMMEDIATELY start yanking chunks out of you. Probably stuff you really liked. Like maybe your job and your family and your health and pieces of YOU that <u>seemed</u> fine. The fire will get VERY hot!

If you even so much as TRY to do this in your own power, you're gonna be toast! <u>ONLY Jesus in you can get you through this.</u>

Last chance. Get out now!
ALL the darkness WILL come for you!

**We've seen it over and over.
We <u>ARE</u> <u>NOT</u> kidding around!**

If you miss a step or make this about YOU, you could end up on crack or beating your wife or drinking like a fish or in jail – or <u>worse</u>, the pastor of a thriving mega-church with pews full of dead bodies and you'll think you're the hottest ticket ever! We've seen it happen to good, Jesus-loving people who weren't <u>all</u> <u>the</u> <u>way</u> sold out. God will get you through, but it will hurt even more if you bail out. You BETTER mean it! We're serious.

We love you very much. We want to see you refined and purified and REALLY dangerous to the enemy, but we want you to be <u>FULLY</u> <u>READY</u> before you pull into the <u>Fast</u> <u>Lane</u>!

DANGER! DANGER!

STILL HERE? GOOD.
MORE PRAYER WOULD BE NICE.

Pick the prayer that suits you best. Not judging you. Just trying to give you options. Everybody is at a different place and that's just fine. You don't have to tell anybody which one you prayed. Maybe after the book or later on you can come back and pray a "hotter" one. Nothing special about these, pray your own if you like. But pray.

Prayer Option #1 – Mild

Dear Lord Jesus, please cover me during this time and bind up anything of me or anything of the enemy that would keep me from hearing You through this. I'm not sure about all this, but I know that what I want is pure Truth straight from the Throne of God. Please help me to hear You and You alone through this. Please don't let the enemy do anything to keep me from getting what You want me to have out of this – and please let everything else drop to the ground harmless. I trust You, Lord. In the mighty Name of my Lord Jesus Christ, Amen.

Prayer Option #2 – Medium

Dear Lord Jesus, I know that demons are real and that I should be making more of a difference but I'm kind of scared. Please hold my hand and help me to be stronger when it comes to dealing with the darkness around me. I trust You. I know You're bigger than they are. I do want to know more about this war. Please help me to hear Your voice and no other. Please bind up anything of the enemy or of me that would try to keep me from learning what You want me to learn. I trust You, Lord. In the mighty Name of my Lord Jesus Christ, Amen.

Prayer Option #3 – Hot

Dear Lord Jesus, I need more than I've got. Please give me more Discernment of Spirits so that I can see the bad guys and tell the difference better. Please help me hear You really well so that I can follow Your directions in all things. Give me Wisdom and Fear of the Lord so that I will know the right thing to do when the moment comes. Please bind up everything of the enemy that might still be messing with me and bind me up too, while you're at it. I just want Your will, not mine. Please help me to be more dangerous to the forces of darkness. Please bring people into my path that I can minister to and begin to practice the things You have taught and are teaching me. You are a great Dad and I trust You. I know You'll get me through anything. I'm not afraid. Show me some bad guys whenever You think I'm ready. In the mighty Name of my Lord Jesus Christ, Amen.

> # READ WARNING LABEL!!
> # READ WARNING LABEL!!

Prayer Option #4 – NUCLEAR

Father God, I want to do as much damage to the badness as I possibly can. I know there is a war and I said I would go, so please use this – and anything else You want – to equip me in the best possible way. Whatever it takes, whatever it costs, whatever I have to lay down or repent for or give up, I don't care. Have Your way. If there is something that I love that is standing between me and You, show me and I'll lay it down. If I can't lay it down, then just rip it out of my grip. I appreciate what You've given me, but I feel like I have a pop gun and I want a NUKE. Not for my glory, but for Your kingdom and to free the captives. Please do whatever You have to do to me so that I can do as much damage to the enemy and his forces as possible. Make me dangerous to satan. Whatever it takes. I'm writing You a blank check. I mean it, Father. Load me up and show me some bad guys. Let me see them and don't let them hide anymore. Please give me more

Discernment of Spirits and more Wisdom to know what to do with it. Give me the authority to rip and shred and crush them and spit down their throats. I want to be heaven's pit bull. Help me to hear Your directions really, really well and obey all the time. Break me into little pieces so that I'll be humble and will never make this about me. I'm also asking that the demonic strongholds on all the people around me would manifest as soon as I come into a room so that we can deal with them right away. Flush them out into the open and I'll pick them off. Bring it on. I'm not scared and I'm not going to back down no matter what. Give me a rock and show me to Goliath! I want to take out some big ones for You! I trust this prayer is inside Your will, so I'm expecting that You're going to answer it. Please, Father, I come in the Name of Your Son, Jesus Christ, making my petition directly to the Big Throne. Amen.

DEFINITION OF TERMS / PROCEDURES

Characters

Host/Subject This is the person being afflicted. The person that needs deliverance.

Demon This is the fallen spirit that is doing the afflicting. These are the bad guys. Of these, the one in charge is satan – who I don't capitalize because he doesn't deserve it.

Jesus Christ If I have to explain Jesus, you're not ready for this. Stop now and go read the Bible.

Holy Spirit This is the Spirit of God through whom all power comes. He is the good guy. There is no "spirit of strength" or "spirit of kindness" or "spirit of discernment" or "spirit of repentance" - there's just the One Spirit and He does all those things. Those are Gifts of the Spirit, not independent spirits. Don't pray for a "spirit of reconciliation" to come, just pray for the Holy Spirit to give a gift of reconciliation or to pour it out.

Angels Angels are the good guys that are provided by God as messengers, warriors, helpers and healers. They are bigger and stronger than us, but they are at the disposal of God's people (at least some of them are). They are real and we need them. Be polite to them. Everybody has some assigned to them. They may show up in human form occasionally. Expect them to look like "the least of these."

Things

Blood   This is the Blood of Jesus that was shed for us at Calvary and is the atoning sacrifice for our sins. It is what vanquished satan and his hosts and is confirmed when we take Communion in proper order. It is a Blood Oath contract between us and Him. Our salvation and our power over the enemy comes from the Blood shed.

Ports   We use this to mean the place on the body of a person where a particular kind of demon is typically attached. Like on a computer, you can't plug a serial cable into a USB port. There are all kinds of these doorways or ports on a person that must be shut (or the polarity changed) so that the enemy can't gain access. There may also be physical damage to the host on or around this port if it's been open a long time.

Defensive Actions

Cover   Covering in the Blood means to, in the spirit, put a thick coating of the Blood of Jesus over something. You can just say it, but in the spiritual realms it's actually happening. So if you see really well, you can even watch as a fire hose or a cup (or however the Lord shows it to you), pours out this patch or coating or band-aid of the Blood of Jesus over an area that needs healing or binding or restoring. You can also take what is in your own "cup" and pour it out – that, too, is the Blood of Jesus.

Bind   This means to tie up, wrap, muzzle or otherwise incapacitate a demon by covering them in the Blood of Jesus in faith and authority. This means immobilizing them until you've done what you need to do to get them off, which may require education of the person, or more prayer or anointing, etc. May be a short term solution for someone that isn't ready to have something particularly nasty removed yet for fear that it will come back worse. But not a long-term solution. You can't bind things indefinitely. Can also bind things on a larger scale if you have authority to do so.

Pearl /
Cocoon
This is essentially to completely surround or coat a demon with the Blood. In the case of the tiny Jezebel, you make a pearl. In the case of the Witchcraft, a cocoon.

Offensive Actions

Weapons
We have the Sword of the Spirit, which is the Word of God, that is described in Ephesians. If that Word is living in us and active and alive and we are in obedience, it has great power. It cuts even between soul and spirit, bone and sinew. That is, it can slice a demon right off of somebody like a razor blade. You can take your Sword in the hand of the Holy Spirit in you and just strip them down to nothing. Then cover them in the Blood, seal up all the doorways, get their cup full and see what happens. If you have authority and a need, the Lord is perfectly willing to give you other weapons or adapt the Sword to the situation. If you're facing something smaller, it's smaller. If you're facing a principality, it's bigger. This flaming Sword is alive with the power of the Holy Spirit and demons HATE making any contact with it. It is torture to them to make contact with the Holy Spirit. So covering them in the Blood or poking them with the Sword is a good way to get their attention. If you need other weapons that you don't have, it's because you haven't asked – or don't have enough wisdom or authority yet. (Ephesians 6:17, Hebrews 4:12)

Slice
This means to take your Sword of the Spirit and cut between the demon and the person at the port (or wherever). To remove all residue of the enemy in one swipe.

Blast   Sometimes you might want to just concentrate all the power of that Sword into a blast that just takes a particular enemy out in one shot. Some fast movers may require blasting instead of slicing. Don't think that the Sword of the Spirit has to be chronologically specific to A.D. 30. It's a weapon and it's from God and He's very creative. If you ask Him to update it to something you're more comfortable with (like a flame thrower or a shotgun), He can do that. Just ask and see what He says. He may tell you you're not ready for that yet. I've seen that happen, too. :-) David's slingshot worked just as good as a sword against Goliath. You could rightfully say it was a Slingshot of the Holy Spirit. What's the difference really? It's all in the spirit.

Rip and Toss   The hand of the Holy Spirit wields the Sword. The hand of the Spirit, the spirit man in you that is powered by Him, can reach out and grab or bind or sever or shred or otherwise do damage to the demons that you have to face. If you see them or know where they are, you can grab them. Then rip them off and cast them to the Abyss (or Dry Places, whatever you have authority for and the Lord tells you to do).

Torture   Which brings us to this one. If you want the enemy to know your name, then get a reputation for inflicting pain. The demon in Acts 19:15 knew Paul's name. The demons in Mark 5 begged Jesus not to torture them. Why would they ask Jesus not to torture them? Probably because they believed He might torture them. How do you torture demons?! Well, they don't like leaving and they don't like dry places, but they REALLY don't like being in contact with the Holy Spirit. And you have a big Sword of the Spirit (and whatever else), so just make them hurt. Make them remember that dealing with you is not a good thing. Have them tell their friends. Even more effective if you have authority to cast them to the Abyss. We need a BUNCH of people that see really well, are deadly serious, like inflicting pain on demons and have a reputation for finding them, making them scream and ripping them off with no hope of return. If they've been torturing you for years, wouldn't it be great to hear THEM scream for awhile? God doesn't mind. He established a place where they will scream for eternity. He's not bothered by you hurting them. They've been torturing God's children long enough. Now it's our turn. "But," you say, the Lord says, "Vengeance is mine." Yeah, that's what's happening, it's His Spirit, reaching out with His weapons, through His children and turning back the tide. Unless you're rebuking them "in the name of Susie" it's pretty much God getting vengeance. Maybe this is what He's been training you for? Been playing "God of War" for endless hours? It's pretty much like that, except for Jesus' team.

Fill   We use this term to talk about filling someone's cup – by that we mean impartation of whatever good thing will help them be strong, have patience, peace, self-control or whatever else is needed. Basically, doing deliverance by praying that they would be SO full of Jesus that nothing else could fit. If you jam your cup full of Jesus, the bad stuff just has to ooze out the top and run scared.

Places & Stuff

Dry Places   I don't really care to debate this theologically, but essentially this is a place the demons can go where they may still be able to come back. They don't like it, but it's not terminal. It's like taking combat soldiers off the battle field for awhile. They aren't happy about it and they don't want to go, but it doesn't particularly scare them because there is no shortage of people with open doorways and the Christians right now are not likely to be able to keep the doors shut and their cups full, so it's a pretty sure thing they'll be back – and probably with big, mean friends. (Matthew 12:43-45)

Abyss   This is terminal. The Abyss is the pit of Hell. This is a one-way trip and Jesus holds the keys. If they get cast here, they're not coming back. This is a place of constant torture and the Dry Places are WAAAAY preferable to this! This isn't just getting the enemy soldiers off of the battlefield temporarily, this eliminates them from coming back at all. I see them well enough to be able to identify individuals – and I've never seen one come back from the Abyss. Jesus Himself cast them to the Abyss, even though He instructed His disciples that typically they just go into Dry Places. (Luke 8:31) I'm not sure why something changed, but it did, because in 2004 the Lord told me very specifically to cast them to the Abyss. This is one REALLY good way to get them to know your name. The really big ones probably won't come around and mess with you or your house. The Lord told me that the best thing He could do to keep me safe from constant harassment was if they knew that I had the authority to make it a one-way trip if I caught them. Since it's Jesus in me that does every good thing anyway, and Jesus clearly has authority to cast them to the Abyss, then I have no problem with it. Don't take my word for it, ask the Lord if He told me that and I have that authority. (At a certain point in Revelation the Abyss is opened, but I'm not sure who is getting out exactly. Rev. 9:2)

Authority   This is important. I just covered it above, but God is VERY specific about authority lines and legal ground. If you expect to have a real impact then you need to have authority to confront whatever it is you're confronting. For example, if you have an active Lust, and you go to try to rebuke one off of someone else, it may Flare and Duck (p. 33), but it won't be really gone – you don't have authority. You may not have authority to do deliverance of strongholds over a city or people group. Even if I have enough authority, if there is a God-anointed authority in place, the Lord leads me to them to check in before He'll let me pull stuff off of their city. I have to get permission, because it's not my land. Just because you're a pastor, doesn't necessarily mean you're an Elder in God's eyes in the city – or even in your own congregation! There may be others stronger.

As for spiritual authority to cast them to the Abyss, I had a sister who had done a lot of deliverance in prison that I told this to and she didn't believe me. She said that it does not say in the Bible that we could do this and she had read in the books that we could not cast them anywhere. She hears God, so I asked her to ask Him if He really told me that and I really did have authority to cast them to the Abyss. She came back and said she had prayed and asked the Lord if she had authority for that and He said, "No." I said, "Now that's not what I asked you to pray about. I asked you to ask Him if I had that authority." So she went and prayed for awhile and came back and sheepishly said, "Yeah, He says you do have authority for that."

So I said, "Great! Do you want it?" She said, "Sure!" So I laid my hand on her shoulder and prayed and asked the Lord to give her whatever I had. Then I asked her to ask the Lord if NOW she had authority. "Yep! Now I do." Great! Why not share? I do it a lot. What good is one person with that kind of authority? **So here you go:**

Lord, whatever authority I have from You, if this child of Yours is willing to receive it and can use it for Your kingdom and you say they're ready for it, give it to them. Confirm it to them and make them mighty. In the Name of Jesus. Amen.

PERSONAL-SIZED DEMONS WE'VE FACED

In general, these are placed in order of badness, sneakiness and general destructiveness. Although any one of them can wreck your life, this is just a sense of the seriousness with which we handle them. These are individual manifestations of these – that is, these are what they are like on a PERSON. We're not meaning this to be comprehensive; people have written LOTS of books about just about every one of these. This is more of a thumbnail type checklist. We reserve the right to modify or add to this at any time. Some of these we've seen dozens or hundreds of times, some only once or twice. We're still learning and as our sample size increase, I'm sure we'll have new data to add. This is not comprehensive or definitive or final, it's just what we know as of now.

Some of these manifest on places or regions, but those are different. Those are the principalities or strongmen set over the foot soldiers that oppress the individuals in their region. The focus in this writing is on the application to individuals. The actual principalities look much different. You may or may not be able to extrapolate this to a larger application. Listen to God really well and do whatever He tells you.

If you pull a demon off of someone that hasn't learned their lesson from it yet, the person is just going to have to go through it again (probably harder) and you're getting in the way of God's refining of them. So always check with the Lord before doing anything. Don't even try to lift a yoke of oppression off of someone when God put it there to humble or chasten or teach. Don't assume that everything that is messing with someone needs to be or can be removed at that moment. Just like not everyone is going to get physically healed just because you pray for them. Sometimes God is up to something and it's not time. Just listen carefully and do what HE tells you – don't act out of pity or guilt or desire to help, or even worse for financial gain or acclaim or attention.

Red Dragon

The nastiest of all. The sneakiest, the ugliest, the most deadly. When it talks to you it will sound just like God and convince you that everything is OK and you're right on track. Covered in detail at the end of this document. (Appendix B) Worst of all, if it's on a child of God, it cannot be rebuked and cast off – it is a curse from God for going your own way and can only be removed by repentance – but it supernaturally suppresses repentance! No spear or sword can hurt it. No man can remove it or tame it. Biblically it's referred to as "Leviathan." Very, very bad.

If you're cut-and-pasting the Bible or you're following Man instead of God or you are going your own way and making your own rules, then you have one already and you're in big trouble and you're probably unwilling or unable to receive ANY of this because you're supernaturally blind and stupid and you're "ever hearing but never understanding, lest you repent and be healed." It is capable of completely blinding you until the Lord says you've had enough. You can get a Red Dragon with a denominational face on it or even one from a person – by following a man (or woman) instead of obeying Christ. You can get one with your own face on it, if you have made yourself your own god.

Jezebel

Description: Nearly invisible microscopic worm, no teeth, no claws, no defenses.

Port: Pituitary Gland (the Master Gland)

Characteristics: Master controller – the Wizard of Oz man behind the curtain. The real brains of the operation that pulls all the levers and coordinates all the attacks. Most active with Psyphon, Witchcraft, Fear, and Loneliness – but gets them all working together to control and manipulate and wreck lives of host and others.

Removal: See detailed Jezebel writing. (Appendix C) Not a simple thing. Requires much authority and substantial spiritual preparation of the host. Requires replacement with alternative. The short term solution is to bind it all the time by making a "pearl" of the Blood of Jesus around it.

Cautions: See detailed Jezebel writing. (Appendix C) The endless Jezebel witch-hunts have wrecked many congregations. If they just understood that everybody has one, it might make them more merciful and more aware of the big picture and of the ways in which their <u>own</u> Jezebel is squirreling with the situation and encouraging the constant finger pointing and malicious talk. (Isaiah 58:9)

Frequency: Everyone has (or had) one. It is the "seed" from the snake in the Garden of Eden. It is the worm in the fruit from the Tree of Knowledge of Good and Evil. Unless it is replaced by the positive alternative (a seed of pure Love), that port will ALWAYS suck in another Jezebel, usually within hours or minutes. All it takes is getting an instruction or a word from the Lord and turning it a degree or two off-center to get a Jezebel back.

Psyphon / Python / Kundalini

Description: Dragon with a long neck that attaches on the back and its neck wraps repeatedly around host's neck and comes up trachea and out mouth to strike at others. Well camouflaged and hard to see. Usually see it as golden or reflective or skin colored. VERY well camouflaged.

Port: Latches onto back and has a single talon on each of four legs embedded in heart, lungs, and/or kidney or liver (or other lower organs). Barbed tail embedded in the spine is hard to remove. Neck wraps around throat of victim and then head comes up and through and out the mouth. Like a hangman's noose. Because it manifests in multiple places, may not get dealt with as a single entity. *(See Gossip and Strife on page 40 & 42.)*

Characteristics: It "surfs" the words of the victim, especially spiritually powerful, anointed words. It will wait until just the right moment, then strike like a viper and grab ahold of someone through the words from the mouth, then latch on and reel them in and feed them poison. It's that thing that hold back until just the right moment and then strikes and hits people right in the heart. It also cranks down on the throat and restricts airflow – apnea, bronchitis and other related things. It can also create a hypoxia that makes people feel lightheaded and/or pass out. The Psyphon is responsible for many of the manifestations of people being "drunk" or "slain in the spirit". There IS a real equivalent when God overloads you and knocks you out to get your full attention, but you rise up from those a changed person. The counterfeit is this restricted airflow or oxygen level that creates a simulated "buzz" but isn't really God's anointing. It is a dragon and it is very smart and very sneaky. It will adapt and hide. It has scales that can be shed and ANY part of it that is left behind will regrow the whole. It carries a Fear with it and that will have to be removed as well (independent of the hosts' main Fear port). It can afflict a whole bunch of organs at once and affect all kinds of biological responses alone or in tandem with the Jezebel.

Removal: Requires someone that either sees VERY well in the spirit or hears God VERY accurately – or both. Requires substantial spiritual authority to deal with and requires someone who has their own Psyphon either WELL-bound or preferably removed altogether. It can be minimized and controlled by Godly tongue control – keeping a tight reign on the tongue and speaking only what God wants spoken – but it's only a control, not a removal. To get it off, the main body needs to be ripped off. The talons in the organs need to be identified, removed, and the physical damage addressed as the Lord leads. The barbed tail needs to be removed by pushing it on through and out of the spine. The neck needs to be unwrapped from around the victim's throat and pulled out of their mouth (or throat). It will most probably shed all of its scales when it sees you coming, so those will have to be washed out by a thorough whole-body "gargling" of the Blood of Jesus to flush them all out. If residue of ANY kind is left, it will regenerate. Continue praying through until the Lord says that all parts have been eliminated and the person is clean. We've also seen it break up into lots of little snakes that were harder to find and to catch. Don't rely on what you see, listen to God's leading about where any bits might be hiding. Cast it into the Abyss, not dry places – or hand it to an angel. If you're ready to do a replacement, then pray that their port be filled with Brotherly Love and then seal it over and pray a turtle-like shield all over their back and neck.

Cautions: Expect it to morph and change and move. Once identified, it will likely adapt quickly. Equip a person as much as possible beforehand about what it is and how to keep the doors shut. Repeated removals are going to get harder and harder. This is the second in command after the

Jezebel. It is VERY sneaky and VERY dangerous. If you deliver parts – like a lying tongue or gossip – but leave the whole, it will just regrow.

Frequency: Everybody has one, unless a replacement has been done. Controlling or minimizing its effects is not the same as replacement. It is VERY common in church leadership and those with prophetic anointings.

Ways other people have seen it: Like the layers of gold rings used for stretching the necks of African women. Like a hangman's knot roped around the throat. Like a boa constrictor around the neck. (Also called **Python** – but folks that aren't seeing in the spirit well may pull the neck off and leave the body, and so it will grow back.)

Loneliness / Despair

Description: Little blue puff ball with a sad look. No real defenses that we've seen.

Port: Hides behind the heart.

Characteristics: VERY dangerous. FAR more dangerous than we usually give it credit. It motivates FAR more behaviors than you would expect. It is the ruling spirit in most bars and night clubs and dating services and clubs and associations of all kinds – and even churches. It hides pretty well and looks harmless, but, like the Jezebel, the enemy hides in little packages that don't seem too dangerous. The reality is that in almost every destructive human behavior, at some level, loneliness was pulling the strings. It can spiral men or women up into anorexia, abusive relationships, addictions to numb the pain, manipulation so as not to be alone, "buying" friends, promiscuity and seduction, cutting, suicide, necrophilia and dozens of others.

Removal: Rip and toss. Cover wound in the Blood. Replace it with daily intimate relationship with Jesus. Nothing else will cure it permanently. You have to teach them how to hold His hand all the time.

Cautions: It hides behind other things, so look hard.

Frequency: Much more frequent then you would expect. Many people with crowds around them are actually VERY lonely. Marriage isn't always a solution, neither is the church.

Pride

Description: Really hard to target and see. Different on each person.

Port: Can be just about anywhere and look lots of different ways. Can be pride in the work of the hands or pride in brain or talent or physical assets. Can be a shroud of pride that wraps the whole person. Can be hard to target, like a pride in a family name. Watch for manifestations, as it will pretty quickly let itself be known.

Characteristics: That which sets itself above God. An exaggerated sense of self-worth and personal power or authority. Can manifest as a spectrum – if you think very poorly of yourself and that God can never heal or deliver or love you, that's still pride. You believe that you are SO bad and so unique and such a special case that even the God of the Universe will make an exception for you and not love you. That's still pride and it still sets itself against God and depreciates the people around you. Remember to watch for the inverse of these. They'll polarize either way and get your eyes off of God.

Removal: Need to identify as clearly as possible so the person can see it and hate it and keep the doors shut. Much more enmeshed with the YOU in you than just the demonic. The hardest of all to deliver permanently because it's ingrained with our nature. C.S. Lewis calls it the "Great Sin." This one has to be crucified daily.

Cautions: Expect it to be a battle to fully identify it and to get them to keep it out. And don't expect that there is just one or one layer of it.

Frequency: Pretty much universal. God wants broken and contrite vessels, a humble people. The "world" wants us to believe in ourselves – instead of God.

Fear (Anxiety)

Description: Snarly, black nasty snake that sits on top of the head, like a periscope watching for things to fear and whispering them to the head. May be really old and long and twisted down around the spine.

Port: Upper neck, base of the skull.

Characteristics: Constantly on the lookout for input from the environment that it can feed back to the victim in the worst possible way. Watches TV or reads the paper with you and whispers that that could be YOUR child or maybe YOU have that disease or maybe YOU could get mugged at the mall. It is constantly searching for things that initially sound reasonable, but by repetition and exaggeration can be turned into full blown phobias. And they always whisper to you with an "I" in front so you think it's you. Works in cooperation with the Condemnation and the Lust (and others) to keep a person constantly off-balance. "I want chocolate. Now I'm fat and nobody likes me. I'll probably end up alone and have a heart attack. More chocolate will make me feel better." On men it's often a fear of man or a fear of looking weak. On women it's often a fear of man, fear of being alone or a fear of losing stability. In prophets it's a fear of the consequences of speaking what God tells you or a fear of admitting you hear God's voice. Can also be the inverse – a rejection of Fear so much that the avoidance of Fear and proof you're not is still the idol and true motivator. (Example: "Fear Factor" or the dopes on "Jackass")

Removal: Rip and toss. Check for related physical damage – particularly brain chemical imbalances. Cover the wound in the Blood and seal the port. Replace with knowledge of God's promises and faithfulness. We have found that THIS is primarily the one that keeps people from being able to commit fully to God. If their hearing is clear and their mind is clear, but they still cannot bring themselves to leap, it's because of the fear. We've seen hardened groups break and beg for Jesus when you bound up the fear on each of them. This is a BIG DEAL. Please hear this! Your ability to get someone to hear the Gospel or a message of repentance, receive it and act on it will increase DRAMATICALLY if you bind up the Fear and the Jezebel first. And YOU need to be Fear-free.

Cautions: Binding it up may keep it from manifesting so that you think it's gone when it's not. Seal over the wound. (NOTE: The Psyphon carries a Fear of it's own, independent of the normal port. Be sure and look for that one as well and deal with the Psyphon (if you can). The Psyphon's fear is not as strong and not as generalized, but will help reopen the door to the original, if it can.)

Frequency: Very common. The higher it dials up the more it goes from a generalized concern to unreasonable phobias and panic attacks. Medications for depression and anxiety are just going to create dependencies on something other than God and open more doorways by acknowledging that it's real and reasonable and something we have to mask – but can't remove. This is direct disobedience to how the Bible says we're to handle Fear. It's a crutch so that you don't have to take every thought captive and keep your cup full of Jesus.

Lust

Description: Fat black frog with a long tongue that shoots out to find food.

Port: Over and/or around the heart (depending on size).

Characteristics: Not just for sex, the Lust is really about self-gratification and anything that gives a "buzz" that makes a person feel good or be numbed. Could be porn, drugs, alcohol, cigarettes, caffeine, sugar, a Corvette, shopping, television, politics, food, image, appearance, power, structure – even things that seem safe, like cleanliness or serving the poor at a soup kitchen or giving money to charity. You can even give the enemy ground by lusting after an experience with God – if you crave being "drunk in the spirit" for the buzz, that's VERY bad. Anything that becomes an idol will stand between you and God, and it's probably the enemy taking something that is OK in the right circumstances and conditions (like sex within marriage or a donut) and turning it into something else. God commands us to care for widows and orphans, but if we do it more so that WE will FEEL good, then we did it so that we will get a reward – and it's void. And the Lust got us.

Removal: Preferably name it and acknowledge it and keep the door closed. Rip and toss. Check for related physical damage. Cover the wound in the Blood and seal the port. Replace with Self-Control.

Cautions: This one is very sneaky and delivering a person of ONE of their lusts will leave the door open and another will replace it. Stop smoking and you'll probably start over-eating. The portal for ALL lusts needs to be shut and ALL self-gratifications that are outside of God's instructions should stop. (Some things are lusts that you wouldn't expect, like Anorexia, Bulimia, Cutting, Tattoos, Piercings, etc. All for self-gratification in one way or another, even though it seems backwards. You have to remember that demons are in charge and it doesn't have to make sense – it's designed to kill, steal and destroy AND convince us it was our idea and makes sense somehow. The more the doorway to Lust is opened, the deeper the generational curse, the more the perversion and deviancy that's going to manifest in horrific ways. Read Deuteronomy 28.)

Frequency: Pretty much universal.

Witchcraft (Control, Manipulation)

Description: Black, scraggly grizzly bear that's biting down on the back of the neck. Size depends on how big it needs to be to control the head. That is, the more a person resists, the bigger it needs to be to turn (control) them whichever direction it wants to go. If you like it and cooperate with it, it doesn't have to be very big and beefy. (That's why Hillary Clinton's is like a Chihuahua.)

Port: Back of the neck, so as to control the movement of the head. Like the rudder on a ship.

Characteristics: This can range from full on occultism to just a controlling pastor of a Christian church. Even a little old lady that makes people pies so that they will feel guilty and do what she wants. It's not just about sorcery, it's about controlling and manipulating others to get what you want. "Unbelief is as the sin of witchcraft" because you're taking matters into your own hands instead of trusting God. This thing will try to use whatever it can – position, money, charisma, spiritual authority, spells, curses, apple pie, whatever – to get someone to do what it wants them to do. This grizzly bear works in tandem with a bunch of other stuff like condemnation and seduction and loneliness and anger and lust. It's really nasty because it disrespects others by trying to enforce its will on them. When you reach out to get what you want from others, instead of waiting on God to provide what you need, you disbelieve that He is able and you take matters into your own hands. That's witchcraft. And God HATES it. (They are HIS kids, not yours – get out of His way and let Him fix them in His time and in His way. He doesn't need your help.)   This is really dangerous for Christians to play around with – and it's RAMPANT in the "church" structures that we have. They are all about control and manipulation – either through marketing or timing or design of systems and programs. It's all about jamming people into your mold by whatever means necessary.

Removal: Wrap it in the Blood like a cocoon and slice it off right against the port. If it's really big and nasty, then put a tourniquet around where it's biting on and crank it down until it lets go, then cast down the whole cocoon. If it's REALLY nasty, then keep cranking down on the tourniquet while you beat on it like a boxer on a heavy bag. Check for related physical damage. Cover the wound in the Blood and seal the port. Replace with Faith. (**Optional:** Especially with this one, but it works with others as well, if you don't believe they will be able to keep the door shut and you don't want it coming back worse and they're not ready for a replacement with Faith, then put on a tourniquet, but slice the demon off behind its head and leave it embedded, but covered in the blood. Like the head on a tick, it will stay put and be brain dead, but won't grow back so long as the Blood is bandaging it. But at least the port is covered for awhile so nothing can load back on. You'll need to put a big bandage of the Blood over it and maintenance it regularly, but it will buy you a few days of clear thinking while they get stronger. This is NOT a long term solution! NOTE: you can't do this with a Jezebel.)

Cautions: DO NOT blast it or hack at it! It will explode and leave bits all over. It will try to get on everyone nearby like shrapnel. It is sort of a compound demon because it has lots of little parts that do different things. Make sure you got ALL of it off. Sometimes it has "suckers" – like the parasite fish under a shark – that will ride along and help. Bundle it all up and pull it off in one chunk.

Frequency: Very common, especially among church leaders. Very common among business leaders and politicians as well. Very common among people that have been abused or assaulted, as they try to control the people and situations around them to keep from being hurt again. Watch for frequent horizontal applications of force to get people to change, instead of vertical (intercession to God). Watch for family history of Jezebel-ridden and controlling mothers or fathers.

Self-Condemnation (Shame/Critical Spirit)

Description: Greasy black crow

Port: Sits on right shoulder. (But could be big enough to totally encompass them.)

Characteristics: Feeds a constant stream of negativity, usually about self, but also about others. Whispers in the ear with the goal of destroying a person and keeping their focus on their own faults or those of others – instead of looking to the Cross of Jesus. As with all the others, it really enjoys it's job and gleefully cackles as it destroys someone. If it's been there a long time, it may not even have to say much at all because it's trained the victim to speak critical things to themselves. It can take a break while you do it's work for it. It also is critical of others so as to make the person seem to feel better, but all they end up doing is grieving God by doing one or more of the things that God hates and bringing curses on themselves. (Haughty eyes, disunity among brethren,lying tongue that spreads gossip, etc.)

Removal: Rip and toss. Check for related physical damage to shoulder, neck or ears. Cover the wound in the Blood and seal the port. Replace with intimacy with God and teach them to take captive every thought and to recognize the voice of the enemy. They have to stop this voice before it gets going and recognize that God would never say those kinds of things to a person. They need to keep their cup full all the time and use this as an indicator that their cup is just not all the way full. (www.FellowshipOfTheMartyrs.com/rain_down_now.htm)

Cautions: The presence of this one is an immediate indication that they are not taking captive every thought and have lots of other open ports. If you see evidence of this one in abundance, start looking for all the other ports that are probably wide open. It probably also means that they do not know how to differentiate between the voices in their head. They're hearing God, but dismissing it because His voice conflicts with the self-condemning things they're used to hearing and saying about themselves.

Frequency: Very common. Especially among women who have been abused or those subjected to a person with a large witchcraft/control. The media helps with a constant barrage of commercials and input telling you that you're not thin enough, white enough, rich enough, popular enough, or have teeth white enough. (That's because the media is mostly run by demons.)

Sorrow / Self-pity

Description: Blue puff ball that is always crying.

Port: Behind heart.

Characteristics: No teeth, no claws. No overt defenses.. Very sneaky. Very difficult to completely eliminate. Works with fear and loneliness. NOT to be confused with Godly sorry or repentance! It's the counterfeit.

Removal: Rip and toss. Cover in the blood. Replace with rejoicing over affliction and true repentance.

Cautions: Very difficult to keep door closed. Fellowship with believers helps. They have to learn to keep their cup full all the time.

Frequency: Very common. Watch for loneliness.

Lying/Deceit (I Tim. 4:1)

Description: Forked tongue, snake

Port: Tongue

Characteristics: This will not just lie to others but to self as well. Any of the other demons that gets a lot of control (Self-condemnation, Lust, Fear, Pride, Guilt, etc.) and can get you to speak forth out of your own mouth the lies they are whispering to you, will get the port open for the Lying spirit to take hold. That is, if they tell you that you are stupid and ugly and no one likes you – and can get you to say it out loud with your own mouth – then you have given that port over to a lying tongue. Then they can probably get you to lie as much as they want, as it gains more and more control. At the extreme, a person can be so controlled and given over to it that they can't even tell the truth anymore at all.

Removal: Rip and toss. Check for related physical damage to throat, gastric and other organs. Cover the wound in the Blood and seal the port. Replace with Truth and a commitment to NOT open the mouth unless God opens it and speak only what He says to speak. Be sure to do follow up and to test the spirits regularly.

Cautions: Make sure and deal with whatever other spirit is opening the door – wherever the lies are coming from that the victim is speaking out (like the Fear or the Self-Condemnation). Close all the ports that assist in giving it room. NOTE: This can be a Lying spirit or it can be a Psyphon. Be sure which you are looking at.

Frequency: Our American propensity for "spin" makes it very common that we would allow this in and give it room to grow. Certainly not unique to Americans, anyone that tells "fish stories" and exaggerates about events is allowing this to creep in in ever increasing measure.

Worry / Stress

Description: Black band like a money belt. (Snake, constrictor.)

Port: Around waist/stomach.

Characteristics: Keeps stomach/bowels churning and eating on themselves – ulcers, irritable bowel, sensitive stomach, bladder problems, kidney problems, etc. Very closely integrated with Fear and a Time Obsession.

Removal: Rip and toss. Check for related physical damage to gastric and other organs. Cover the wound in the Blood and seal the port. Replace with peace and patience.

Cautions: If you see evidence of this one in abundance, start looking for all the other ports that are probably wide open. It probably also means that they do not know how to differentiate between the voices in their head.

Frequency: Very common, especially among hard-driving professionals and single moms and people in other stressful jobs. The aged are also very susceptible to this as they find more and more things to Fear.

Lethargy (or reverse - Constant Motion)

Description: Black Tick – size depends on length in place and efficiency. (Some have seen a black box or a greasy coating on the same port that keeps getting thicker – like a layer of fat that immobilizes the victim. I think that's just a really bloated tick that is working fast.)

Port: Middle back, one side or the other of spine, just below rib cage. (Usually on the right.)

Characteristics: General depressing and slowing down of bodily functions. Sleepiness, sloth, constant lack of energy. Works with the Psyphon to create and keep Sleep Apnea and other physical problems that depress energy levels. May have plenty of motivation, but feeling constant drag on resources. It sucks out and feeds on physical energy.

Removal: Rip and toss. Seal over wound with the Blood. Folks with this one often report a lot of back pain and feel an instant release when it is removed.

Cautions: As with all others, learned habits and behaviors have to change to keep it gone.

Frequency: Very common, especially when a Lust is present to help feed it. (Could be Lust for food, soda, beer, fishing, TV, Playstation, chocolate ice cream, whatever.)

Confusion

Description: Black spider/octopus

Port: Side of face. Usually on the right – haven't ever seen it on the left, but not saying it couldn't.

Characteristics: Digs in to eyes, sinuses, ears and brain and scrambles signals. It may result in physical issues like migraines, sinus pain, ear problems, facial rashes or inflammation. It is responsible for Dyslexia, ADHD and other types of mental or auditory or visual garbling.

Removal: Rip and toss. Seal over wound with the Blood. Reverse any physical damage.

Cautions: Urge them to immediately stop speaking anything detrimental about themselves from past "labels."

Frequency: Getting more common as general societal, religious, media and educational confusion increases. Drugs intended to combat it will actually mask it, but open doors for it to root in deeper. By the time that it results in Alzheimer's it has become very powerful and deeply rooted. See Deuteronomy 28 to see if it is a curse from God – as with some of the others, it may not be removable without repentance for having let it in by disobedience to God (and a commitment to turn from your wicked ways – 2 Chronicles 7:14). May also be a generational curse or a word curse effect.

Double-Minded

Description: Like a metal plate through the head going vertically from ear to ear – dividing the brain into front and back.

Port: Brain/head.

Characteristics: Used by the enemy to keep a person shook up and in motion. God hates a double-minded man, so the enemy wants to try to get us to be that so that God's blessings won't flow and His protection won't cover us. This can range from a slight waffling on decisions to a full blown psychosis and dementia (like bi-polar or schizophrenia).

Removal: Rip and toss. Seal over wound with the Blood. Reverse any physical damage – which it most likely DID cause if it's been there a long time. Explain to victim and spend extra time explaining the importance of not leaning on your own understanding. That will keep the halves of the brain from arguing with each other – if you just ignore both and obey God. Teach them how to keep their "cup" full ALL the time.

Cautions: Expect resistance. This one is particularly well-rooted and will likely require behavioral/habit changes. It's really important that the person be shown that it's NOT them and that it must be stopped in order for them to walk in the fullness of what God has for them. Requires fasting and prayer. It works most actively with Confusion and Fear and Self-Condemnation and the Wings on their feet.

Frequency: Rampant in America. In fact, so rampant that a person that sets their face like flint and will not turn to the left or the right is seen as a rare exception. (And/or a close-minded, fundamentalist freak.)

Gossip

Description: A function and component of the Psyphon

Port: Tongue

Characteristics: Because the Psyphon is a multi-component dragon, if you address individual pieces it will just grow back. I have never seen anyone effectively and permanently deliver someone of a spirit of Gossip. They might get better tongue control, but unless the Psyphon as a whole is removed (which can only be done under certain conditions), it's just really likely that they'll have to continue fighting this. Listen carefully, you CANNOT deliver someone from just a spirit of Gossip without addressing the whole Psyphon. It will lay low for awhile and make you think you got it, or by the force of will-power and tongue control you could suppress it, but it's still in there waiting for a chance.

Removal: See Psyphon

Cautions: See Psyphon

Frequency: Pretty much universal.

Dementia

Description: Really a combination of things all dialed up really high.

Port: All around the head and brain.

Characteristics: Is most likely a combination effect of the following really well-entrenched demons; Double-Minded, Confusion, Fear, Lying Spirit, Pride, Sorrow, Witchcraft and the Psyphon. Could surely include others as well. When multiples of these are really well dug in and dialed up to a high level, they will kill, steal and destroy any quality of life possible – including mental functioning. A person fully handed over to this will become a burden on family and a constant stressor and will steal the family's quality of life as well. Medication rarely does any good in the long term, and in fact, will open more doorways so the person has less and less control to keep these things out.

Removal: Identify all the culprits. Get them off as directed by God. Seal it all over with the Blood and reverse any physical damage done. Teach the person how to keep their cup full ALL the time and fight these off. (The Jezebel is the one coordinating all the attacks from multiple directions, so binding it will help isolate them.)

Cautions: Keep checking with the Lord to see if you got them all.

Frequency: As demonic activity increases, the number of people totally turned over to dementia will increase. As it is, we have them pretty much around us all the time. Either warehoused in institutions or sleeping under bridges or hidden away in the attic. Please listen, it doesn't have to be that way. They're just waiting for someone to go free them and fill their cup with Jesus. Some of the best evangelists and pastors and radical, John the Baptist repentance preachers are pushing shopping carts and talking to themselves, just waiting for us to come free them! It will be a fight, but isn't it worth it? Do you know who was the very FIRST missionary Jesus ever sent out? It was the MOST demonized guy in the Bible! (Mark 5:19-20) He covered TEN cities alone!

Strife

Description: Component of the Psyphon.

Port: on the tongue. .

Characteristics: See Psyphon.

Removal: Cannot be permanently removed independent from the Psyphon. See above.

Cautions: See Psyphon above.

Frequency: See Psyphon above.

Forgetfulness

Description: Really fast moving thing that looks like a cheetah but with back legs reversed like a grasshopper.

Port: Affects the mind and speech, but doesn't really port up anywhere.

Characteristics: Races by at top speed and grabs a thought and rips it out of your mind. Just races by in a blur. (Had to catch one to get a good look at it.) Some folks say they just lost a word or lost their "train of thought." But especially when it's about God, it's probable that this thing is behind it. If they just accept it, or worse – expect it – then they open the doors more and more until swarms of these things just circle and steal everything. Then you have Alzheimer's or other dementia that will actually result in eventual organic damage.

Removal: You have to refuse to accept them when they attack and you have to rebuke them. If you can, you need to catch one and crush it. They won't be afraid of you if you show yourself open to an assault from this direction. Once you've beaten a particularly flavor of demon, they'll be more cautious around you or stay away.

Cautions: Do not just assume that it's you when you "blank" on something important at a key moment.

Frequency: Very common and getting more so. Drugs open the doors even more.

Sexual Abuse (physical, emotional, verbal, spiritual or other)

Description: Horns (or handles) – could be layer upon layer of different "flavors" of them.

Port: On either side of lower back, just above or on the hip bones.

Characteristics: These can range from verbal abuse, to physical, emotional or sexual. When there is a long string of them, they look like stacked ice cream scoops of different colors. That is, the "horns" get larger and fatter and multi-layered. If you see them this way, you're just going to have to have the Lord explain to you what each layer is so you can help the person peel it all back like an onion. These horns are markers – they are tags. The spiritual realms see them and know that this is a person that has been abused in the past and that there is still unresolved pain and hurt – which means it really isn't washed away, which probably means the person got away with it somehow or the host hasn't really forgiven it – so the demons send people with abuser demons TOWARD the people with these markers so that the demons can cackle and laugh while they ruin both lives. A woman with a history of sexual or physical abuse as a child is VERY likely to end up with boyfriends and husbands that will do the same kinds of stuff. In fact, they may be a guy that would NEVER think to even do such a thing, but the demons on HER will whisper to him that she's the kind of person that needs to be beaten into submission. Then another layer is added to the horns and they get more and more entrenched. Please understand, it's NOT her voice, it's not her personality, it's not HER asking for it – it's the demons and the generational curses and the doorways that were opened by these acts of violence or incest or abuse. Someone forced these doors open, probably against her will, and the spiritual head of the family didn't slam them shut and repent and wash them away. Or worse, the spiritual head of the family was the one responsible and it really mangled up her "Dad Filter" and squirreled with her view of God. When you remove these markers, the person will not attract the same kind of people anymore. They will REALLY be a new creation, just as the Lord promised. If they're not already, it's because they didn't know about the horns or didn't believe He could really wash it away – or have an unforgiveness they won't lay down and that still binds them. Be gentle.

Removal: Identify them to the person as the Lord leads and say whatever needs to be said so that they will want the markers gone and believe in faith that they will be gone. Grab them and snap them off and cast them to the Abyss. Cover the wounds in the blood of Jesus and smooth over and scrub off any scar tissue.

Cautions: If there is an active, ongoing abuse situation right now – do as the Lord leads. Armor them up really good. Expect the enemy to try to get them back. Watch for the demons that were inserted by the acts committed and deal with them as well – particularly Lust, Seduction/Prostitution, Homosexuality, Bitterness, Anger, Murder, Loneliness, Guilt, Confusion, Self-Condemnation and Control/Witchcraft. Might even be some REALLY ugly ones like the Dominatrix or Suicide or Self-Mutilation or Anorexia/Bulimia or a full-blown Dementia. They almost certainly have a mangled "Dad Filter" and may even have a bitterness and unforgiveness toward God that restrains Him from swooping in to the rescue because they don't believe He can, or are binding God by their unforgiveness toward Him. They almost certainly have a very active Witchcraft that tries to control and manipulate people and situations so they won't get hurt that way again. Either by building up walls and keeping distance and running when someone gets too close (Wings) – or by manipulating people and situations so that they can always keep the upper hand and nobody will sneak up on them. Please deal with them with mercy and love and gentleness and look for the root causes – how they got mangled as a kid and what to do about it. My experience is that the meanest, most hateful, most controlling, most obnoxious people are really just little kids that got hurt REALLY badly and nobody has ever helped them peel off all the layers of demons that have been oppressing them ever since. The little kid inside is begging for someone to give them a hug and kiss their boo-boos, but the demons built these walls that keep it from ever happening and it makes them more and more bitter and lonely until the demons have succeeded in killing, stealing and destroying any quality of life or fullness in Christ they might have had – and probably done real damage to that of the people around the abused little kid that's all grown up now and is a boss or a grandma or a pastor. (NOTE: The Lord may not want you to remove the markers. Sometimes they need to minister to people who have been through the same things and those markers are spiritual proof that they know what they're talking about. God has had me leave them sometimes.)

Frequency: VERY, VERY common. The enemy always wants to wreck the little kids. As soon as he can get to them, he wants to insert every possible kind of ugliness into them. Especially these last generations that have such a promise and such a calling. Please be merciful and don't blame the person, blame their rulers and the rulers of the people that messed them up in the first place. (Psalm 141:5-6)

Seduction / Prostitution

Description: A shiny, black snake – the front half is Seduction and the back half is Prostitution.

Port: Ported inside vagina or scrotum, but snakes up the front and stares out from the cleavage under the chin, trying to get the attention of someone else's Lust demon. Breast implants really make its job easier. Current clothing styles SUBSTANTIALLY help it along.

Characteristics: Wants to get your attention, then the snake will strike and reel you in. First it tries to get your attention drawn toward the cleavage, then the Prostitution will try to reel you in to the privates and create a soul tie. If it can sink it's teeth in by intimate contact, then it creates an illegal soul tie that it can draw upon to wreck both people's lives – and maybe children, too. The goal is to get as many people as possible under the worst curse in the Bible – the ten generation bastard curse for sex outside of marriage (Deut 23:2). This curse keeps any offspring from this couple (and themselves) from being truly fruitful and from entering into the Holy of Holies and having real intimacy with God. This can be present on anyone that uses their body or their femininity (or masculinity) to get what they want. It's NOT just about sex. A grandma that uses her baking ability to get people to like her and meet her needs can have a spirit of prostitution. It's about using your body to get what you want, it doesn't require intercourse or sexual contact. Lots of Christian girls don't realize that by listening to the "world," they have allowed this Seduction and given it more ground by their clothing and other choices. They are attracting the wrong kind of attention and using their parts to get affirmation or attention. The enemy WILL use it to get them away from God, if at all possible. People don't need to dress seductively for this to be in play, it's not just about skin showing, it's about a spirit that whispers to others and tries to get them to gratify it.

Removal: Show it to them (if adults). Rip and toss. Seal over with the Blood. Reverse any physical damage. Ask the Lord to reverse mental and emotional damage and teach them to seek His direction on everything - like clothing and language and friends and input (TV, magazines, music, etc.). Prostitution is harder to remove as it is wrapped up and around the private parts and needs to be sucked out and fully removed.

Cautions: You CAN tear loose from Prostitution and handle separately, but don't leave one or the other or it will return as a unit. Look for old Abuse scars that might have activated sexuality too early in a child. Watch for Self-condemnation and Lust and Loneliness. Check for generational curses in play. Check for Homosexuality. If you are a man or woman of God, be VERY careful about the situations you put yourself in. Particularly if you have any open doorways and are in a situation with someone with an active Seduction.

Frequency: VERY common right now. Pretty much everybody on TV that isn't a Muppet has one (and even Miss Piggy!). The media wants to objectify our bodies and teach us how to use them to get what we want. There is implicit teaching from birth that attractive kids are more likely to succeed and are more favored by teachers and parents and employers and the "in" crowd. If your kid has a gift for drama or the arts, be VERY aware of how body performance and using what you have to get attention can open the door to gratification and allow this in. MANY "performance" people in the churches are riddled with this.

Procrastination

Description: See Double Minded. (p. 39)

Port: See Double Minded.

Characteristics: See Double Minded.

Removal: See Double Minded.

Cautions: See Double Minded.

Frequency: See Double Minded.

Time Obsession

Description: Black or silver snake

Port: Wrapped around the wrist and down the forearm where you would wear a watch.

Characteristics: Tries to get eyes off of God and focused on time. It could manifest a whole bunch of different ways – as a fear of your biological clock running out, a fear of old age, a constant emphasis on time pressures and deadlines and a life driven by appointments. Could be a constant background whisper that no matter how much you have to do there's not going to be enough time to do it. Another sneaky one is that you're not doing enough for God and you're a failure and you better hurry because you're running out of time. It works in conjunction with Self-Condemnation and Stress and Fear especially. It tries to get people to ignore the specific commands of James 4:13-17 and thus causes them to sin.

Removal: Show it for what it is, encourage habit changes, rip and toss. If God gives you something to do, He'll allow enough time to get it done. God doesn't "hurry". Seal over with the Blood. Look for associated strongholds and deal with them as well. Reverse any physical damage – particular stomach and intestine damage from the Stress/Worry thing.

Cautions: Expect that certain jobs actually force this demon on people and it may require them to completely change attitudes or even job situations to really be free of it. Like money, it's not a sin to have time, it's a sin to love it. It's not a sin to be on time and structured, it's a sin to do it outside of the directives and peace of God. It's a sin to put all your focus and attention on the clock and make it an idol.

Frequency: Constantly increasing in America. Technology actually makes it worse. Pretty rare in Latin America and Hawaii and equatorial regions and places that are a lot more laid back. VERY common in Japan. Very much a component of the "Protestant work ethic" - and I believe, the curse of Adam in Genesis.

Deaf and Dumb

Description: It is a very high level Cut-and-Paste that seals off information completely. Input AND/OR output.

Port: Looks like earplugs, or a black tub stopper in the back of the throat.

Characteristics: Just like the cut and paste or garbler that filters information. This one can cause complete information back up and clogging. Those with Alzheimer's suffer with this one a lot. They can see and hear but they can't get anything out. May manifest as spiritual OR physical deaf and dumbness

Removal: Rip and toss, cover it in the Blood.

Cautions: May require fasting. Look for generational curses and word curses.

Frequency: Spiritually very common. Less common in the natural.

Homosexuality (Sodomy, Lesbianism)

Description: Nasty, fat, toothy, multi-colored snake with a big knob on its tail. (Mostly green and purple.)

Port: Anus

Characteristics: Very gross, very stinky, can vary in size and length depending upon severity and duration. Seems to be the same regardless of male or female host. Can come from abuse or from consensual act – may even come without physical contact (from visual or mental stimulus – fantasy, porn, etc.). But most often a door was already opened by some instance of abuse. Can even come from generational curses in the family line. Watch for abuse handles. A spirit of Pride can be present on hands or brain or elsewhere – but when a spirit of Pride is wrapped around the homosexuality snake, there's big trouble cause it's real unlikely to want to budge.

Removal: Hard to remove because it may be very strongly embedded and has a knot at the end that doesn't want to pull out. In order to be permanently removed may require substantial habit/behavioral/environmental changes. I don't know how you could possibly remove one that had a Pride around it because it is a curse from God and without repentance probably can't be lifted. Worse still if there is Pride that really <u>likes</u> defying God! Certainly the enemy wants to not just cause people to sin, but to encourage them to do so flamboyantly and proudly so as to further distance them from God and from any hope of healing or forgiveness. Even if a tiny minority, this can result in God pouring out judgement on whole cities because the majority didn't put a stop to it.

Cautions: Be gentle with people if you suspect abuse is at the root. (Be gentle with everybody for that matter.) Find the pride. Watch for a big self-condemnation. Look for a deep loneliness. (**NOTE:** I've pulled this off of people without them knowing it or approving of it and seen changes in demeanor nearly immediately, particularly kids under generational curses that hadn't fed it, but it was there. But I don't see any way that you could expect the door to stay closed on someone really proud of it. Nevertheless, the Lord has had me deliver it off of some of that group anyway. I suspect it came back even worse and even more entrenched, but maybe it will make them break and beg for God.)

Frequency: Increasing substantially.

Dominatrix/Perversion

Description: A combination effect of Lust, Seduction/Prostitution, Abuse, Witchcraft, Pride and a really strongly entrenched Psyphon. (And maybe others like Homosexuality, Bestiality and even Cannibalism and Murder.) And naturally, the Jezebel is coordinating the attacks.

Port: All over.

Characteristics: Each individual demon is stinky enough, but all together, this person just REEKS of badness. This isn't just a person that is deviant and hurting, they really, really LIKE it and don't want to change. We first saw this on a girl we believe was actively involved in incest with her male relative(s) and liked it and used it to get what she wanted and had no motivation to stop. It had then extended to sadistically dominating ANY male that she could get her hands on. She had turned the tables on the abusers and it had become blackmail and control and prostitution – and now SHE was in control of the relationship and got whatever she wanted.

Removal: To date, that I'm aware of, we have never removed this from anyone. They are very, VERY sold out to the badness and are really unlikely to want to let it go. The only hope is Salvation and a complete renouncing of ALL of it. Without Jesus, I don't think this person will ever get free. If you insert someone like this into the church, or into church leadership, they will leave a massive trail of devastation behind them. (And they ARE in the churches.)

Cautions: Bind the Jezebel and Psyphon, See individual components. Expect lots of resistance. Fasting is probably required. Check for familiar spirits and generational curses – particularly the Bastard curse – and LOTS of open soul ties. This is going to require lots of changes and LOTS of sincere repentance! Be ready to help.

Frequency: Increasingly common as evil thrives and good doesn't put a stop to it.

Garbler

Description: It looks like a large clear helmet with a filter in front of the mouth.

Port: Over a persons head. Like a really big, clear, Darth Vader helmet.

Characteristics: Like a speaker in the glass at the bank or the movie theater. It mangles input and communicates it on. It's intent is to muddy communication to suit it's purposes. A person with a garbler may have a really hard time being understood or understanding others or both. When you find that everything you say to someone is misunderstood, or it is received with the worst possible spin, then look for the garbler. Maybe selective to some, and more potent to others. Lots of pastors have garblers.

Removal: They need to see it. And acknowledge it so they can regularly pray against it. Otherwise, just rip and toss. Cover in the blood. It would never have had legal ground to get on if the person only opened their mouth when Jesus opened their mouth for them.

Cautions: Avoid idle words. And useless fighting and quarreling.

Frequency: Very common. Especially among those with deep theological, scientific or political histories,

Cut-and-Paste

Description: A sort of gray censor bar or fuzzy dot like those used on TV to cover up nudity.

Port: In motion. It's not on you, it just filters input and create blindspots.

Characteristics: It picks and choses what can be let through. It will mess up reading, hearing, sight. It will censor out anything that the Red Dragon (see Appendix B) doesn't think you need to know to break the box you've got God in.

Removal: Acknowledge it, repent for putting God in a box and/or allowing your filters to modify the Truth. Desire the whole TRUTH. Rip and toss, cover it in the Blood.

Cautions: Very unlikely you can get out from under this if you're still under a Red Dragon (See Appendix B.) May also be a product of a Confusion.

Frequency: Practically universal in some degree or another. We all like to pick and choose out parts of the Bible that we don't like – or eliminate people or situations that might challenge us. *(Like stoning prophets.)*

Pain

Description: Black fur ball with two long fangs. Size depends on level of pain. May have multiple Pains or a whole cloud of little ones in the case of something like full body Arthritis.

Port: Fangs biting into the area of pain.

Characteristics: Not particularly offensive or difficult to remove. See Cautions.

Removal: Rip and toss. Make sure to pull the teeth out, don't break them off. Cover in the Blood and seal over the wound. Believe in faith that it's gone. If the person can see and believe, let them hack on it with their sword of the Spirit a little bit themselves so they'll feel better. :-)

Cautions: Pain is used to teach us something about Jesus. Probably how to share in His sufferings and really appreciate what He endures for us. Maybe to teach us patience, perseverance, long-suffering, gentleness, etc. The demons don't like to be used to teach us lessons about Jesus – they want us to focus on THEM and the pain and get our eyes off of the Cross. But if you will ask the Lord sincerely, "Lord, why am I going through this? What am I supposed to learn?" He will probably tell you pretty quickly and as soon as you learn it, the Pain is probably going to be released and you can move on to some other lesson. Sometimes we are just supposed to share in His sufferings so we can appreciate and understand better what He did for us. Even so, our eyes should be on Him, not on the Pain. If you try to pull a Pain demon off of someone that hasn't learned their lesson from it yet, they're just going to have to go through it again (probably harder) and you're getting in the way of God's refining of them. (If He'll even let you pull it off.) So always check with the Lord before you do anything and try to show the person what the point is/was. If they get it, they may just find that it was released on the spot. If not, and the Lord gives you permission to handle it, them pull it off as directed. Check for generational or word curses. Check to see if it's the Psyphon or some other stronghold that is causing the pain and not just a loose Pain demon. (For example, a broken toe is probably just a Pain. An ulcerated stomach is probably a Stress/Worry at the root, even though there may be a Pain helping at the moment of acute pain.)

Frequency: Very common. All kinds of pain for all kinds of reasons is rampant in our society.

Love of Money

Description: A sort of green, slimy blob – like a tick

Port: On the thigh around the knee, usually the right leg (never seen it on the left so far)

Characteristics: Whispers about money constantly. Works with the Lust to waste it on gratifications or with the Fear to obsess about not having it. There is nothing wrong with having money, but we're not to love it! If we do, God will make it a curse. The enemy knows this and tries to get us to go our own way where money is concerned so that it can't be really used to store up treasure in heaven. Even in a church, they will buy a new chandelier or a sound system or build bigger buildings rather than feeding widows and orphans. If we begin to love our "stuff" we're in big trouble. This thing draws it's power from getting us to get our eyes off of God and onto cash or stuff. Again, it could manifest on those with lots of money who love it or on those who have none and lust after it. The desperately poor are just as likely to have a Love of Money. Where is your focus?

Removal: Recognize, repent, rip and toss, cover in the Blood. May require lifestyle changes.

Cautions: There is a background Love of Money in America that we don't even see. Practically everyone has this without even realizing it. Unless you've really seen the difference between our lifestyle and other countries, you can't really even understand how much we expect and take for granted that isn't really necessary. Our kind of "suffering" is NOTHING like in other places. It creates a panic if our electricity is out for two or three days! Half the world has an average daily income of less than $2 per day. Half the world has never slept on a bed <u>once</u> in their whole life. At any given moment 200 MILLION Christians are starving – while Christians in America control tens of trillions of dollars of assets – far more than the total annual income of the United States Government. You can feed an orphan in Ghana for $50 for a year. Your iPod could have fed four orphans for a year – assuming you got the cheap one. The insitutional churches in America are spending over 90% of all of their budgets on their own comforts and shows. If we stopped loving it, there's more than enough to share. Christians average 2% in giving to church and charity and 50% on discretionary spending (feeding wants).

(Go read www.fellowshipOfTheMartyrs.com/scary_stats.htm for more on that stuff.)

Frequency: Pretty much universal in America since we are the greatest producers and exporters of Love of Money on the planet. All of our television programming is about why you will be happier if you have money and are pretty. Even the news reinforces that the inner city where the poor are is dangerous and the suburbs where the money is are peaceful and pleasant. Rampant in the churches. The Prosperity Gospel feeds and nurtures this particular demon really well, but nearly all of the denominations are implicitly about money. People are offended sometimes when you bring this to their attention, but it's pretty much impossible to grow up in America and not have one. Unless God has broken you and taught you how to trust Him for every penny – and probably had you walking penniless and hungry at some point – then you may not even get how much it's messing with you. When people begin really laying down all their stuff and sharing, it will change the whole economy.

Wings (Running)

Description: Little wings on the heels like the mythological god Mercury (or Hermes).

Port: Heels.

Characteristics: Creates a constant desire to flee somewhere else. It makes it very hard to stand where you are planted - a "grass is always greener over there" kind of thing. This constant motion keeps a person all shook up and probably unable to hear God or be productive in any one place. Probably results in rotating jobs, marriages, churches, relationships, etc. Any time conflict or discomfort arises, the person will be urged by the Wings to flee. The word *mercurial* is commonly used to refer to something or someone that is erratic, volatile or unstable.

Removal: Rip and toss. Seal over wound with the Blood. Reverse any physical damage. Sooner or later, these will definitely affect your "walk" – physically, emotionally and spiritually.

Cautions: If they're not present, watch for recent scar tissue or "buds" that may indicate it's not all the way resolved. This demon will whisper that they have to run – usually so as not to get hurt or have people too close.

Watch for Abuse scars and a Witchcraft/Control. Probably also a Loneliness or Recognition-Seeking in play.

Frequency: Very common. It is especially common in people that have been abused. Very common in the church where people hop from one place to another looking for something "comfy".

Restlessness

Description: Black tick with a LONG "tongue" that goes all the way up the spine to the brain.

Port: Base of spine – tail bone.

Characteristics: Seen on little kids that just wiggle all the time and can't sit still. They may stay in their seat, but they're in constant motion. This manifests in adults who stand where they are planted, but they are constantly stirring and spinning and wiggling. They don't necessarily have "Wings" on their feet looking for another place, but they're not content with resting in the place they're planted either. This tick actually creates this discomfort and then sucks from that nervous energy. The lies it whispers aren't about the grass being greener elsewhere, but about a need for constant improvement or movement in the place where you are. This perpetual motion results in no rest and peace incites sin by a lack of faith in God's plan and His timing. You can't wait on the Lord because you get too "twitchy" and you just have to DO something.

Removal: Acknowledge and repent. Rip and toss. Seal over wound with the Blood.

Cautions: Don't just slice it off, pull it out and make sure you get the whole "tongue" that goes up the spine to the brain. Then wad it up and toss it – or hand it to an angel.

Frequency: Pretty common in Americans who are taught constant dissatisfaction and that there's always a "better mousetrap" to be invented.

Recognition-seeking

Description: Can range from a little, fake-smile puff-ball to a really all-consuming nasty black frog.

Port: Behind the heart when small – in front when full blown.

Characteristics: Creates a desire to be recognized and rewarded for performance or work done. Constantly comparing against others and pointing out how much YOU deserve more than they got. Doesn't quietly and patiently serve sacrificially without thought of acknowledgment as Jesus commanded, but like the Pharisees wants to sit at the head of the table and be recognized in the marketplace. This is behind hot-rod cars and $3000 wheels and fancy paint jobs and big houses and extra large breast implants and all kinds of things that people do to show others how great they are or to reward themselves with a "trophy" for being great, powerful, successful, cool, anointed or whatever. (Don't miss how much Loneliness motivates and strengthens this one.)

Removal: Rip and toss. Seal over wound with the Blood. Reverse any physical damage – probably to the heart.

Cautions: Behavior has to change. Past awards and honors have to be renounced. Future honors have to be dedicated to God alone. Look for Pride. Watch for a Lust too, but they don't just do these things quietly to self-gratify, these are big public demonstrations so people will notice. This is also in play in exhibitionism and Gay Pride type events.

Frequency: REALLY common in America and we're teaching it to all our kids at a record pace. When schools award every kid, they teach them that they DESERVE recognition, not that they have to earn it. Worse still, Jesus says to sit at the end of the table and serve, not to seek recognition at all! Rampant in the churches and church institutions. If we're not even supposed to let the left hand know what the right hand is doing, then why do we give people a plaque with their name on it over the new gymnasium? Every new building should be Jehovah Jireh Library or Jehovah Jireh Chapel. Who really provided it? (OK, now I'm preaching again. Sorry.)

Obsessive-Compulsive

Description: Throbbing, snarly, black slimy, sticky coating in the back of the throat, tonsils and tongue.

Port: Back of throat and tongue

Characteristics: Urges repetitive and/or obsessive behavior. Could be practically anything. Works closely with Fear and Self-Condemnation, but also Lust. Performance of the desired behavior results in a desperately needed endorphin release by the Jezebel, Psyphon and the Lust – but it gets increasingly more difficult to achieve. As with any drug, the demons on the victim will require increasing levels of obedience to get the desired biological response – which THEY tell you that you HAVE to have or you'll die. People with this one get itchy and start having withdrawal-type symptoms if you disrupt whatever it is they are obsessive about. (See "Monk" TV show or "Rain Man" movie.) Some drugs can really open up this doorway – like Meth and Cocaine.

Removal: You need to be fasted up for this one. Rip and toss. Seal over wound with the Blood. Reverse any physical damage – probably to the throat, tonsils, sinuses or tongue. May be brain chemical damage from medication to "control" it or from drugs that introduced it.

Cautions: Always remember that it's not the victim that is the problem, it's the demons that have been ruling them. This one is a complex, coordinated attack, but the Obsessive-Compulsive is the one that opens the door more than any other. I don't know if you can expect it to stay gone if you don't handle the Lust and the Fear and the Self-Condemnation. They HAVE to learn to take captive every thought and ask if what they are about to do brings glory to Christ. If not, they need to rebuke it instantly, even if it's their OWN thought! Look for generational curses. This is the counterfeit of a true Gift of Administration. Folks with a detail focus and organizational skill for small details are needed, but it has to be the real thing, not the Obsessive counterfeit.

Frequency: Increasing in America. Often can become it's own religious spirit. That's why the Lord cautioned against vain repetition and meaningless mantras that open the door to this AND combine it with religion.

Mischief

Description: Only seen a couple times. Usually around the hands, but sort of transient, like a fast shadow. Like it hands you a knife and tells you who to stab, but convinces you it's just a joke and they'll like it.

Port: Mostly seen around the hands.

Characteristics: Can be small or large. Just wants to cause trouble and stir things up. May convince someone to do something that sounds like a funny practical joke, but is actually very hurtful or insensitive or outright dangerous to life and limb.

Removal: Identify and stop before it gets moving. Rip and toss. Preferably make it hurt so it won't come back around too much.

Cautions: It's a fast mover. It likes to get you to do something before you can stop to think about it. Be deliberate, avoid idle words, pray about everything and let the Lord direct all your paths. Don't be hurried into any action that doesn't feel right. The Lord rarely speaks with that kind of urgency.

Frequency: Not really on a person as much as transitionally around. If they give it a home, I suppose it would get entrenched and stay around more. I've never seen a person with one embedded. Who could stand them?!

Familiars

Description: These are typically invited, welcomed demons that are actively used and consulted and they teach and train and direct. This is full-on witchcraft when it's conscious and intentional. (It's still witchcraft – even in Christians – when it's just control and manipulation, but you aren't on a friendly, first-name basis with the demons that are telling you what to do. But that doesn't mean that they are any less in control of you.) Looks the same as the Witchcraft grizzly bear. It's not a different demon at all, it's just that if it's a familiar, you are more aware that it's there and want it and welcome it. In fact, any or all of your ports can be filled with "familiars" if you've invited them, got upgrades to the strongest one you can find, like them and use them.

Port: Same port as Witchcraft – at the back of the neck/head. (Typically.)

Characteristics: If it is trying to stay hidden, it will have to operate in subtle ways and make you think it's YOU being controlling and manipulative. If it's a familiar and you invited it because you want the power and authority and direction it can give, then it doesn't have to hide at all. It can talk to you directly as an independent entity, tell you its name, what it does, what it wants you to do, operate through you, speak in demonic tongues and cast spells and curse – whatever.

Removal: You can slice them off and cast them down, but the person will likely go get another one. But as an offensive move against witches and warlocks, it's very effective. They will either be forced to rely on a lesser familiar or will be out of commission until they recruit another. It may free them enough for God to get through to them. Or may show them that they're on the wrong team.

Cautions: If you start messing with true Familiars on occultists, you're in the big leagues. If you start trying to slice them off of witches and warlocks, you better be squeaky clean and ready to fight whatever comes. Be very prayed up and stay that way. Keep your house and family covered at all times. They will fight back. (In the spirit and in the natural.)

Frequency: Very common, even in churches. Full out satanists have infiltrated the leadership of most Christian organizations. Some very sincere people have Familiars and don't even know it. Generational curses or family history of occultism can place Familiars on children from birth. Dedication to idols or directly to satan can also do it. Free-Mason membership may also do it – including any of the associated organizations (Eastern Star, DeMolay, Shriners, etc.). These ARE NOT safe for Christians! I don't want to argue with you about it, God has sent me to pray against too many Masonic temples for you to convince me differently. It's a very old Babylonian mystery religion that has a worldwide influence and is a big part of the badness that's coming for us. REPENT!

PLEASE!! LISTEN TO ME!! If you adopt a kid from China (or somewhere else), DO NOT go to a Buddhist Temple and have the priests or monks pray for them!!! Good grief!! Are you goofy?! That's not our God!! It's NOT cute! It's NOT OK! This isn't a matter of being culturally sensitive – that's a false religion to a foreign god! If you do adopt a kid that you think has been prayed for or dedicated like that, break that curse off immediately in the Name of Jesus and don't let that stuff come into your house. They're in your family line now on your land, so they are going to be subject to your headship and you have authority to sever any old family stuff. But be sure you're not replacing a Chinese generational curse with an American generational curse! Make sure YOU are squeaky clean first. My daughter was adopted at 3 1/2 years old from China and was untouchable and uncontrollable until we got her home and delivered her of a whole bunch of nasty stuff. Radical behavioral changes resulted nearly instantly – especially with fear and obedience and mischief and obsessive behavior. The very next day she got dressed and held our hand and behaved and we went to church and dedicated her to God. (Even so, it's still a fight with her until she's old enough to accept Jesus and keep her own doors shut.) If you've been into witchcraft, or were when your kids were young, but now God's got you, go back and make sure you've scrubbed down your whole bloodline – physical AND spiritual children. Make sure every soul tie is broken and all generational curses are cleaned off. Get the idols and dragons and phoenix's and religious symbols all out of your house. Even if you think it's just cultural, it's not – these are idols and religious symbols with power and this is worship of a foreign god and the Lord really hates that. Cleanse your temple!

Drills

Description: Drill

Port: Probably on the "cup" – not sure about a "natural" port. Could be used against any closed door over a port. A desperate attempt to force entry.

Characteristics: Used to penetrate armor (break into a sealed cup).

Removal: Rip and toss. No resistance or defense that we have seen. Reverse or reseal whatever it did. Check for physical damage (like in the heart or deafness or blindness). Sooner or later, these will definitely affect your "walk" – physically, emotionally and spiritually.

Cautions: Sometimes sort of like the sacrificial pawn in a chess game used to get things into position for a bigger kill. Watch for the strategy in play, not just the presence of the thing.

Frequency: Rare. (Thus far.)

Bitterness

Description: Black cloud (haven't seen it more specifically as yet) – One of us sees it as gross, disfigured hunchback that wraps you in chains. Doesn't particularly do anything, just binds you up in chains.

Port: Gall bladder usually

Characteristics: Tries to keep unforgiveness alive so that you won't be forgiven by God either. (Matt. 18:35)

Removal: Recognize, repent, rip and toss, cover in the Blood. Keep the door shut. Replace with forgiveness.

Cautions: They need to REALLY get it and really lay it down all the way. May require personal follow-up with those that were harmed or who harmed host. May require substantial repentance. Take care of any physical symptoms, as the Lord allows. Also look for Witchcraft/Control and Fear and Wings.

Frequency: Very common. How could we have 37,000+ denominations and endless church splits without this?!

Slimers

Description: Layers of goo

Port: All over

Characteristics: Purpose is to disrupt communication with God. Results in heaviness and more "static" in the connection with God. Feels gross and stinky. Like a wet, dirty, acid rain, thick fog.

Removal: Hose off with the Blood of Jesus.

Cautions: Get ALL residue off. Look for whatever is spitting it at the person and deal with that as well. Usually a Confusion octopus type thing that is nearby, but not ported up. Usually bigger than a personal-sized one.

Frequency: Pretty rare. An attack against someone that isn't otherwise vulnerable internally. Frequency will probably increase as more people are well armored and sealed.

Wedges, Plugs, Scales

Description: Practically inert demonic blockages that are used to clog up hearing, vision or other faculties or defenses. May be jammed into armor to widen a smaller opening. May be wedged under the lid of a cup to allow access for other things

Port: Anywhere – ears, heart, eyes, brain, legs, hands, etc.

Characteristics: It's a demon, but it's not really even sentient (that we can tell). It's like it's just a brain-dead tool like a door stop or a paper weight. Something else probably has to run by and insert it or jam it into place.

Removal: Rip and toss. No resistance or defense that we have seen. Reverse or reseal whatever it did. Check for physical damage (like in the heart or deafness or blindness). Sooner or later, these will definitely affect your "walk" – physically, emotionally and spiritually. Check to see if they've cracked a hole in a cup or a shield or pried up a lid.

Cautions: Sometimes sort of like the sacrificial pawn in a chess game used to get things into position for a bigger kill. Watch for the strategy in play, not just the presence of the thing. What are they after?

Frequency: More common than we might think – particularly ear plugs and eye scales. It may be one of the only things to use against someone VERY strong who has all the ports well guarded.

Self-pity

Description: See Loneliness/Despair (p.13)

Port: Hides behind the heart.

Characteristics: Haven't seen it (as yet) as a separate entity than the Loneliness/Despair. When the Despair is working with the Self-Condemnation you get the effect of Self-Pity, but it's really the two working together.

Removal: See respective demons.

Cautions: See respective demons. Don't expect that dealing with one component is going to stop it.

Frequency: Very common. Look for Abuse scars and Wings. Maybe also be some inverted lusts– like anorexia.

Barnacles

Description: Barnacles - like a whole bunch of big ticks.

Port: All over. Like a slimer.

Characteristics: Sort of parasites that suck and reproduce. Tries to clog up hearing and break communication with God by smothering. Result is a feeling of increasing heaviness and distance from God – but also saps energy.

Removal: Hose off with the Blood of Jesus.

Cautions: Get ALL residue. Look for whatever is spitting it at the person and deal with that as well.

Frequency: Very rare. An attack against someone that isn't otherwise vulnerable internally. Frequency will probably increase as more people are armored and sealed. Watch for the strategy in play.

Guilt

Description: We know it's out there, but we haven't seen it yet enough to describe it as an independent entity.

Port:

Characteristics: I believe it's a compound effect of several others – Self-Condemnation, Self-Pity, Fear.

Removal: Address each individual stronghold.

Cautions: There are certainly larger ones of the non-personal sized variety. Some religions are governed by the principality of Guilt – particularly the Catholics and the Jews. It self-reinforces by a constant emphasis on works in order to clean the slate, but an expectation of the constant need to continue doing so endlessly.

Frequency: Very common.

Hate

Description: A combined effect of a number of things if seen on a person regularly. Like all the dials are pegged at once. Pride, Fear, Lust, Loneliness, Bitterness, etc. Like the Jezebel just turns them all to "High" at the same time.

Port: Could be anywhere, but usually visible in the eyes or a "mask" over the face.

Characteristics: Wants to do damage – LOTS of damage – and inflict pain. Self-seeking.

Removal: Bind up the Jezebel first, then the Witchcraft. Slow everything down and start putting up your own shield extra beefy. Don't let it suck you into a response in anger. Start covering everything in the Blood and listen to God really well. Speak Peace over the whole situation.

Cautions: There is also a much larger, transient one that can come and take over – like in a riot or mob situation when the crowd just flips out at a referee or the opposing team. Heightened emotional states and not making slow, deliberate, prayerful decisions make it easier for this one to get in and throw a punch with your own hand before you even know it. There is a Principality of Hate that is seen over some groups or cities or nations (or religions) – they have made it their god.

Frequency: More common all the time. Killer, bloody video games and movies help objectify people so we have less restraint and think of them as objects that can be hurt without consequences. It's conditioning. Increasing worldwide – especially against Christians.

Murder

Description: An overwhelming desire to do serious and permanent damage immediately to another life.

Port: don't know or multiple

Characteristics: We've seen this as a transient mid-level demon that comes and oppresses for a particular reason, but we haven't seen this on a person as a regular state of being. That is, we've seen it show up and contort someone's face up and glare through their eyes, but we haven't seen it ported up. More likely it's a combined effect of a

Witchcraft/Control, a Lust, a Fear, a Pride and other things all dialed up really high. It could be a self-preservation lie to eliminate someone that has or could harm you. That's still Witchcraft because it fails to trust God to be your defender. We might have more experience with the personal-sized one if we had been doing more prison ministry. We have seen it on a really vicious German Shepherd and rebuked it off with instant results. Animals can have familiars, too. Usually from abuse.

Removal: Name it and rebuke it and rip and toss it. Cover in the Blood. May require prayer and fasting depending on its size. As with Hate, there is also a much larger, transient one that can come and take over – like in a riot or mob situation when the crowd just flips out at a referee or the opposing team. Heightened emotional states and not making slow, deliberate, prayerful decisions make it easier for this one to get in and do something crazy before you even know it. All of a sudden you just ran over your husband and didn't even know it! There is a Principality of Murder that is seen over some groups or cities or nations (or religions) – they have made it their god.

Cautions: Very, very dangerous. Listen well and obey instructions.

Frequency: Increasing worldwide – especially against Christians. Praise God! We're getting more like Jesus!

Anger

Description: A compound effect of Witchcraft/Control, Lust, Jezebel, Psyphon and Fear. Maybe Loneliness, too.

Port: don't know or multiple

Characteristics: Can manifest as passive or active. Silent sabotage or frontal assault. Either way grieves God.

Removal: Identify and cover in the Blood,

Cautions: Much like Hate and Murder, there are large ones over groups or cities or religions. Some cultures just seem to have more Anger waiting to boil up at any moment.

Frequency: Very common and getting more so all the time. Sadly, all too common in the church.

Cannibalism

Description: Pretty much says it all, doesn't it?

Port: don't know or multiples   (The Lord says in the teeth. But I've never seen it.)

Characteristics: We've never seen a personal-sized one, but did deal with a larger flying African one that was city/tribe sized. It's a specialist and works with Lust and others. Biblically it is one of the most nasty things God will force on you if you disobey Him – Deuteronomy 28. We do have it in America as evidenced by a whole host of serial killers and satanic blood drinkers and obsessions with vampires. Present in other societies and cultures as well.

Removal: Much prayer and fasting. Identify, seek the Lord, do as you're told.

Cautions: Look for all the other doorways that are probably wide open, including Abuse scars. Watch out for Hate and Murder and Lust. Get armored up all the way and take all your angels with you. (May manifest spiritually in the ripping and tearing of our own sheep to feed ourselves. See Ezekiel 34.)

Frequency: No idea.

Physical Illness Attacks

Description: Black clouds or masses or Pain demons on, in or over particular organs.

Port: Whatever is sick and being attacked.

Characteristics: This is a spiritual attack that is having physical manifestations. How it might manifest depends on the organ or place of assault. It could be shutting it down or eating it or dissolving it or cutting holes it in or whatever. Could be acute or dull. The acute ones are a lot easier to see and easier to remove. The chronic pain has probably gained a lot of legal ground and has been accepted and the host is used to it and resigned to it. The person with an immediate acute pain is more likely to want you to rebuke it and believe that it will go. We're such stupid sheep – if you just dial it up slowly we'll learn to live with it.

Removal: Identify, build faith, rip and toss, cover in the Blood. Pray about reversing physical damage already done.

Cautions: Listen really well. It may be a refining that you shouldn't get in the way of. Check for generational or other curses and open soul ties. Make sure that you know what the Lord wants done.

Frequency: Very common in America since we depend on Man to heal us and not God. Since we are a Christian nation going our own way and not obeying God, He says that all the diseases of Egypt – and new ones that He will invent – will stick to us and no one will be able to heal us. Thus we give the enemy more and more room to afflict us and see fewer and fewer miracles.

Death

Description: Black cloud over a residence – or a persons cup with black stuff in it.

Port: Could be over a specific part that has died – necrotic tissue or dead limb – or over the whole person as an indication that it's coming for them. Sometimes a spirit over places, like funeral homes and retirement homes – and some institutional churches. Once saw, in the spirit, piles and piles of dead, rotting bodies with demons eating them stacked up in the gymnasium of a Spirit-filled ministry here in Kansas City. They were the souls of the people in the pews that think they are just fine, but they're really dead. They can fall down and giggle, but they can't repent for anything. (See Ezekiel 9 and the Red Dragon info in Appendix B) The whole place had a spirit of Death over it.

Characteristics: Not necessarily unavoidable, depending on how much ground it has taken. Prayer and fasting is required usually to push this one back. Find out if it's from God and His will, in which case, don't resist it. If it's their time, let them go home. If the enemy is trying to take something that doesn't belong to him, then snatch it out of his grip.

Removal: Listen to the Lord and do whatever He tells you. Pray hard.

Cautions: Make sure you're fully cleaned out and armored up. Make sure your house is well covered.

Frequency: We're living in a giant tent full of dead bodies (Numbers 19). If the Tribulation is coming (or here) then we're going to see 2/3 of the world die and there's really no stopping it. Better learn how to handle this one without it getting on you.

We'll update this as we learn more.

Reminder: This is NOT a summary of what OTHER people say in their books. I'm only writing about stuff that I've personally faced either alone or as part of a team.

BIG ONES WE'VE SEEN OR FACED

Full descriptions and stories about these are beyond the scope of this book. This is mainly focused on personal deliverance so that people can walk free. Regional and group deliverance is a lot more advanced and it would be better if God explained it to you Himself. He's probably raised up lots of people that have been doing that already without anyone else explaining it to them. This isn't about us, it's all about Jesus..

Congregation / Group / Building Sized:

- Sloth / Lethargy
- Division / Faction
- Witchcraft / Control
- Mammon (Love of Money)
- Fear
- Lust
- Loneliness / Despair
- Pride
- Jezebel
- Competition / Recognition
- Murder
- Pharmakaeia (Drugs)
- Death
- Antichrist
- (and others)
-

City Sized:

- Sloth / Lethargy
- Fear
- Loneliness
- Murder
- Witchcraft
- Love of Money
- Stupor
- Lust
- Pride
- Mammon
- Pharmakaeia
- Mocking / Mimic
- Death
- Antichrist
- (and others)

State / Province / Regional Sized:

- Sloth / Lethargy
- Witchcraft / Control
- Love of Money
- Lust
- Destruction
- Fear
- Mammon

Country Sized:

- Ruling Principalities

Mega Sized, Head Honchos:

- **Mammon**
  Compound demon - a bull and a bear. The bull is an empty illusion, the bear is where all the money is.
- **Abortion**
- **The Goetia (look it up)**
- **Satan**
- (and others)

When the Lord shows me and says to, I diagram out the twin pairs of major (outer) and minor (inner) triads over a city.

HOUSTON, TX

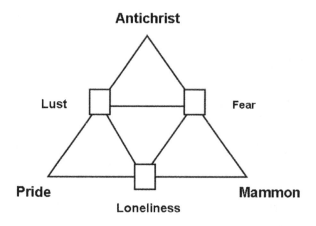

NASHVILLE, TN

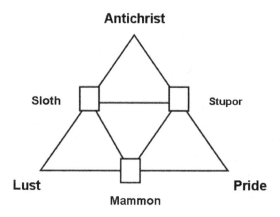

DEMONIC STRATEGIES

Bait and Switch

Description: There are lots of deliverance ministries that will have you fill out a questionnaire ahead of time so that they can tell by your own self-revelation what demons are messing with you. OK, I have a Psychology degree and ANYBODY with any sense at all should be able to tell you that if you let someone with lying spirits SELF-DIAGNOSE you're not going to get any usable information! Give me a break! And they are ALL lying spirits! That's what they DO – all the time. I don't know who started this method of demonic identification, but I'm pretty sure some demon whispered it in somebody's ear and it took root.

I'll tell you exactly what will happen. If you haven't bound up everything on them ahead of time, they will let you get a bead on SOMETHING so that you will feel like you accomplished something – maybe a fear or a seduction or a lethargy. The lying spirits will use the "Sacrificial Lamb" strategy to give you something, but it won't be anything really big and really deep and it won't be something that is likely that they will be able to keep the doors shut well enough that the enemy will permanently lose that ground.

Are you getting this? Why would you have someone with a demon tell you what demons they have – and you're just going to believe them? This is a war! The enemy is sneaky! If you're not hearing God really well – and preferrably SEEING the bad guys for yourself – then you're just going to have to take the word of the person that you KNOW needs deliverance.

Can you see the problem there? If you can't walk up to a person that you've never met, never spoken with and know nothing about and immediately diagnose the things on them and start getting them off, then you're not really ready for war. Pray hard and ask the Lord for a LOT more discernment and to hear His voice a lot better. I'm not trying to be harsh and I don't mean to belittle the success and effort of all the folks that are trying hard – I'm just trying to raise the bar and tell you that Jesus NEVER had someone fill out a questionnaire! And neither should we if we want to be like Him. Ask to see through the eyes of Jesus, not through the eyes of a 50 question survey.

Solution: Pray for more discernment and more accuracy. Do whatever you have to do to get your pipeline unclogged so that you can hear God really, really well. Don't just blast away in the dark at anything that pops its head up for a moment. And understand that the really dangerous stuff, the brains behind the operation, will probably NEVER pock its head up so you can get a clear shot at it.

Flare and Duck

Description: This is probably the most common one used against people doing deliverance. We're such suckers! It's sort of like the Bait and Switch. What they will do is that when it's clear that someone is going to do deliverance on the host, one or more demons will make a big fuss – they'll scream and shake and spit and cough, maybe even throw up or curse or something really showy. Then, at the moment for best effect, they'll duck and hide so that you think you got them off. They might lay low for a few minutes or for days or weeks. Then, when you let your guard down, they will flare up again at the moment that will do most harm to the faith of the host – and hopefully the deliverance minister. Then accusations will fly, that they didn't keep the doors shut and it came back worse or that they were never really delivered in the first place – or even that this one is too tough to get off and they'll just have to live with it! The result is frustration, hurt feelings, division and maybe even more pain and suffering than before! And the demons just laugh and laugh and laugh.

The real problem is that the person doing deliverance didn't SEE the bad guys well enough to know if they were really gone. And they weren't really gone probably because the deliverance minister didn't have proper authority to get them off. Maybe they themselves had a lust problem – and didn't have legal authority to get a lust off of someone else. Maybe they weren't standing before God cleaned out and had things against a brother that they should have settled before they came to the altar to offer sacrifices to help another.

I have seen this repeatedly when I've been around people that were delivered by this or that ministry. The person didn't even mention what they had been delivered from, but I still saw it there, crouched down and hiding, waiting for just the right moment to pop back out and wreck something. They weren't fully delivered – or were, but couldn't keep the door shut all the way. But without hearing God well enough to ask "Did I get it all?" and KNOW that you're getting a reliable answer – or seeing the bad guys – you're just going to have to go on how they are ACTING. And that is the worst of all possible kinds of feedback, because the DEMONS are dictating the feedback that you get – and they're liars. And really good ones, at that.

Solution: Make sure you have FULL authority and legal ground over whatever you're going after and make sure that you're hearing God really well and letting Him direct your paths and methods. Preferably, you're seeing the demons really well so you can tell if they are still there or not. You'll also need to brief the person about what to expect and check in regularly to make sure they're not sneaking back in.

Sacrificial Lamb

Description: They will offer up something that is relatively inconsequential, in order to keep the truly dangerous strongholds. They'll self-reveal or manifest something that seems like a big deal and seems like it requires urgent attention (and it may well), but the other things will duck for cover and hope they don't get noticed. This often leaves things like the Witchcraft and the Jezebel and the Psyphon and others completely unnoticed and untreated. But we took care of the Stress or the Fear or the Gossip! But they won't stay gone as long as the root command and control structures are still place.

Solution: Get them squeaky clean and hear God well enough or see the bad guys well enough to know that they are truly clean. Don't listen to the demons or to the person about what requires attention first. Listen to God and He will direct your paths. There may be something that is in the way that keeps them from being able to be delivered at all. Usually a Dad Filter or an unforgiveness or something that will keep the Lord from coming to their rescue. Teach them to keep their cup so full of Jesus that nothing else can fit.

Divide and Conquer

Description: Some of the demons will "shed" or split into pieces or do whatever they can to leave a residue in place that can regrow and retake the ground. I don't know how it works, that's just the way the Lord shows it to me. The dragons especially are very sneaky and will shed scales or break into pieces and regrow, like pulling the tail off of a lizard.

Solution: Listen to God and get a countdown. "Lord, did I get 100% of it?" Nope, 92%. Then go find the leftovers and scrub it all out. It may be that the person is holding on to a piece of it and won't let go. That is particularly true of someone that has an entrenched compound Lust (say porn, crack and cigarettes) and they want to be delivered of the crack but they really like the porn and the cigarettes. You might as well not bother. It's all part of one Lust doorway. If you don't shut it all the way, it's not really going to result in holiness. If they're not going to lay it all down, then what's the point really? (Do whatever the Lord says. He may need it to be gradual.)

Redundant Backups

Description: You need to understand that the enemy has been at this a long time and doesn't want to give up a single inch of ground. The Jezebel is the main command and control center, but the Psyphon can handle it all if the Jezebel is removed or bound up. Fear is a powerful stronghold, but the Psyphon carries a backup with it. Other things, like Loneliness and Bitterness and Lust can all mimic each other and overlap so that one can pick up where another leaves off. If a person has ANY open doorways, whatever has access will try to "morph" and crack open the other doors from the inside so that the others can come back.

Solution: You need to get completely and totally cleaned off and armored up. Things will still try, but you have to take captive EVERY thought and keep moving forward taking the ground until the enemy doorways are all closed. The hardest to remove are often the ones that hide the best and look the most harmless. (Particularly Loneliness is far more dangerous than we realize.)

Merry Go Round

Description: In this one, multiple demons will manifest in sequence to keep you off balance and keep you from getting a bead on what the real issue is. Some may curse or blaspheme or spit up or get seductive or something. Some will speak in other languages. But they'll keep moving so no single one can be targeted. They like to show off, so if you allow it, they'll make a big presentation out of the whole thing. My experience is that this GREATLY diminishes around people who have lots of authority and see the bad guys. In those cases, mostly they just lay low. You don't HAVE to scream and yell and hack and cough and curse when you get deliverance. Typically that kind of showboating should be stopped immediately by the person doing deliverance.

Solution: Handle them one at a time and assume that there may be multiple "personalities" involved. Deal with them individually, one stronghold at a time. Understand that the master command and control center is what is organizing a coordinated attack like this. So bind up the Jezebel and Psyphon first and they will have a lot harder time coordinating their responses. Then pick them off one at a time.

Suppression

Description: The goal is to stop whatever good is happening or about to happen. If they can't just twist it outright or put a stop to it, then they'll try to suppress it somehow. One of the most common is with lethargy – sleepiness. You'll see a pastor preaching and it's great and affecting lives and you look over to the person you brought to hear it and they can't seem to keep their eyes open. Afterwards they can't even remember what was said. Things could be suppressed by a person constantly bringing up side issues and diverting the conversation to some pointless "rabbit trail." But they burned the clock until time ran out and what needed to be said didn't get said. Other ways to suppress include confusion or garblers so people end up offended at a misspoken word and miss the whole point of the teaching.

More to come, I'm sure.

I don't want to give any impression that I know or have seen it all. This is an ongoing curriculum with all of us!

CONCERTED DEMONIC ATTACKS

Fog

Essentially just a blockage to keep you from hearing God. Like throwing flack up into the sky hoping to hit an attacking airplane or lighting fires on the ground to create smoke to obscure a target. Like a jamming signal or static noise on radio transmissions. It's intent is to block out the sun (Son) so you can't get a clear signal from Headquarters. The solution is just to burn through it with a really focused beam of prayer. Just press in really hard and ask the Lord to clear it away or cut through it. Praying in tongues works best.

Musical Chairs - (Tag)

We've seen this one repeatedly, especially on little kids. Basically, demons are manifesting or speaking through a person and you're ripping them off, but it doesn't seem like you're getting anywhere. The goal of this kind of attack is to wear out the victim and the person doing the deliverance. Especially to get you to doubt that you have authority and that you're getting anywhere. What happens is that the enemy sort of plays "musical chairs" by rotating through the open port at a high speed. That is, one will jump on and start manifesting and hop off real fast and another will take their place and manifest in a similar way. If you grab one and crush it and cast it down, there's another right behind it that looks just like it, so it doesn't seem like you're getting anywhere. They accelerate the pace and urgency of everything so you can't slow down and hear the Lord well. They are perfectly willing to sacrifice lots of their own in an effort to keep the victim or to demoralize the deliverance expert.

If you command the victim in the name of Jesus Christ to tell you who is in charge, they will speak the name of the demon that is then controlling at the moment, but it will continue to rotate. You need to listen to whatever comes out of their mouth first when you ask that – and don't expect that a demon has to have a name like "Fred". Sometimes it's a guttural sound like a grown or growl, sometimes it's just a vowel like "Oo". The most annoying (to me) is that there are demons named "Mommy" and "Jesa Christ" and all kinds of variants that sound like Jesus Christ. Also, understand that they are not unique. I have crushed and cast down MANY demons named "Mommy" - but never the same individual twice. Don't get demoralized if you believe you cast down "Mommy" but they are saying that "Mommy" is in charge again. It's not necessarily the same demon. (Momi, Mahmi, Mahmmi, etc. See how sneaky they are?! They don't play by our rules!) Under NO circumstances should you stop doing deliverance if you ask who is Lord and they say, "God is." Technically just about ANYTHING can count as "god". It's hard to capitalize things out loud.

There is ONE name under heaven by which we are saved – "Jesus Christ is Lord" is the right answer (unless God clearly endorses some very close variant as being sufficient – don't get legalistic.). You need to keep pulling stuff off until they give the right answer – and it's clear and distinct, but mostly you have to keep pressing through until the LORD says that you're done. If you can't hear God, you're going to just have to hope you can outsmart or outlast the demons (and that's a real long-shot!). When confronted with a revolving attack like this, start looking for why the port or doorway is open and what you need to do to shut it so that the flow can be stopped. Something is letting them whip through there unhindered. Probably a generational curse or an illegal soul tie to someone else. In the case of kids, it's nearly always something that the parents are doing that is in direct disobedience to God or a generational portal that the parent(s) still have open. You need to sever the illegal soul tie or break the generational curse (and cover it in the blood of Jesus), so that the portal slams shut and the attacks from that direction are cut off.

If a person undergoing this kind of attack does NOT know Jesus, they may never get to a place where they can spontaneously say Jesus Christ is Lord. Truthfully, every time we have dealt with this kind of attack it was on someone that does know Jesus. Christians are NOT immune to attacks from the enemy! How you can get a non-believer to this point, I don't know exactly. I suspect that they are so oppressed that when you get all the stuff off, they'll be fully convinced that they need Jesus and will be happy to declare Him Lord! There is no way for them to keep the doors shut and keep the ports closed without the Blood of Jesus. Willpower will NOT keep you from having these things come back seven times worse. Only the Blood and being filled with the Holy Spirit and walking in holiness can give you what you need to guard the gates well enough.

Black Hurricane

This is essentially a Musical Chairs attack escalated to a gigantic level. It may look like a giant black tornado or hurricane funnel cloud (or dark rain storm) swirling around the target, which could be a person, a business, a congregation, or a city. It just looks like a black hurricane, but you can't get any detail because of the massive scale of the attack. If you "zoom in" and get a closer look, you'll see that the "rain drops" are actually individual flying demons all in formation creating this devastating force by their unity. (It's really a shame that demons can work together so much better than Christians!)

This is a massive assault and we've only seen it once or twice. It requires tens of thousands of demons that have all stopped whatever else they were doing so as to work together on this attack. It creates a weight and an oppression that is practically impossible to describe. I don't think any person could survive it. Only by the Blood of Jesus can we war against the forces of darkness, and this is a great example of our desperate need if the enemy decides to gang up on us in a frontal assault kind of a way.

There is no way to individually grab them and squish them and cast them down fast enough. It's like taking a bath towel out into a rain storm and trying to dry your car off before another drop hits it. This attack is going to require a massive offense. A defensive maneuver like putting up a tougher shield will help, but is not a long term solution. They have to learn that you're on to them and that you are capable of thwarting this kind of attack – or else they'll just keep coming until you're squashed.

The first time I faced this one, the weight was unbearable but I was with a group of brethren who could also see what was happening – but were told by God not to help me (I had to learn how to handle it alone). They helped bear the burden and could advise, but couldn't directly assault the hurricane themselves. I couldn't get focused on anything and the noise of all these demons screaming and blocking out the Son was keeping me from hearing God about what to do next. I launched a giant spinning Sword of the Holy Spirit offensive into the hurricane long enough to slow it down so I could get some clarity. A sister felt to read a verse from Revelation 6 about the angels that stood at the four corners of the earth restraining the winds. The Lord was using this to show me not to fight this in my own power, but to rely on Him. So I requested four BIG angels to stand at the corners and restrain the wind. They flapped their wings in the direction opposite to the rotation of the hurricane and it stopped spinning and then retreated and dissipated. (It's so much easier when you just ask Him to fight your battles!!)

I'm not suggesting that is the only way to handle it, that's just what He showed me at the time. I know it works, so if you're under this kind of attack and can't hear God well enough or no one is around to help, ask the Lord if you can do that. I would prefer to have just incinerated them all and cast them en masse to the Abyss – and probably could now – but I wasn't strong enough at the time for anything but a defensive response. (Eventually we did deal with all those demons as a group.)

Create a Lid

One of the curses in Deuteronomy 28 for going your own way is that there will be "brass over your head." One way to understand that is that the heavens will not be open to you, your prayers will not be heard. I have seen demons pack tightly and form a sort of "lid" over the city that would make it harder and harder for true prayers for revival to get through. Think of it like a large stone disk like what the enemy used to try to keep Jesus in the tomb. The enemy will use whatever resources are necessary to build a sort of shield to block prayers. The right solution is simply to jack-hammer away at it with your prayers until it's just rubble. That happens by concerted intercessory prayer – hopefully from as many people as possible, until there is an open heaven. Don't let them get in the way between you and your Dad!

Yeah, I know, it's hard for <u>me</u> to believe I'm saying stuff like this, too. This is a LONG way from my Southern Baptist roots, believe me. But I know it's real. I felt the effects of it, I saw it and others with me were seeing the same things. It's just real common for those of us who have "poured" our spiritual gifts back and forth into each other to have the same Discernment of Spirits – to see the enemy through the same lens. And it works really well and there are lots of folks that are free because of this and walking in holiness and victory. So I'm not really trying to make excuses, I'm just acknowledging that I'm well aware of how crazy this sounds. But the Bible is clear that our battle is NOT against flesh and blood but against power and prinicipalities and wickedness in high places. You can de-spiritualize it if you like, but He's talking about demons of all shapes and sizes – and they are real and they are nasty and they work together REALLY well. We need to know our enemy. That's what I prayed for and that's what I got. (Thanks, Lord!) Ultimately, I can't really care what <u>you</u> think of me, I just have to please my Dad.

Empty-White-Space-Filler Personal Story

A dear, sweet sister came into the furniture store one time. She didn't even know why she was there – the car just drove itself. I talked with her for awhile and prayed with her. I wasn't getting too much to do specifically, but I knew she had issues. This sister came back a week or so later and let me know that when she had come in the first time she had been hearing voices, couldn't keep a job, was on medication for schizophrenia, was hearing voices tell her to kill herself and other people, and was at the end of her rope. All her relationships were unraveling and she was living with her sick mom. She came back in to thank me because she was off her meds, full of Jesus, not hearing voices and just about to get a great new job as a paralegal and preparing to complete the Bar exam she'd had to put aside years before when this had started. Praise God! He did it, not me. But this <u>is</u> for real. There was so much praying going on in the furniture store during that period that some people would hack and cough up black stuff and get deliverance as soon as they walked in the door!

HUMAN ATTACKS

Astral Projection

Description: When a person's soul leaves their body and travels elsewhere to spy or to curse or attack.

Characteristics: This is a common element of witchcraft and meditation of all kinds. This is FOR REAL. There are surely fakers and posers, but this is absolutely for real. Witches and satanists (and others, but they're all ultimately satanists no matter what you call it cause there's only two choices) use soul-force to enter an altered state where their "soul-man" can travel outside of their body connected by the "silver cord" that binds them back to their physical body. We have had them come into homes and manifest as cats or other things that looked like they were there, but weren't really. We have seen them (in the spirit) flying over houses or places where meetings were going on. Sometimes out of curiosity to see what we were doing – or to do harm and place curses. You have to understand that if you're having a really powerful time with God and you're no well cloaked, you're sending up big flares in the spiritual realms. It's like a big beacon, a spotlight of goodness blasting up into the heavens. And the enemy may send somebody to try to stamp it out.

This is a real thing – it is the cheap, knock-off counterfeit to what God can do when He takes someone in the spirit to heaven or elsewhere to give them a vision or dream or see the enemy on a battlefield, etc. There are LOTS of Biblical examples of God picking people up and taking them elsewhere, like John, Philip, Elijah, Daniel, Ezekiel, etc. The difference is that for witches this requires a LOT of effort and will substantially wear them out and tax them. Many die young from being "burnt out" by this kind of stuff. But when the Holy Spirit does it, it doesn't tax any of our resources because it's HIM doing the work. (We may be in bed for weeks because of what we saw, like Daniel, but that's not because of the effort of the trip, it's because of the close encounter with God's bigness. - Daniel 8:27) The enemy will force them to use up their own soulish and physical resources to make this happen, but it IS for real. The brighter your light gets, the more you have Discernment of Spirits, the more likely that you're going to encounter people attacking you by this method, not just demons. Mostly they do it because they suspect that it's a "safe" way to approach Christians and do harm because we're all so dumbed down that we won't see them or catch them. It's far less risk than breaking into your house and planting a fire bomb or some physical attack with legal risks (but you need to watch for that as well). But they're going to need to learn that we're on to them and this isn't going to work anymore.

Defense: Do whatever the Lord tells you. But you may want to make sure that you're shielded from any outside ears hearing what's going on – or cloaked so that nothing of the enemy can even see that you're there. (More on that in the Shields, Spheres and Cloaks section following.) In one instance He had us reel in and trap some witches that were overhead and preach the Gospel to them while some of us read all the verses in the Bible about what God says about witches (and we just happened to have a list handy at that meeting, Thank You, Lord!) They were VERY unhappy, but eventually we let them loose and they took off like a shot. If you are having trouble inside your house with spiritual eavesdroppers or with things moving around or missing, make sure your house is anointed and that you've closed all the doorways that would allow entry. Seek the Lord about any objects that might be opening a door (religious objects, symbols, gifts from others, TV, etc.).

Offense: If, _and_ ONLY _if_, the Lord tells you to – I'm serious here – do you handle them offensively. By "offensively" I mean in keeping with what God's Word says to do to witches (See Appendix F). And I'm talking about SPIRITUAL warfare, not carnal! Our battle is NOT against flesh and blood, but against spiritual wickedness in high place. I'm going to contain myself here to JUST offensive responses to Astral Projection. For my definition, in this case, binding or trapping or preaching to them is really more defensive. The offensive move would be a terminal solution. That is,

God has had enough with that person, none of the preaching is having any effect, and God has given them their last chance – and IF and ONLY IF HE tells you very clearly and in NO uncertain terms – then you cut their silver cord with the Sword of the Spirit. I'm not an expert on what exactly happens next, but I'm sure that you should ONLY do this with MUCH fear and trembling. Basically that soul is lost. My understanding is that if the cord is broken and you can't get back to your body, you're dead. That is confirmed in the Bible in Ecclesiastes 12:6-7. You can find that same diagnosis from any number of witchcraft and new age sites if you go looking. Even Wikipedia - http://en.wikipedia.org/wiki/Astral_projection .

Cautions: If you have people astral projecting against you, REJOICE!! You got somebody's attention! And then get VERY serious and find out what the Lord wants you to do next. Make sure your armor is fully intact and you have no open doorways. Get your house in order and keep it guarded all the time. They'll wait for an opening for you to let down your guard. If you act offensively, expect a backlash – maybe even in the natural.

Curses

Description: Curses can include all kinds of things, including the talk of Christians and family and friends. Our words have power and when we speak things out, that word takes on life. If people wishing you harm or projecting failure or collapse or disgrace, they give those things life. You may even be speaking them over yourself. The more spiritual authority and faith that you have, the more likely that your words are going to have effect. In the case of satanists and witches, they may invoke all kinds of curses and spells against you – whether you know they're doing it or not. On one occasion, the Lord alerted us to a witchcraft session in progress at that moment with bunches of folks in black robes, pentagram on the floor, candles and the whole deal. He instructed us to slice everything off of them, nuke it with the Blood of Jesus and break up their party. This was confirmed by more than one person. In fact, God sent a prophet to the furniture store who had seen the face of the warlock in question. I pulled up a website and sure enough, that was the guy – a major, well-known businessman in Kansas City from a famous, powerful banking family who had been a major spiritual annoyance to us for awhile. This is not your tattoo-covered, angst-filled, Buffy the Vampire Slayer, kid with a magick book and collection of Goth figurines, variety – this is an ivy-league, multi-millionaire, Skull and Bones, international contacts, powerful Familiar, seriously <u>bad</u> guy. I met him in person once at a business event, but he wouldn't shake my hand. I'm not naming him here because it doesn't matter, but he knows who he is and I'm believing that he's going to come to Jesus and lay all his money and stuff down and be a big help to God's kingdom one day soon. I want him free, not dead – and not shackled to satan. I'm not mad at him, I just want him free.

And someone that didn't know him came in and told us that this guy (and his "team") were at that moment cursing us and <u>then</u> identified his picture and confirmed that THAT was the guy God had showed him. So we thrashed them and asked the Holy Spirit to just flood their whole place in the Blood of Jesus. I haven't found out yet what exactly the consequences of all of that were, but I'm sure I will someday. At one point we had someone ritually sacrifice a cat in front of the furniture store, spells, curses, death, disaster, the whole deal. I've had Tarot cards jammed in the back door of my van. I had business cards of psychics placed on the van. I found brownish spit on the van repeatedly. The Lord was always good to alert me when there was a "tag" or a curse of some sort and have me neutralize it. Like a dog peeing on a tree, this kind of stuff is about marking territory and claiming the ground. If we don't claim it back, they get jurisdiction. A big part of my trip to 32 states was reclaiming the ground. I did a lot of anointing and spitting on things myself. (So did Jesus, look it up.)

Characteristics: My advice never really changes, does it? Get armored up, close all the doorways, walk in holiness, hear God really good and do whatever He tells you. And by all means, STOP speaking curses over yourself!! Watch your words and don't bind things. If you say you're stupid and nobody likes you enough times, you'll BE stupid and nobody will like you.

Defense: Keep your house and your cars and yourself anointed as the Lord leads. Don't get "religious" about it, just do whatever He tells you. Sometimes He has sent me to somebody else's house to pray up a bigger shield, just before some major attack on them we didn't see coming. Don't worry. Don't look over your shoulder all the time. Our God is bigger. Just keep your eyes on the Cross and do whatever He tells you.

Offense: Do whatever He tells you. If you find something that is evidence that someone has cursed you – like the cat or the Tarot cards – then bless them. Ask the Lord to deliver them of everything messing with them, slice all their familiars off and cast them to the Abyss, pour every good thing out of your cup into theirs and ask the Lord to fill them so full of Jesus that nothing else can fit. That will REALLY mess with them – but it might just free their mind long enough to repent and come to Jesus. You can fill them full of Jesus without them being saved, it will just drain out eventually. I shook hands with a psychic at the Kansas City Psychic Fair one time and even though he had walked away, in the spirit, he reached out to me so I was still holding onto his hand spiritually. So, as the Lord directed, I sliced everything off and cranked him full of the Blood. Five minutes later he's back with an official from the event to have me thrown out! What fun! So we put a sphere of the Blood of Jesus around the whole thing, cranked it all full of the Spirit, filled it with warrior angels and let them slice and dice all the badness inside. We'll see what happens. They weren't directly attacking me personally, but they were doing harm to my God and my town, so the Lord sent us there by divine appointment to do some damage.

Cautions: Don't freak out. Don't worry. Our God is bigger. Keep your doorways shut, keep your cup full, listen real good and do whatever He tells you. Find some folks to hang with that are full of Jesus and can help defend you or warn you. Don't obsess about this stuff. They can't do anything unless the Lord allows it – and if He allows it, it's only to help you build spiritual muscles so you'll be a big strong warrior for Jesus and bring God glory, not to crush you. (Uh, but you might also want to make sure you don't have a Red Dragon and it's not actually a punishment for going your own way. Deut. 28 says He'll turn you over to other nations.)

Cursed Objects

Description: Something that was used in worship of anything that wasn't Jehovah or something that depicts, symbolizes or exalts something that is a false god. Some occultists and new agers pray over amulets and rocks and crystals and all kinds of things that are supposed to carry good luck or magic or power. If you have a really highly tuned "demon scanner" most major bookstores are just going to set you to buzzing like a four alarm fire – even the Christian sections that have all kinds of idolatry and lies mixed in. But this is specifically about items that are carrying demonic signatures or opening doors.

Characteristics: Could be any kind of object or symbol, jewelry, clothing, art, etc. Might be an item or a gift that was prayed over to impart power to it. This is a real thing. Harry Potter, Pokemon, and lots of others are very bad. Could carry disease or pretty much any kind of demonic oppression on it. Curses could be placed on things of yours, like my van or my furniture store. If those things are not cleaned off, they become "dedicated objects" and "abominations" which is a very bad thing Biblically. See the references in Appendix E.

Defense: Check everything in your house. Have the Lord walk you through room by room and check everything. Remove anything that is questionable or has a demonic signature. I threw away over $10,000 worth of comic books. He wouldn't let me sell them and keep them in circulation, they went in the dumpster – titles included Ghost Rider, Dr. Strange, the Eternals, and lots of others that are all about magic and demons. Be careful about gifts or things you bought at garage sales. One brother had a constant lust for his ex-girlfriend and couldn't get over her and couldn't walk right with the Lord. He knew she was a witch and he still had some things in his house he was storing for her. Those were left there on purpose so that she could maintain a soul tie and control over him. When he pitched them out, he was freed. If you know that an item is cursed, but God says you can keep it (like my van), then claim it, anoint it and cover it in the Blood of Jesus. Pray against any damage they already did – physical harm or embedded oppression. If you need someone stronger to come scan your house, contact whoever the Lord tells you to. I have no idea who is capable in your area, but the Lord will send someone or do it Himself if you're over your head and you ask Him nice – and repent for making this mess.

Offense: Ask the Lord to bless the pants off of whoever cursed you. If it's just a generalized thing, like Pokemon, ask the Lord to crush the whole company and tell all your friends. Stop spending money on witchcraft.

Cautions: Be very careful about accepting gifts. Always check with the Lord. If you receive something from someone, it creates a tie. Even if it's your mom or whatever, always check with the Lord. I don't want even a cash donation from someone that wasn't told by God to give it. I don't want their guilt or their gratitude or their curses or whatever. I just want them to be obedient. Check all objects in your house. Lots of dolls and statuettes and art and things are NOT OK with Him. Get out all of the Harry Potter and Pokemon and YugiOh and masonic stuff and new age stuff and Halloween stuff and anything else the Lord says. Preferably burn it. See Ephesians 19. Don't open doorways with the TV (psychics, mediums, ghosts, dragons and other shows).

Trackers

Description: These are basically cursed objects that are used specifically for the purpose of keeping tabs on someone and knowing their movements.

Characteristics: When they cursed my van, it wasn't necessarily so that I would die in a huge fireball when the engine blew up in traffic, it might have just been so they would know where I was going and who I was talking to. The more dangerous you are, the more the enemy wants to know where you are at all times so that they can spoil whatever you're doing or wherever you're going.

Defense: See "Shields, Spheres and Cloaks" on page 108. Listen well enough to know you've been tagged and ask the Lord what to do. Cover it in the Blood and cancel it in the Name of Jesus.

Offense: Pray that God would bless the snot out of whoever did it. That He would just flood them with His Spirit until it runs out their ears and from under their toenails. That's fun. Sometimes He may also have you feed misinformation or misdirection.

Cautions: Again, we're talking about full-on witchcraft, so you got somebody's attention. It doesn't necessarily require people involved, it could just be the rulers and principalities in the locality you're in, but this is the big leagues. Keep all your doors shut, walk in holiness, stay prayed up. Our God is bigger.

Eavesdroppers

Description: These are like trackers except they listen. They create a portal through which someone can listen in – like two tin cans with a string between them. Or they are recording devices that can be replayed later. They are demonic attachments to items that might be given to you or something you already had that was used for the purpose.

Characteristics: We never did figure out what was being used this way, but we did have an instance where we were being VERY quiet about something we were doing and a brother's wife told us what we were up to. She was dead set against everything God was doing and had been a real enemy to the whole thing (tried to physically kill me with her car at one point). I know that she got the information spiritually, but I'm not even sure if she knew how she had gotten it. We were a lot more careful to stay cloaked and shielded after that.

Defense: Cloaks and shields are the only real defense. You may not see an eavesdropper, it could be a thing or a spirit. You have to just listen to the Lord really well all the time and He'll alert you if it's a problem.

Offense: Same general recipe. Romans 12:20-21. Give your enemy to drink and to eat and that will heap burning coals on his head. Well the best food we have is the Bread of Life and the Living Water so jam them so full they want to throw up and see what happens. Pray sacrificially and with love that God would give them any good thing that you have, if only He would free them – and that will be more likely to break things. Remember the point here is humility and love. You can torture the demons all you want, but with people, we're talking about living souls that might still have a chance to come into the kingdom. I want to be very clear about the difference. Smothering a demon in Jesus is going to hurt. Smothering a person filled with demons in Jesus might hurt the demons on them (who will make a big fuss), but it might just free the person, too.

Cautions: See above. Take this seriously.

Familiars

Description: See "Familiars" elsewhere (p. 28). Pretty much the same thing but on an object – or could be an animal as well. All kinds of purposes and reasons.

Characteristics: Witches often use animals that have familiar spirits. It mostly just means that it's one you know and is working with you. I've seen animals freak out in the presence of spirits. At one sister's house, she's having some time with the Lord and an otherwise pleasant and loving cat jumps up behind her on the sofa and bites her right on the head!

Defense: Keep your house anointed. Be careful about any new things that come into your possession.

Offense: See previous.

Cautions: See previous. Take this VERY seriously. But don't panic. Get help if you need it. If the Lord says to, contact us and we'll do what we can.

Empty-White-Space-Filler Personal Story

When daughter #1 was three and a half years old she started seeing monsters in her room. Before she could write her name or make a circle, she was drawing pictures of big snarly things with teeth and with PERFECT upside down five point stars in their eyes. She couldn't draw a circle, but she could make a half-inch tall perfect satanic star with a crayon! We sure didn't teach her that! This was not imagination, she was seeing demons and the Lord was letting us in on it so we could start anointing the house better and teach her what to do.

She would call out calmly from her room at night,
"Daddy, there are monsters in my room."

"You know what to do, honey."

"In the NAME of JESUS, go AWAY!"

"Are they gone?"

"Yep, they're gone. Good night, Daddy."

And she'd fall right to sleep. This isn't about fear.
This is about <u>confident</u> <u>warfare</u>. And this is real.

(At five she was seeing angels. "Wilbur" taught her how to read in one day before she even started Kindergarten.)

NON-DEMONIC "FILTERS"

Dad Filter (God in a earth dad-shaped box)

Description: A black "hockey puck" looking mass, like a lens on a camera.

Port: So far, always seen in their hip/pelvic area. Usually on the right.

Characteristics: This is in the hip because it affects their "walk" with God. In essence it is a lens through which they look at God that limits Him in some (or many) ways. Usually this cookie-cutter "box" in which they have placed God is shaped like their Earth Dad. **This is one of the most critical things that needs dealing with because so much of the other deliverance they may need hinges on this.** For example, if your father died when you were young and you learned how to be the "man of the house" at a very early age and depend on yourself and your own strength, you probably have a "filter" that says that God is unavailable and you pretty much have to depend on yourself. If your father was abusive, you probably have a filter that says God is a vengeful, angry God waiting to strike you with lightning at the slightest little sin.

The most common one is that people don't believe that God can be Abba Father and pull them up on His knee and speak sweetly to them and kiss their boo-boos because they have absolutely NO experience with an earthly father that is like that. I've seen Dad Filters of all kinds. One young man could not be delivered of the fear and anxiety and other things. When I asked the Lord why, He said, "Because of His Dad Filter." This young man had lost his father at an early age and had been through all kinds of bad things and no one came to his rescue. Deep inside, he didn't really believe God was the kind of Father that would help in his time of need. He knows what the Word says and he tells other people that God will rescue them, but he didn't really believe it for himself. When I named it and showed it to him, he acknowledged it and then I had him repent for putting God in a box like that, then take his Sword of the Spirit and hack that lens into a million pieces. When he did that, the Lord had me pounce on him and give him a huge hug and speak all kinds of loving things to him that the Lord had been UNABLE to say to him because he didn't believe God loved him like that. Then we pulled all the fear and everything off and showed him how to keep his cup full of Jesus all the time. I could NOT do **any** deliverance on him until he stopped believing that he had to do everything in his own power and he laid down his belief that God was not the kind of God that would come and rescue him when he was in trouble. Now, had I not been seeing the demons and hearing God about the Dad Filter, I would have rebuked the Fear and made a lot of noise – and then both he and I might have been demoralized later when it didn't really leave (or didn't stay gone for long). But he gave the Fear legal ground and would have kept giving it legal ground to oppress him until he stopped putting God in a box and started believe that God's power would fight his battles instead of his own. You can't rebuke demons in the name of "Fred" - only the name of Jesus will work! But if you don't believe God will come to your aid, then just keep rebuking them in your name and see how that goes for you.

I have seen this RADICALLY transform people and their walk with God. It's always a bad thing to put God in a box, but particularly a box shaped like a person. Some people I've ministered to had dads that threw them into the trunk of a car with dead cats, or sexually abused them, or invited friends over to sexually abuse them, or were totally unavailable, unreliable, unloving, or otherwise generally a stinker. It's practically unavoidable that a child will look to their father as a hero and put him on a pedestal. It's hard-wired into us and a dad has to do some pretty amazingly awful things to negate that fully. And it's also practically unavoidable that when that kid prays, "Our Father who art in Heaven" that they will have a flavor in their mouth (or flashbacks) to what Earth Dad did to them. The Word says that what we bind on Earth will be bound in Heaven, so if we put limits on God or force Him into a cookie-cutter mold shaped like Earth Dad, God will go along with it. He would really rather you didn't do that, so you can experience the fullness of all He has for you, but He'll take whatever He can get.

Removal: They need to see what they've done. They need to acknowledge that they have put God in a box and say they're sorry. Preferably they really hate it and hunger for more of Him. It's enough for them to pray and acknowledge it before the brethren (even one), but usually I'll have them take their sword of the Spirit and whack it into a million pieces (or some other creative way to destroy that lens). Just so they will have seen it happen in the spirit and can believe in faith that it is done. Usually that results in almost immediate changes in the depth of their relationship with God. The more they have Him bundled up, the more visible the difference will be. We all put Him in a box. If we didn't, then we'd probably BE God. We can't possibly get our heads around how big He is and the depths of the ways that He wants to relate to us. All of us need to regularly check to see if we're limiting Him in any way – and say we're sorry.

Cautions: They need to expect changes in their walk with Him. If it freaks them out and they shove Him back in a box again, that is going to go very badly. They need to keep moving forward, even if it's hard. We've seen people regress substantially when they let God out of a box so He could be more involved in their lives and speak to them more, and then they didn't like what He was asking them to do and they shoved Him back in.

Mom Filter

Characteristics: Probably replaces or impacts the Dad Filter in situations where there was no Dad at all. Have not seen it as a distinct thing but a sort of "coloring" or flavor of the Dad Filter. There are surely lots of impacts and bad doctrines and views of things that affect God and relationships and money – particularly generational curses handed from the Mothers may be in play – but I'm not aware (thus far) of a specific Mom Filter.

Body Filter

Characteristics: A focus on your own body or that of someone else that is based on lies. Like a 90 pound girl standing in front of a mirror and seeing a 300 pound girl. Or a guy that can't look a woman in the eye because he can't take his eyes off her breasts. False lenses placed there by society, media, abuse, or other experience or cultural influences.

Self

Description: Yellow stuff in your cup. (See Appendix E.)   Just you and your own nature. This the Law of Death. (The red stuff in your cup is the Law of Sin, but YOU are your own worst enemy – not satan. It's the YOU in your cup that invites the SIN to come in.) (See "Spiritual Tuneup" or "Rain Down NOW, Lord!" on the website.)

Port: You

Characteristics: This is self, this is your own flawed human nature. This is the flesh that needs to be crucified daily so that Christ can live. You decrease so that He can increase.

Removal: You can lay it down or He can slice it off and rip it out. Those are the choices. Usually you need a combination of both. But you need to be willing to let Him do it. Anything you hold on to is an idol and will stand between you and God and clog up your hearing. There ARE ways to speed this up.   Your growth in Christ is directly proportional to your willingness to run headlong into the refining fire and give it a big, wet, sloppy kiss. You can walk slowly toward the refining fire, but this is a war and we can't have you taking ten years to get out of Boot Camp. You can run away from the refining fire, but it's still coming for you anyway.

Cautions: When God flushes icky pieces of YOU up to the surface, it's just so you can see it, hate it and ask Him to kill it and expel it. Then replace it with Him. Sometimes you'll feel like a dirty aquarium with dead fish floating on the top. That's just cause He's been flushing up dead pieces of you and you need to ask Him to get you all cleaned out and refilled with His living water. He'll explain how to do that. (It would help if you asked Him to let you see your "cup". Lots of folks around here do and it really helps.)

Doctrine Filter – traditions, generational, institutional

Description: Could be any system, doctrine, dogma, tradition of Man. Sometimes things you don't even notice because they've been there so long – like denominations or steeples on churches or passing an offering plate or Christmas, all of which are recent inventions and not in the Bible.

Port: Could be tied up with anything. Could be attached to pride or lust or fear or guilt or anything. The enemy will use all available demonic strongholds to reinforce systems of Man so as to keep our eyes off of Jesus. Christmas has become as much about lust as it is about anything else. The enemy will use fear in the pastors or leadership to tell them that they HAVE to continue in traditions that they know are meaningless because if they don't, people will leave and they won't be able to pay the bills. We fail to rock the boat, even though the boat is sinking.

Characteristics: Could be just about anything, but the worst ones are the ones that lie about the very nature of God and the way He relates to His people. The most dangerous of all are the "once saved, always saved" theology that fails to require constant obedience and results in fat, lazy, spiritually weak Christians that think they're safe no matter what they do. Another is the "Pre-Tribulation Rapture" theology that says we will escape any persecution or danger because Jesus doesn't want us to suffer. That is directly contrary to scripture where the Lord makes it clear that if we are like Him then we WILL be persecuted and killed. Again, this results in fat, lazy, spiritually weak escapist Christians that are unprepared for any real suffering. Another is the theology that the Gifts of the Spirit ended and they're not for today and God doesn't speak to His people any more. That is directly contrary to God's nature and to His Word. He says that in the last days He will pour out His Spirit on ALL flesh and they will prophecy and dream dreams.

Removal: You have to see it for what it is – man-made – reject it and seek only God. You have to repent to Him for holding to something that wasn't pure and you have to try to make it right with the people that might have been deceived or kept in the dark because of your support, or deliberate spreading, of a doctrine of Man.

Cautions: Those who are unwilling to let go of their doctrine of Man are going to really, really hate you and try to stop you. Jesus said that's what would happen when you were like Him and spoke Truth. Be ready and DO NOT back down. If you haven't, pray for the filling of the Holy Spirit in the biggest possible way. Ask for a bigger cup of Jesus so that He can fight your battles. Just shut up and listen really good and do whatever He tells you.

Others ... (as we find them)

GENERATIONAL AND OTHER CURSES

We'll start with the easy ones, OK? Probably not going to get any argument from you on these. Let's not argue right now about whether these will pass down spiritually to your children someday, let's just agree that if you DO this stuff and you have children, it will affect them negatively right now – including their relationship with God.

Unforgiveness

Verse Reference: Matthew 18:35 - *"So likewise shall my heavenly Father do also unto you, if ye from your hearts forgive not every one his brother their trespasses." Mark 11:26 - " But if ye do not forgive, neither will your Father which is in heaven forgive your trespasses."*

Way to Get Under Curse: By not forgiving someone for something – worst of all by being angry at God and not forgiving HIM for something!! Like taking your Dad away when you were two or raising you in a rotten family or not rescuing you from that guy that raped you. VERY bad to have unforgiveness. Worst of all to have it toward God.

Effect of Curse: God will not forgive you for anything during the time you're not forgiving others. You may or may not be His anymore. He may not come and rescue you from demons that are oppressing you. This is a BIG wall standing between you and will likely clog up your ability to hear with God a LOT.

Way to Get Curse Off: Forgive them all the way and mean it. Ask God to help scrub it out. Say you're sorry for disobeying Him and not acting like Jesus – especially if you told people you were a Christian. Ask Him to forgive you. Look around your environment to see if you've opened the door to this and taught it to you children – that would make it a generational curse.

Length of Curse: Indeterminate – it's up to you.

Does it Affect Christians: You betcha. No exceptions. It doesn't look like there is any Biblical exemption that says that if you are "saved" and then later start holding an unforgiveness it's OK. By all indications, during the time that you are holding on to unforgiveness, you will not be forgiven by God. If you die with unforgiveness in your heart, you can't Biblically be sure you're going to heaven. I don't see any other way to read that.

(This might help you see the danger here – http://www.shepherdserve.org/special_reports/daniel_main.htm)

Illegal Soul Ties

Verse Reference: I Corinthians 6:15-17 - *"15 Don't you realize that your bodies are parts of Christ's body? Should I take the parts of Christ's body and make them parts of a prostitute's body? That's unthinkable! 16 Don't you realize that the person who unites himself with a prostitute becomes one body with her? God says, "The two will be one." 17 However, the person who unites himself with the Lord becomes one spirit with him."* (God's Word)   Genesis 2:23-24 - *"24 Therefore shall a man leave his father and his mother, and shall cleave unto his wife: and they shall be one flesh."* Exodus 20:14-17 - *"14 **Thou shalt not commit adultery.** 15 Thou shalt not steal. 16 Thou shalt not bear false witness against thy neighbour. 17 Thou shalt not covet thy neighbour's house, **thou shalt not covet thy neighbour's wife,** nor his manservant, nor his maidservant, nor his ox, nor his ass, nor any thing that is thy neighbour's."* (KJV)

Way to Get Under Curse: Sex before marriage – or during marriage with someone other than your spouse. Because Jesus says that if you even THINK about having sex with a woman, you're guilty of adultery, it's possible to have soul ties with people you only fantasized about. What happens in your mind is very powerful. God holds you responsible. Spiritually, you became one flesh with that girl in the centerfold when you had sex with her – you created a soul tie and God will hold you responsible for fornication (or adultery).

Effect of Curse: Going to taint future relationships. Maintains a connection to a past love that can reestablish – in person or in the spiritual (thought life). If it happens after a time that a person has become "saved" there is no indication that it's consequences are invalidated. You became one with some flesh other that the one you were supposed to. That spot is taken and the right person can't fully fill that spot. And God is mad at you because you're unrepentant. Because of the effect it may have on marriage relationship, may also have substantial negative impact on children. If they grow up seeing illegal soul ties and lust and unrepentant hearts, they will likely respond to God likewise. (I see black umbilical cords coming from a persons back or neck.)

Length of Curse: Indeterminate – it's up to you.

Way to Get Curse Off: Repent to God and to others as needed, break the ties completely in the natural and in the spirit, make life changes as needed, cover in the Blood.

Does it Affect Christians: Surely. Yes, they are a new creation in Christ and these are broken and washed clean if they repented - but if the ties are new, then they're still active. It's a multiple violation of the Big Ten. If a kid grows up in a lust-filled home, it's likely that they'll related to God like this and be adulterous and disobedient.

Sin

Verse Reference: John 8:34-35, 44-47 - *"34 Jesus answered them, Verily, verily, I say unto you, Whosoever committeth sin is the servant of sin. 35 And the servant abideth not in the house for ever: but the Son abideth ever." "44 Ye are of your father the devil, and the lusts of your father ye will do. He was a murderer from the beginning, and abode not in the truth, because there is no truth in him. When he speaketh a lie, he speaketh of his own: for he is a liar, and the father of it. 45 And because I tell you the truth, ye believe me not. 46 Which of you convinceth me of sin? And if I say the truth, why do ye not believe me? 47 He that is of God heareth God's words: ye therefore hear them not, because ye are not of God."*

Way to Get Under Curse: By sinning – in any of it's flavors or frequencies.

Length of Curse: Indeterminate – it's up to you.

Effect of Curse: Will make you the son of satan and you <u>will</u> do the lusts of your father the devil. Because you're no longer <u>of</u> God, you can't really hear His voice and understand Him anymore. It may not be coincidence that the denominations that say you can't stop sinning also say God doesn't speak to us anymore.

Way to Get Curse Off: Repent, if you can, and ask the Holy Spirit to help you stop sinning once and for all. Believe that it's possible and stop cutting and pasting parts like this out of the Bible. If you are doing this in your house and your children are watching, you're probably going to pass it down to them and it will affect their relationship with God and thus become a generational curse.

Does it Affect Christians: Not if you stop sinning. You're exempt and you will abide in the house forever if you are a servant and stop sinning. If you're a son of the devil, then you're in outer darkness. Unlikely you'll have peace and joy and victory and walk in the fullness of all God has for you – you can't drink from the cup of demons <u>and</u> from the cup of the Lord. Pick a team and stick to it.

Hate

Verse Reference: I John 4:20 – "If a man say, I love God, and hateth his brother, he is a liar: for he that loveth not his brother whom he hath seen, how can he love God whom he hath not seen?"

Way to Get Under Curse: By hating your brother – any brother.

Length of Curse: Indeterminate – it's up to you.

Effect of Curse: God hates liars. And you're a liar if you say you love God and yet you hate your brother – PLUS you're hating your brother! This will REALLY clog up your pipeline to God. It's unlikely you'll hear His voice at all. Then you'll just have to lean on your own understanding and direct your own paths. You'll probably end up surrounding yourself with other men that will tell you what to do, who are also full of hate. If you raise your kids up around this, it will probably affect their relationship with God, fill them with hate and become a generational curse as they grow up being like <u>you</u>.

Way to Get Curse Off: Repent to God and to the people involved. Make changes in keeping with repentance.

Does it Affect Christians: Not unless you're hating somebody that you're supposed to be loving. You <u>are</u> acting like One Body with all the other Christians in your city, aren't you?

Fornicators, Idolaters, Adulterers, Homosexuals, Thieves, Greedy, Drunks, Haters, Slanderers, Extortioners

Verse Reference: I Corinthians 6:9-11 - *"9 Or know ye not that the unrighteous shall **not** inherit the kingdom of God? Be not deceived: neither fornicators, nor idolaters, nor adulterers, nor effeminate, nor abusers of themselves with men, 10 nor thieves, nor covetous, nor drunkards, nor revilers, nor extortioners, shall inherit the kingdom of God. 11 And such were some of you: but ye were washed, but ye were sanctified, but ye were justified in the name of the Lord Jesus Christ, and in the Spirit of our God."*

Way to Get Under Curse: Doing any of those things.

Length of Curse: Indeterminate – it's up to you.

Effect of Curse: You will NOT inherit the kingdom of God. That means you can't walk in the fullness of what He has for you right now and you won't go to heaven. Is there another way to read that?

Way to Get Curse Off: Repent to God and those harmed. Make fruit in keeping with repentance.

Does it Affect Christians: Not unless they do any of those things. And if they do, they stop being washed, sanctified and justified and they get dirty again. They will get separated from God by their sin and it will clog up their hearing really good. If they have kids that watch them and grow up around this as they get more and more depraved, but think they're fine because they go to "church" - the kids will surely grow up with a whacked relationship with God and will probably do many of these things themselves. Then it becomes a generational curse. Know any greedy Christians?   Seen any on TV?   Any drunkards?   Doesn't have to be alcohol. You can get drunk on donuts or fried chicken or chocolate.

Are you getting this yet? You'll find lots of websites and authors and pastors that say that talk of Generational Curses is a heresy because once we're washed with the Blood of Jesus none of that stuff can stick to us. I hope I just showed you that it can clearly still affect Christians. If you raise your child in a home full of rebellion, you can expect a rebellious child. My point is that people may want to dismiss Old Testament curses, but they don't get the very practical, real world FACT that family systems cycle and repeat. There HAS to be something in play here. Never mind your theology and your interpretation and your desire to diminish and dismiss the Old Testament – what's happening in the REAL WORLD?

In a previous career I was Director of Residence Life and Student Life at a small private college. We had a freshman girl who was having a horrible time. She had attempted suicide twice (mostly to get attention), she was cutting herself, she started a fire in the student union. She had decided she was gay, but that was only because the idea of being with a man disgusted her so much. The lesbian students didn't want to have anything to do with her because she was so mangled up. She had been raped by her older brother from when she was five to about fifteen (as I recall). Nobody in the family had ever done anything about it. Mom was oblivious. Now, finally, just before she went to college, it all came out and the family was torn into pieces. The father was defending the brother, it was going to court, the brother was in jail, she was going to have to testify against him, and she was a wreck. I told the father that we couldn't have her on campus anymore because she was just too big a mess and we weren't equipped for that. She was consuming six or eight hours a day of staff time by herself without any progress! He looked me in the eye and said to me, "We sent her to college here, now she's your problem." Then the mother, between tissues, looked at me and said something I'll never forget. She said, "I just don't understand how this could have been happening all those years right under our noses. I should have seen it! The same thing happened to me!" And they were ALL church members.

OK, so what is that?! Is that a bunch of demons in a family tree or what?! Is that a house full of lust and adultery and rebellion or what? If there is such a thing as a generational curse, they got a big one. Way back then, I had no idea how to handle anything spiritually, so I recommended they put her into residential treatment and medicate her. That's probably what they did, because I never saw her again. I pray to God that she's still alive and there's a way for her to find peace and joy and victory in Jesus. And I'm sorry for not being better prepared to handle that as Jesus would have and really free her – instead of turning her over to Man's medicine.

Those same people that say Generational Curses aren't real, also probably don't believe in witches or cursed objects or that satan has ANY effect on us anymore. They probably think the war is over and done with and there's nobody left to fight. Or you can just quote the Bible to anything that comes for you and they'll run away. I got news for you, they'll quote the Bible right back to you! If you're not walking clean before the Lord, you don't have any authority to be throwing around the name of Jesus any more than the sons of Sceva did. (Acts 19)

Here's another shocker for all those folks that don't believe Generational Curses are real.

The word "heresy" means "a difference in doctrine" or a "faction" and those who participate with them will not inherit the kingdom of heaven.   For example here -

Galatians 5:19-21 (KJV) - *19 Now the works of the flesh are manifest, which are these; Adultery, fornication, uncleanness, lasciviousness, 20 **Idolatry**, witchcraft, **hatred**, **variance**, emulations, wrath, **strife**, **seditions**, **heresies**, 21 **Envyings**, murders, drunkenness, revellings, and such like: of the which I tell you before, as I have also told you in time past, that they which do such things **shall not** inherit the kingdom of God.*

Galatians 5:19-21 (Amplified) - *19 Now the doings (practices) of the flesh are clear (obvious): they are immorality, impurity, indecency, 20 Idolatry, sorcery, **enmity**, **strife**, jealousy, anger (ill temper), **selfishness**, **divisions** (dissensions), **party spirit (factions, sects with peculiar opinions, heresies)**, 21 **Envy**, drunkenness, carousing, and the like. I warn you beforehand, just as I did previously, that those who do such things **shall not** inherit the kingdom of God.*

Galatians 5:19-21 (Darby) – *19 Now the works of the flesh are manifest, which are fornication, uncleanness, licentiousness, 20 **idolatry**, sorcery, **hatred**, **strifes**, jealousies, angers, **contentions**, **disputes**, **schools** **of** **opinion**, 21 **envyings**, murders, drunkennesses, revels, and things like these; as to which I tell you beforehand, even as I also have said before, that they who do such things **shall not** inherit God's kingdom.*

So try this Generational Curse on for size:

Denominationalism

(Factions, party spirit, heresies, disputes, strifes, envyings, idolatry, hatred)

Verse Reference: See Galatians 6:19-21. I Corin 1:12-13, I Corin 3:1-4

Way to Get Under Curse: By being a part of, supporting, encouraging, agreeing with, or otherwise fomenting a division/sect/denomination within the Body of Christ.

Length of Curse: Indeterminate – it's up to you.

Effect of Curse: You WILL NOT INHERIT THE KINGDOM OF HEAVEN. How much more clear does a verse have to be? And that's the New Testament by the way. You are carnal and you are worldly and you will not inherit the Kingdom of God. If you have made up your own doctrine and dogma that explains away this CLEAR, UNAVOIDABLE instruction in the Bible, then you have cut and pasted the Bible and you're **also** subject to the curse in Revelation 22:19 that says you will be erased out of the Book of Life. You have created your own mystery religion, set up your own idols, followed men instead of God and you're off the reservation. You will not inherit the fullness of what He has for you right now and Biblically it seems clear that you're not going to go to heaven. Since it's likely that you will take your children into that same cult you joined and indoctrinate them into your mystery religion, it's likely that this generational disobedience and rebellion will continue and become a curse upon you and all your children. You are also under a Red Dragon curse from God (See Appendix B).

Way to Get Curse Off: If you can and you're eyes aren't still blinded, repent to God for not obeying Him and His Word, repent to all the people that are also trapped because of you, put all sects behind you and produce fruit in keeping with repentance. Listen to Him really good and do whatever He tells you.

Does it Affect Christians: ABSOLUTELY NOT. Biblically speaking as soon as you joined a "Faction" you went your own way and stopped inheriting the Kingdom anyway. So you're not really a Christian anymore and you're not in the Book of Life. Is there any other way to read this? If I were you, I'd be VERY afraid, just in case.

I Corinthians 3:1-4 (KJV) - *"1 And I, brethren, could not speak unto you as unto spiritual, but as unto carnal, as unto babes in Christ. 2 I fed you with milk, not with meat; for ye were not yet able to bear it: nay, not even now are ye able; 3 for **ye are yet carnal**: for **whereas there is among you jealousy and strife, are ye not carnal,** and do ye not walk after the manner of men? 4 **For when one saith, I am of Paul; and another, I am of Apollos; are ye not men?"***

Rev 22:19 (KJV) - *"And if any man shall take away from the words of the book of this prophecy, God shall take away his part out of the book of life, and out of the holy city, and from the things which are written in this book."*

Did that get your attention?   You don't think there are Generational Curses? Go look at what people that said they were Christians have done to oppress and dumb down and make sure whole family trees were on the Broad Path to Hell while they were all being told they could be absolutely sure they were "saved" and safe.

Now, if you don't mind, I'm just going to proceed with my discussion of Generational Curses from the Old Testament. Just in case they might also be affecting people spiritually.

Witchcraft

Verse Reference: Exodus 20:5 (KJV) - *"5 Thou shalt not bow down thyself to them, nor serve them: for I the LORD thy God am a jealous God, visiting the iniquity of the fathers upon the children unto the third and fourth generation of them that hate me;"*

Way to Get Under Curse: The best way to show that you hate God is by worshiping false gods and messing with witchcraft. I'm not going to quote all the witchcraft verses here because they're in Appendix F. But ANY dabbling with stuff from foreign gods (which doesn't mean un-American, by the way, it means ANY God that ain't Jehovah!) will invoke this curse upon you.

Length of Curse: Three or four generations. About 100 to 150 years.

Effect of Curse: Increasing rebellion and distance from God. Increasingly difficult to turn back.

Way to Get Curse Off: Repent to God substantially and thoroughly. Wash it all in the Blood. Break any ties to Familiars. Get anything out of your house that is related. May require lifestyle or location changes. Repent to all the people you took down a path to hell.

Does it Affect Christians: If they mess with witchcraft, it sure does. Even if they were washed clean before, if they pick it up again, it can still affect them. If a child was dedicated to satan, that child is tagged. The Blood of Jesus can wash it off, but not unless you ask Him to. If you don't have, it's because you don't ask.

Bastard Curse

Verse Reference: Deuteronomy 23:2 (KJV) - *"A bastard shall not enter into the congregation of the LORD; even to his tenth generation shall he not enter into the congregation of the LORD. 3 An Ammonite or Moabite shall not enter into the congregation of the LORD; even to their tenth generation shall they not enter into the congregation of the LORD for ever. 4 Because they met you not with bread and with water in the way, when ye came forth out of Egypt; and because they hired against thee Balaam the son of Beor of Pethor of Mesopotamia, to curse thee.*

Way to Get Under Curse: Sexual illegitimacy either by babies born before marriage or babies born by people you're not married to. The Ammonites and the Moabites were the descendants of Bennami and Moab the sons of Lot's daughters and who were conceived by incest. Later on, God curses them, not just because they are rebellious and fail to come to the aid of family, but also because they are illegitimate, bastard sons to the 10th generation. King David brought this curse on his family line by his relationship with Bathsheba – complicated by his murder of her husband – the result was increasing rebellion and perversion in his house for generations. Even though he repented for the act, and that particular child died, it remains an active curse on the family tree.

Length of Curse: Ten generations – minimum 400 years.

Effect of Curse: Rebellion, inability to get along in fellowship with others, inability to develop intimacy with the Lord, increasing sexual perversion, increasing problems in each subsequent generation. (I see this as a big fat black umbilical cord coming from a person's back.)

Way to Get Curse Off: Repent to God and confess your sins and the sins of your forefathers. Ask the Lord to break it and sever it on you and all of your descendants to the tenth generation. Cover it in the Blood of Jesus. It's important that you have legal ground for this. That means that you need to be the head, or the spiritual leader of the family. If the husband doesn't know Jesus, the wife can do it. It should be the first born or the eldest living male, if possible to scrub it out across all cousins and nephews and all.

Does is Affect Christians: I have definitely seen it affect Christians and make a huge difference in their walk with God when it's broken. The Blood of Jesus is sufficient, but if we're taught to disregard parts of the Bible and that they're not even real, then we don't ask the Lord to apply the Blood to those things and they remain "live". If this is in play, it will really clog up communication with the Throne. It's like a glass ceiling, where people are trying to grow in Christ and have intimacy, but just seem to keep bouncing off of this ceiling and can't get any farther. MANY lives have been changed by breaking this one.

This particular curse is REALLY nasty and satan wants to get it instituted across all the world. The African-American community in America has been decimated by it. This trend of young girls having babies is creating massive spiritual problems and will keep many from the kingdom if we don't start breaking this off of people. This curse can last 400 years!! We're talking about someone in your family tree that was a Christian but misbehaved even many generations ago. This curse isn't on the "world" for doing what the "world" does. This is a curse on the children of God for not obeying His laws about sexual behavior. People that say curses are real, but not on Christians need to explain why God keeps cursing His own children over and over in the Bible – but He won't do it to us? (Read Deut. 28!). He loves us more than He loved the children of Israel? We are the grafted in vine, but THEY are the natural vine! Why should we think we're going to get any more grace than they did?

If He was willing to whack them, He's willing to whack us just as hard. Those curses on natural Israel had natural consequences with spiritual after effects – the women actually did end up eating their babies in the book of Lamentations, just like Deuteronomy 28 said would happen. On spiritual Israel, those curses have spiritual consequences with natural after effects. We're still turning our children over to foreign nations, but we call them MTV and Wicca and Islam and Humanism and Evolution. They may not go in chains marching across the desert, but they're just as much in chains.

Innocent Blood Curse

Verse Reference: Matthew 27:34-35 - *"When Pilate saw that he could not prevail, but rather that a tumult was beginning, he took water and washed his hands before the multitude, saying, "I am innocent of the blood of this just person. See ye to it." Then answered all the people and said, "His blood be on us, and on our children!""* Jonah 1:14 – *"Wherefore they cried unto the LORD, and said, We beseech thee, O LORD, we beseech thee, let us not perish for this man's life, and lay not upon us innocent blood: for thou, O LORD, hast done as it pleased thee."*

Way to Get Under Curse: By murder of an innocent – as King David killed Uriah. May also be brought into effect by murder of innocents in war. Most commonly this comes as a result of abortion. May also be possible to get under this because of murderous words spoken against another. Mark 7:20-23 – *"And he said, That which cometh out of the man, that defileth the man. For from within, out of the heart of men, proceed evil thoughts, adulteries, fornications, murders, thefts, covetousness, wickedness, deceit, lasciviousness, an evil eye, blasphemy, pride, foolishness: All these evil things come from within, and defile the man."*

Length of Curse: Indeterminate

Effect of Curse: Increasing manifestations of death in the family tree. See King David – sons usurping control, then being murdered. More blood (physically or spiritually) flowing all the time as the curse repeats from one generation to another and gets worse.

Way to Get Curse Off: Repent to God and confess your sins and the sins of your forefathers. Ask the Lord to break it and sever it on you and all of your descendants. Cover it in the Blood of Jesus.

Does is Affect Christians: I have definitely seen it affect Christians and make a huge difference in their walk with God when it's broken. If this is in play, it will really clog up communication with the Throne. Many people repent to God for having had an abortion, but they never think to repent to the person they killed. You have to say you're sorry to ALL concerned. Sometimes that's not possible to do in person, but you can still ask the Lord to convey to them how sorry you are for ending their life (or wishing death on them). I encourage all women that had an abortion (or men that cooperated or talked them into it) to say they're sorry to the baby. It is not "fetal tissue" - it's a real person that you killed.

The best resource on the Bastard Curse that I have found on this is from my friend, Paul Norcross.

http://www.kingdomfaith.org

There are seminar notes on this here -
http://www.kingdomfaith.org/LiveFreeContents.htm

And you can order his book about the Bastard Curse here -
http://www.kingdomfaith.org/books3.htm

SHIELDS, SPHERES AND CLOAKS

Let's just start with what the Bible says, so that you don't think I'm making this stuff up. All I'm doing is standing with faith like a child that the Bible is true and this is a real thing, not just figurative.

Psalms 18:29-42 (ASV)

*29 For by thee I run upon a troop; And by my God do I leap over a wall. 30 As for God, his way is perfect: The word of Jehovah is tried; He is a **shield** unto all them that take refuge **in** him. 31 For who is God, save Jehovah? And who is a rock, besides our God, 32 The God that **girdeth me** with strength, And maketh my way perfect? 33 He maketh my feet like hinds' feet: And setteth me upon my high places. 34 **He teacheth my hands to war**; So that mine arms do bend a **bow of brass**. 35 Thou hast also given me the **shield** of thy salvation; And thy right hand hath holden me up, And thy gentleness hath made me great. 36 Thou hast **enlarged** my steps under me, And my feet have not slipped. 37 I will **pursue** mine enemies, and **overtake** them; Neither will I turn again **till they are consumed**. 38 I will smite them through, so that they shall **not** be able to **rise**: They shall fall under my feet. 39 For thou hast **girded me** with strength unto the battle: Thou hast subdued under me those that rose up against me. 40 Thou hast also made mine enemies **turn their backs** unto me, That I might cut off them that hate me. 41 They cried, but there was none to save; Even unto Jehovah, but he answered them not. 42 **Then did I beat them small as the dust before the wind; I did cast them out as the mire of the streets.***

Psalms 35:1-10 (KJV) – *1 Plead my cause, O LORD, with them that strive with me: fight against them that fight against me. 2 Take hold of **shield** and **buckler**, and stand up for mine help. 3 Draw out also the **spear**, and **stop** the way against them that persecute me: say unto my soul, I am thy salvation. 4 Let them be **confounded** and put to shame that seek after my soul: let them be **turned back** and brought to **confusion** that devise my hurt. 5 Let them be as **chaff** before the wind: and let the **angel of the LORD** chase them. 6 Let their way be dark and slippery: and let the **angel of the LORD** persecute them. 7 For without cause have they hid for me their net in a pit, which without cause they have digged for my **soul**. 8 Let destruction come upon him at **unawares**; and let his net that he hath hid **catch himself**: into that very destruction let him fall. 9 And my soul shall be joyful in the LORD: it shall rejoice in his salvation. 10 All my bones shall say, LORD, who is like unto thee, which **deliverest the poor from him that is too strong for him**, yea, the poor and the needy from him that spoileth him?*

Those who say that we only have the Sword of the Spirit mentioned in Ephesians 6, need to note that here we see bows and spears and all kinds of offensive and defensive equipment and maneuvers – including calling up angels to help fight for you. These verses indicate that God Himself will teach you to do war (that's what He did with me). He will defend you. He will hide you. He will confuse them and distract them and have them turn their back and then He will help you smash your enemies into itty-bitty little pieces and grind them into the dirt! He will send them someplace from which they cannot come back. Go God! These are not figurative or theoretical shields or "hedges" - if satan can see them and has to respect them, they are very much real. It should be clear that these are not "natural" or physical enemies – David is talking about things seeking his soul, not just his life.

Job 1:8-10 (KJV) – *8 And the LORD said unto Satan, Hast thou considered my servant Job, that there is none like him in the earth, a perfect and an upright man, one that feareth God, and escheweth evil? 9 Then Satan answered the LORD, and said, Doth Job fear God for nought? 10 **Hast not thou made an hedge about him, and about his house, and about all that he hath on every side?** thou hast blessed the work of his hands, and his substance is increased in the land.*

Satan could not violate that hedge. It wasn't a three foot tall wall of evergreens like we think of a "hedge" out in front of the house. This was a mighty spiritual wall that fully surrounded Job and all of his house and his people. There were no cracks or seams or openings. This was a dome – more than a dome, this was a sphere. Fully compassed round about. More verses about that. We may think of a hedge as a little thing, or a shield as something you hold on your arm that the enemy could get around – but in the spirit, these are spheres that fully surround in every way and leave no access for the enemy.

> **Psalms 5:11-12** (KJV) – *11 But let all those that put their trust in thee rejoice: let them ever shout for joy, because thou defendest them: let them also that love thy name be joyful in thee. 12 For thou, LORD, wilt bless the righteous; with favour wilt thou **compass** him as with a shield.*

Here are lots more, so that you know I'm not just using a couple to make my point.

> **2 Sam 22:3** (KJV) – *The God of my rock; in him will I trust: he is my shield, and the horn of my salvation, my high tower, and my refuge, my saviour; thou savest me from violence.*

> **2 Sam 22:36** (KJV) – *Thou hast also given me the shield of thy salvation: and thy gentleness hath made me great.*

> **Psalms 3:3** (KJV) – *But thou, O LORD, art a shield for me; my glory, and the lifter up of mine head.*

> **Psalms 7:10** (ASV) – *My shield is with God, Who saveth the upright in heart.*

> **Psalms 18:2-3** (ASV) – *2 Jehovah is my rock, and my fortress, and my deliverer; My God, my rock, in whom I will take refuge; My shield, and the horn of my salvation, my high tower. 3 I will call upon Jehovah, who is worthy to be praised: So shall I be saved from mine enemies.*

> **Psalms 33:20-21** (KJV) – *20 Our soul waiteth for the LORD: he is our help and our shield. 21 For our heart shall rejoice in him, because we have trusted in his holy name.*

Psalms 18:17-18 (ASV) – *17 He delivered me from my strong enemy, And from them that hated me; For they were too mighty for me. 18 They came upon me in the day of my calamity; But Jehovah was my stay.*

Psalms 28:6-8 (ASV) – *6 Blessed be Jehovah, Because he hath heard the voice of my supplications. 7 Jehovah is my strength and my shield; My heart hath trusted in him, and I am helped: Therefore my heart greatly rejoiceth; And with my song will I praise him. 8 Jehovah is their strength, And he is a stronghold of salvation to his anointed.*

Psalms 84:8-12 (KJV) – *8 O LORD God of hosts, hear my prayer: give ear, O God of Jacob. Selah. 9 Behold, O God our shield, and look upon the face of thine anointed. 10 For a day in thy courts is better than a thousand. I had rather be a doorkeeper in the house of my God, than to dwell in the tents of wickedness. 11 For the LORD God is a sun and shield: the LORD will give grace and glory: no good thing will he withhold from them that walk uprightly. 12 O LORD of hosts, blessed is the man that trusteth in thee.*

Psalms 89:15-18 (ASV) – *15 Blessed is the people that know the joyful sound: They walk, O Jehovah, in the light of thy countenance. 16 In thy name do they rejoice all the day; And in thy righteousness are they exalted. 17 For thou art the glory of their strength; And in thy favor our horn shall be exalted. 18 For our shield belongeth unto Jehovah; And our king to the Holy One of Israel.*

Psalms 115:11 (KJV) – *Ye that fear the LORD, trust in the LORD: he is their help and their shield.*

Psalms 119:114 (KJV) – *Thou art my hiding place and my shield: I hope in thy word.*

Psalms 144:1-2 (KJV) – *Blessed be the LORD my strength, which teacheth my hands to war, and my fingers to fight: 2 My goodness, and my fortress; my high tower, and my deliverer; my shield, and he in whom I trust; who subdueth my people under me.*

Prov 2:7-8 (ASV) – *7 He layeth up sound wisdom for the upright; He is a shield to them that walk in integrity; 8 That he may guard the paths of justice, And preserve the way of his saints.*

Proverbs 30:5 (KJV) – *Every word of God is pure: he is a shield unto them that put their trust in him.*

Eph 6:11-18 (KJV) – *11 Put on the whole armour of God, that ye may be able to stand against the wiles of the devil. 12 For we wrestle not against flesh and blood, but against principalities, against powers, against the rulers of the darkness of this world, against spiritual wickedness in high places. 13 Wherefore take unto you the whole armour of God, that ye may be able to withstand in the evil day, and having done all, to stand. 14 Stand therefore, having your loins girt about with truth, and having on the breastplate of righteousness; 15 And your feet shod with the preparation of the gospel of peace; 16 Above all, taking the shield of faith, wherewith ye shall be able to quench all the fiery darts of the wicked. 17 And take the helmet of salvation, and the sword of the Spirit, which is the word of God: 18 Praying always with all prayer and supplication in the Spirit, and watching thereunto with all perseverance and supplication for all saints;*

Personal Shields

OK, boy, I really don't want to do this. I've resisted this and it's just about the last thing to write on this book, but I'm told I have to lay it all out there, no matter how crazy it sounds, and I have to finish this today, so here goes.

Because we went through such a radical time of warfare and we were dealing with all kinds of stuff, we got REALLY motivated to understand everything we could about shields! We knew that by anointing the furniture store, we were setting up a wall (or sphere), but as Discernment of Spirits increased, I started actually seeing the sphere – like a shiny, opaque, white dome over the top (and under the ground). Sometimes someone would come into the shop and bring all kinds of nasty stuff in riding on them. And since they were invited to come in, we gave it legal ground to come in. There was no way around that. But we had to keep cleaning out the inside of the shield all the time. Sometimes they would jump on us and we'd have to deal with that. (At the time, I can't say that we all had all of our doorways shut.) If you wanted to blast the sphere out, you could pick the stuff off individually with the Sword, or just dial your light up inside the sphere and find anything that was hiding. Or you could shockwave it with a big blast wave of the Holy Spirit by just taking everything in your cup and compressing it down real tight until it exploded like a supernova. (Well, that's how He taught us anyway.)

We began to also make sure that we each had a good personal shield working. The Word says that if you bind it on earth it will be bound in heaven. I know this is a little touchy, but the key to the spiritual realms and seeing what is happening in the "real" world is through the mind. That is, I asked the Lord for a personal shield and what I pictured in my mind was that it would be a perfectly round, white bubble all around my body. Since that's what I asked for, that's what I got. That was "Personal Shield Version 1.0." If you had two people with bubbles, when they got together, the bubbles would kind of pop together into one, like reverse cell division or when you blow soap bubbles and two of them join together to make a big one. It kept the bad stuff out, so long as we didn't get too close to somebody – like hug them or shake hands – then their stuff would jump into our bubble. That got old really fast. You can't minister to somebody like that!

So we asked the Lord for an upgrade. We didn't really understand that we had dictated the terms of the shield by our own preconceptions of what it would do and look like. But the Lord was patient and walked us up through this progression to build our faith. As we learned more about the personal shields, that naturally influenced the shields we prayed up over the shop or homes or the city – or vice versa.

We prayed for a harder shell so that demons couldn't suck through into our shields from other people. That was Personal Shield 2.0. If they got near enough it either bound them onto the person or pushed the demons off until they got back outside our shield. That worked better and we saw a lot of fruit from that. But we still had to be constantly maintaining our shields because the enemy would beat them down or crack them or sneak in somehow. Sometimes we would make an opening by disobedience or let them in some other way. He says that He compasses the righteous round about, the "mostly righteous" have a mostly intact sphere! Which is like a submarine with screen doors.

We were constantly having to defend the furniture store sphere because it was under attack all the time. I know that sounds crazy, but it's true. Lots of people can testify to it. There was just a constant flow of people needing help and lots of people getting saved and healed and delivered and lots of talk about being one body – even some of the pastors in town that were helping and starting to get on board. The enemy REALLY didn't like it!

At one point, when we were out on the public sidewalk repenting and confessing for the city for two days in the summer heat (another long story there), we were getting spiritually pounded on and the people repenting couldn't really do warfare and repent before the throne at the same time. We had to have someone defending us, while we were crying out to God. At one point the person that was supposed to be doing that got distracted, our sphere got penetrated and repentance stopped. (You can't repent in spirit and in truth unless God pours it out on you and that's ALWAYS what the enemy wants to keep from happening.) Just then I got a cell phone call from a prophet I know from Jerusalem. He prayed for us and without asking or anything he prayed up a shield around us and asked the Lord to surround it with giant rings of Holy Spirit fire! Well, I had never thought of that, but as soon as he prayed it, I could see the sphere and the fire rings! That was COOL! And that sphere lasted a LOT longer than what we were doing before. Eventually the combined force against it got through, but it lasted two or three times longer. So we started praying fire rings around the spheres. That was Personal Shield 2.5.

At one point I was still not satisfied that they required so much maintenance and really felt like there should be SOME way to have a permanent shield. So I pestered God to tell me how to get a shield that wouldn't be able to be compromised. He showed me a picture of the Spirograph game/toy that I had as a kid. Basically they are these little clear plastic gears and cogs that you put a pen through and they make intersecting arcs and spirals and make really complex, intersecting, overlapping flower shapes. The Lord showed me that picture and said, "Call up some fire angels and have them do laps around your sphere like the Spirograph. Overlapping, interlocking, rings of fire that are constantly self-renewing and by the time the enemy gets through one, the angels will be coming back over that area to renew the fire ring." COOL!! But isnt' that kind of boring for the poor angels doing laps around me endlessly? Well, evidently not. They don't really seem to get impatient or bored.

So we started praying that and saw immediate results. No more stuff getting into the spheres, unless we purposely let it in or got in too close a proximity to it. Self-renewing fire rings around the shop also ended the need for constant maintenance on that shield. Made a difference for the city, too. That was Personal Shield 2.75.

Then at one point, the Lord just sort of whispered to me at one point and said, **"You know it's just your brain that thinks shields that "compass round about" need to be a spherical bubble."** Huh? I hadn't really thought through how I was binding that, but I did totally put God in a box and impose my own filter on it.

"Lord, so, a shield could be a square or a star or irregular or anything?"
Yep.
"How do the angels do laps at full speed around something that isn't round?"
Don't worry about it. Physics don't work like that here.
"So the shield could be skin-tight, like spandex, so I can be close to people without them being in my sphere?"
Sure.
"GREAT!! Do it, Lord! Pretty please?"

So He did. We upgraded to skin-tight shields with self-renewing fire rings. If something did get in, it was real easy to spot and feel because there was really nowhere to hide. You could just blast the sphere a teeny bit and clean it out because it was so tight. But it was still possible for stuff to get in. That was Personal Shield 3.0.

During all of this we're also getting instruction and revelation about how to get personally cleaned out. About the cups and the Jezebel and all the other strongholds. We're progressively getting each other more and more shiny by walking in righteousness, crucifying pieces of ourselves daily and pouring out all we have on the poor and the poor in spirit. So it's all sort of interwoven in ways I can't explain. I'm not suggesting that you take this path or that God will do it this way with you. I'm, frankly, hoping that you just skip right over all the intermediate steps and ask Him for the best possible shield right away. I'm just trying to show you how He built our faith and proved to us OVER and OVER that the shields work and that it's not Him that fails, it's us. When we were ready for an upgrade, He suggested to us that we ask and what to ask for. He directed all of the steps in ways I can't even describe.

Anyway, about this time He puts us through a deep, gut-wrenching, tearful curriculum about witchcraft and manipulation and how VERY, VERY dangerous it is to be a person with a prophetic calling and a big anointing (or just the average person made in the image of God) and to then speak words that aren't from God. You can REALLY do a lot of damage and bind things that shouldn't be bound. At one point, my two little girls are fighting at home on either side of a door, both tugging on the doorknob. I said, "Be careful, somebody is going to get hurt." BAM!! Just like that one of them catches the doorknob in the eyeball! And the Lord says to me, "You did that." Huh?!! "Yep. You said someone WOULD get hurt, so they did. If you had said someone might get hurt you would have left my options open. But I'm going to honor the words of your mouth. You did that to your daughter." OUCH!!

Then at work one day, I'm walking one of the sisters to the front of the store as she's leaving to go get her kids from school. We're having a prayer meeting that night, so I say to her without thinking, "See you tonight."

She says, "No, I have something with my Mom we've been planning for a long time.... Uh, wait .... Now I'm hearing I'm coming to the prayer meeting. But I was sure that God wanted me with my Mom."

"Huh?! Lord, what just happened?" I say.

He says, "Well you said that you would see her tonight so now you have to see her tonight."

"NO, NO, NO!! That's just not going to fly!! I can't be doing that!! I can't be making other people adjust their lives over an off-handed comment like that! If she was supposed to minister to her Mom and misses it because of this, it's my fault and all the blood of the missed opportunities is on my head! We can't be having this! I renounce that in the Name of Jesus! She can do whatever the Lord wants her to do tonight!"

So she got a confirmation that she was free and off she went to get her kids and see her Mom. (A whole lot of the stuff we learned you could ONLY learn around people that understood the complete meaning of the word "ALL" and didn't take a step without God directing it. I really appreciate them for what they taught me about ALL.)

Do you see how dangerous this is? I asked the Lord if I had been doing that a lot and He said yes. Were people doing it to me? Oh yeah, all the time. Well, that just stinks!! How can anybody have a ministry or accomplish anything or even walk with God if people around them are speaking curses and it's sticking?! I had no idea that I was doing that! I wasn't doing it maliciously or intentionally, but just all kinds of things popped out of my mouth that I know were squirreling with things. We don't get that He will adjust His perfect will to us sometimes. We're joint heirs and adopted sons, He'll give us stuff we want sometimes, even if it's bad for us!

I saw the horrifying, big picture consequences for this kind of stuff if you project it out, realized that it was not pleasing to Him – and impossible to accomplish all that He wants you to do – and I started begging and pleading God for an anti-witchcraft shield – incoming AND outgoing. I didn't want anybody binding me and I sure didn't want to be binding anybody! I didn't want it just as a defense against witches and satanists – but against my own family and friends and others Christians! I don't want ANYBODY speaking words that are going to bind me except God Himself! And I don't want to bind anybody either and keep them from walking in His perfect will. So the Lord granted a really tough, really strong, hard shell, skin-tight, permanent fire rings, anti-witchcraft incoming and outgoing shield of the Blood of Jesus. That was Personal Shield Version. 4.0.

I was at a Sonic with a brother and he wanted to order his favorite – the Super Sonic Extreme Tots with jalapenos and chili and cheese – but he didn't have any Pepsid or Tums or anything and it always gave him heartburn. I told him that when I fast six or seven days without food OR water, I usually end the fast with a double cheeseburger with bacon, onion rings and a shake and I pray on it first and claim God's promises that we can drink deadly poison without it hurting us and it goes down just fine. So he order the Tots, prayed and didn't have any trouble at all.

I think that sort of planted a seed because I started asking the Lord for another shield upgrade that would protect us even more. We had been fighting some internal physical problems as we continued to get more cleaned out. The shields don't really do any good if you've got your own demons on you that you haven't dealt with! I asked the Lord if we could have an all the time internal and external shield. He said, "Yes." But I gotta see it in the Word, so He sent me to this:

> **Mark 16:17-18** (KJV) – *17 And these signs shall follow them that believe; In my name shall they cast out devils; they shall speak with new tongues; 18 They shall take up serpents; and if they drink any deadly thing, it shall not hurt them; they shall lay hands on the sick, and they shall recover.*

I know that there are lots of times where the Bible refers to snakes or scorpions and they're talking about demons. We already had shields that allowed us to handle the "snakes" without them hurting us. We were ripping and tearing the bad guys off of people all the time. But this says that even if you get deadly things inside of you they won't hurt you. So I took this as a confirmation that it's possible to have an internal and external permanent shield. So we asked the Lord for it and He said to just tilt my head back, open my mouth and believe in faith. And then He just smothered me with the Blood of Jesus inside and out. Just poured it in me until it was coming out my toenails and out every pore. Just saturated completely. Then two angels showed up with flame-thrower looking things and heated it up and baked it all down. The end result was that in the spirit, it looked like a solid silver, skin tight shield. Like the "Silver Surfer" in the Marvel comic books (or movie), or the bad guy in Terminator 2. (This is the point at which normally I might apologize again for sounding crazy, but I just don't care anymore. Take it or leave it, that's what it looked like.)

And the shield works really well. It doesn't mean you can't get sick or nothing can still get in, but it's a much better protection that we had before. That was Personal Shield Version 5.0. That was around August of 2006. It held for a long time without any problems and I had no indication there was a better shield – or motivation to ask for one. (Soon after that, I got Version 5.5 that was Red Dragon proof – at least against other people's Dragons.)

Just after Christmas of 2006, I was in Branson when God dropped this HUGE bombshell on me. Practically crippling. There are lots of times that He has put me on my face crying like a baby, but this was almost more than I could bear. The same sister (whom I had bound about going to her mothers) had a good anti-witchcraft shield and neither of us had been binding each other (or others) for months. But all of a sudden she had to drive to Branson to help me with something, but it made no sense. What she said she was coming to do didn't even need doing and I couldn't figure out what God was up to. But it's going to substantially inconvenience her whole family and feels all wrong. I'm on the phone with her about it and seeking the Lord and I don't know what else to do, so I release her from anything in any way that I might have bound her to have to go to Branson to do. And she gets released! I get off the phone with her and start really seeking God and pressing in for answers on this.

"Lord, what the heck was that?! Is my anti-witchcraft shield still holding?"

"Yes."

"So how did I bind her? What was this about?"

"It's a lot deeper than that. You both want to be a part of something, so I'm honoring the intentions of your heart. You want to be a part of a team and build something for me."

"HUH?! I didn't even SPEAK it and I'm binding stuff? I never even once thought that she needed to go to Branson! Was it me or her that did this?"

"Both."

"HUH?! I don't get it."

"I'm going to honor your prayers."

Well, at this point I'm in the bathroom at the hotel on my face crying and groaning like crazy. He gives me the verse that says, "May the words of my mouth and the meditations of my mind be acceptable to you, O Lord." (Ps. 19:14) And that God judges even the intentions of our heart! (Gen. 6:5; Gen. 8:21; Hebrews 4:12)

"Are you KIDDING ME?!! You're going to bind people based on things I'm praying for that are SUBCONSCIOUS?! I'm binding people in ways I don't even know I'm binding them even though I'm not even speaking or THINKING anything?! That's horrible!! I mean, I love You, that's really sweet that you're granting the intentions of my heart and all, but I don't WANT THAT!! This is <u>horrible</u>!! You'll adjust Your perfect will to suit me because I want something I don't even know I want?"

"Yep."

"NO, NO, NO!! That's no good! If I look longingly at my secretary's cleavage without even knowing I did it, You might just grant the intention of my heart and I'll have an affair?! NO! I have no idea what kind of consequences could result from all of this!! This could wreck everything!! How can we get anything done for You like this?!! This is horrible! How much of all of my life and ministry and relationships is based on You answering the intentions of my heart instead of really being in Your Perfect Will?"

"Some."

"NO! NO!! NO!!! Oh God, I'm so sorry!!! That's not going to work at all!! I love You. It's really beautiful that you give us stuff we don't even know we want or need, but this has GOT to stop!! I don't want You to be constantly adjusting Your perfect will to ME – I want you to adjust

ME to YOUR perfect will!! This is horrible! Do whatever you have to do and make this stop!"

"It's your birthright."

"Well, I love You for it and it's really, REALLY pretty that You, the God of the Universe, would allow Your plans to be subverted to please me, even if it's bad for me and works counter to what You want, but NO, NO, NO!! This is HORRIBLE! We've ALL been doing this to You in some way, haven't we, Lord?!"

"Everybody but Jesus."

"Are You telling me that if He had even had an intention of His heart ANYWHERE deep down in there to call up 10,000 angels and get Him off the Cross, You would have answered it?! ANYTHING in Him ANYWHERE? He laid it ALL down, even that deep? He didn't even hold anything subconscious back?!"

"Yep."

"OH, GOD!! OH, GOD!! I had NO idea He was THAT pure!! Oh, GOD!! How is that even possible!?! I had NO idea!! Oh, Thank You, Jesus!! I had NO idea!! Oh, GOD! Bless Your Holy Name!! You're so Holy!! I had no idea!" *(Like that, but with lots of blubbering for a long time. Just trying to be transparent here.)*

"Lord, I know that no man can take this from me. I know it's my birthright. But I lay it down right now. Jesus laid it all down. He said that He only said and did what You told Him to. He totally submitted to You on every possible level. He agreed to let You have Your way and not do anything that He wanted. He prayed that in the Garden with tears of blood! I agree Lord, I lay it down right now. Please, from now on, completely ignore ANY prayer I pray – outloud, mentally or in the deepest intentions or desires of my heart!! Ignore ANYTHING coming from me that didn't originate with YOU. Please ignore everything from me from now on that isn't YOUR perfect, pleasing will! Don't even answer the phone when I call unless it's YOU talking through me! I don't want anything of me to color any of this anymore. Please take everything in my life, every promise You've made me, all of me, my ministry, all of my stuff, my marriage, my kids, my friends – all of it and reboot it to the way YOU wanted it all along!! Whatever it takes. Even unto my own salvation, that You would be glorified in every way and set this right. I'm sorry, LORD!! OH, GOD!! Do it NOW!! Whatever it costs!! I mean it! I'm so sorry!!"

(And more blubbering for quite a while until He told me to get up and stop crying.) But as I was praying, at one point He said to receive it and watch, and He started pouring into me and I saw the silver shield start turning into gold, starting at my feet and working it's way up until I was totally gold all over, inside and out. I had no idea what that was at the time, but it wasn't over yet. Technically, He says that was Personal Shield Version 6.0.

That was December 30, 2006. What followed after that was three days of the worst brain-numbing, mind-pretzel I've ever been through in my whole life. I've been through a lot in this walk with God – I've seen a lot – I've fought a lot and had to work through all kinds of complex things, but NOTHING was like that! EVERYTHING around me looked like it was completely unraveling. I had written Him a blank check and told Him to reboot it all back to the way He wanted it before the intentions of my heart squirreled it up. There is NO telling what that looked like! I could be in the wrong city, the wrong marriage, the wrong ministry. Maybe I was supposed to be dead by now. Maybe somebody around me was supposed to be dead. Maybe I was supposed to be in jail. You can't possibly get your head around how writing Him a blank check like that might throw your whole world into complete chaos until the pieces all get reset! Of course, it's not chaos to Him, but it sure can feel like it to us!

Relationships with EVERYBODY started flipping and convulsing. Plans that I thought were firm were canceled, then reaffirmed, then canceled. Best friends severed ties with me and dusted their feet off - literally! Others the Lord told me I couldn't contact anymore. He wouldn't let me call anyone for help or advice or counsel. "Just trust Me and rest," He said. I wasn't hearing Him the way I used to and there was just MASSIVE static and flux everywhere. For someone that is used to being plugged into the Source all the time (and having peace that passes understanding most of the time), even a momentary signal disruption is distressing, but this was for DAYS while everything did flip-flops in front of my eyes!! And I couldn't get anymore out of Him than, "Rest." I didn't care a whit about the enemy or spiritual warfare! I understood that the biggest enemy to God's plans was ME!! I have a VERY high tolerance for change and for brain pretzels, but at the end of this, I spent about 20 hours sleeping because I just had to shut down before my head exploded. I told everybody and everything to leave me alone and crawled up into a ball in His lap and slept for a day. When I woke up, my shield was pure, spotless white. Not opaque, frosty white – PURE transparent white hot light. I have no idea how He did it, but those three days were like Jonah in the whale or Jesus in the tomb. At the end of it, something new came out.

He swept everything clean. All the way down to the foundation! I had my heartbeat, a van, a laptop and two little suitcases of clothes. That's it. Otherwise I had no idea what was going to be left. Then He started to put things back. This time I knew that if He put it there, it was His perfect will and not mine. Since January 2, my walk has been radically different. Things just happen. Doors just open or close. If I talk too long on the phone, God hangs it up. If I try to check my email when He told me not to, the computer crashes. I haven't seen anyone bind me or me bind them in any way. I can't ask anybody for anything because I have to depend on Him completely. I have a freaky high Gift of Faith that is far beyond what I had before (which I thought was a lot then). I don't understand it and I don't know the limits of it, but I know that I'm ABSOLUTELY confident that I'm in His perfect will and I'm not coloring it or nudging it one direction or the other. Last night I was on a phone call that was about to run too long, so the fire alarm in the hotel went off! I said goodbye and hung up and the INSTANT I put the receiver down the alarm stops! The Lord sort of grinned at me and chuckled. Stuff like that is happening every day. Plus I'm hearing Him really good and it's been VERY reliable. A lot more than before. I don't expect you to believe me, but I know what I know. This is about _faith_ after all. If you _believe_ your shield will hold, then it _will_ hold. If you believe that the enemy will get you and eat you, then he _will_ get you and eat you.

I've seen other people pray the White Shield prayer, but not get to 100% coverage. And we're back to a submarine with screen doors. What good is a shield that blocks 93.5% of the intentions of your heart from binding things? Might as well have not bothered. The problem is that they don't actually want to give it all up or don't actually believe that God could KEEP them from sinning. But the Bible is clear that His intentions and desire is to have people that have such a heart for Him that they will willingly subvert ALL of their will to His and let HIM keep them from sinning. Read Deuteronomy 5:29 – _"Oh, that there were such a heart in SOMEONE that they would let me write my law on their hearts and keep them from sinning that it might go well with them and their descendants forever!"_ He's desperate for somebody to be like Jesus and push ALL their chips – even the subconscious ones – out onto the table and bet it all on God, all the time, every day. So that He can bless them abundantly! That was Personal Shield Version 7.0 and He says that's as good as it gets. Go figure.

That's all I know. If you can and He says you're ready, pray for the White Shield. But be ready for your <u>whole</u> life to be rebooted. There's really no telling how much of everything that you've built was YOU.

Personal Shield Upgrade Path

1.0 Bubbles
2.0 Hard Shell Bubbles
2.5 Fire Rings
2.75 Permanent Self-Renewing
      Fire Rings
3.0 Skin Tight
4.0 Anti-Witchcraft
5.0 Silver Internal/External
5.5 Anti- External Red Dragon
6.0 Gold
7.0 White Anti-Intentions of
      the Heart

Territorial, Regional and City Shields

Basically, the Word is clear that the Lord SEEKS people that will spiritually defend the ground and His people. He will always try to raise up someone that will be instant in season and out of season with a correction or a reproof – so that God's people might grow up and be mature. He is actively seeking people to lay everything down if necessary and stand in the gap to defend the cities (and children and homes and nations).

> **Ezek 13:4-5** (KJV) – *4 O Israel, thy prophets are like the foxes in the deserts. 5 Ye have not gone up into the gaps, neither made up the hedge for the house of Israel to stand in the battle in the day of the LORD.*

> **Ezek 22:29-31** (KJV) – *29 The people of the land have used oppression, and exercised robbery, and have vexed the poor and needy: yea, they have oppressed the stranger wrongfully. 30 **And I sought for a man among them, that should make up the hedge, and stand in the gap before me for the land, that I should not destroy it: but I found none.** 31 Therefore have I poured out mine indignation upon them; I have consumed them with the fire of my wrath: their own way have I recompensed upon their heads, saith the Lord GOD.*

Here He is clear that even ONE MAN would have kept Him from having to pour out His indignation on the city and the nation. If ANYBODY had put Him first and believed in faith that God would be their rear guard, there's no telling how it might have been different. I believe God is finally raising up those people to save this generation. People that understand that SOMEBODY has to stand in the gap or we're all toast. "Saved" or not, if you're not standing in the gap or helping rebuild the wall, then you're not obeying Him. Odds are good that you're a friend of the world and not really as "saved" as you think you are.

You need to keep your own house, business, cars, etc. fully armored up. That means get it cleaned out, anoint it, ask the Lord to put up a shield and station angels round about and keep the sphere cleaned out. If something comes in, you need to be sensitive enough to the Spirit and to the environment (and the people in it) that you know something is wrong and you seek God about what to do about it.

I'm not going to deal with city, regional or national shields here. If you're qualified to do anything of that scale, then you're capable of having Him explain it to you Himself. (But If you're not walking in holiness, your prayers are probably bouncing off of brass. The enemy will try to get you to launch off on some critically important quest to save the world. Just make sure it's God and don't make it about YOU. If you have a Red Dragon, you're probably off track and don't even know it – and probably can't be convinced of it. See Appendix B.)

Cloaks

2 Kings 6:13-23 (KJV) – *13 And he said, Go and spy where he is, that I may send and fetch him. And it was told him, saying, Behold, he is in Dothan. 14 Therefore sent he thither horses, and chariots, and a great host: and they came by night, and compassed the city about. 15 And when the servant of the man of God was risen early, and gone forth, behold, an host compassed the city both with horses and chariots. And his servant said unto him, Alas, my master! how shall we do? 16 And he answered, Fear not: for they that be with us are more than they that be with them. 17 And Elisha prayed, and said, LORD, I pray thee, open his eyes, that he may see. And the LORD opened the eyes of the young man; and he saw: and, behold, the mountain was full of horses and chariots of fire round about Elisha. 18 And when they came down to him, Elisha prayed unto the LORD, and said, Smite this people, I pray thee, with blindness. And he smote them with blindness according to the word of Elisha. 19 And Elisha said unto them, This is not the way, neither is this the city: follow me, and I will bring you to the man* *whom ye seek. But he led them to Samaria. 20 And it came to pass, when they were come into Samaria, that Elisha said, LORD, open the eyes of these men, that they may see. And the LORD opened their eyes, and they saw; and, behold, they were in the midst of Samaria. 21 And the king of Israel said unto Elisha, when he saw them, My father, shall I smite them? shall I smite them? 22 And he answered, Thou shalt not smite them: wouldest thou smite those whom thou hast taken captive with thy sword and with thy bow? set bread and water before them, that they may eat and drink, and go to their master. 23 And he prepared great provision for them: and when they had eaten and drunk, he sent them away, and they went to their master. So the bands of Syria came no more into the land of Israel.*

That's one of my favorite passages! We get to see how Elisha sees in the spirit, how he imparts that gift to his servant (by intercession), how he prays specifically against the enemy, how he marches out in faith to meet them believing God answered his prayer, we get to see how easy it is for God to blind His enemies, then we get to see mercy in the handling of them. And victory because they leave Israel alone after that!

Here we see a great example of a "Cloak" in action. Elisha is right there in front of them, but the Lord blinds them. I've seen that happen personally. I've been standing in front of someone for an hour and they never saw me at all. There are lots of examples of that in Brother Yun's life. ("The Heavenly Man" by Yun and Hattaway.)

Richard Wurmbrand was the founder of "Voice of the Martyrs" and was imprisoned and tortured repeatedly over the course of decades in Russia for smuggling Bibles and for preaching the Gospel. He tells stories that he used to drive a car across the border with a special hidden compartment under the trunk to smuggle two or three Bibles at a time. God told him to fill the trunk and trust Him. So He did and the guards eyes were blinded. Then he would fill the whole back seat as well. The guards would say, "What are you coming in for?" He would say, "I'm smuggling Bibles." And they would laugh and laugh at his funny joke and wave him through! THAT is a Cloak! Christians in countries undergoing lots of persecution absolutely stand in faith and depend on that God can hide them from the eyes of the enemy. I could give you LOTS of stories. Do a Google search for Richard Wurmbrand and read some of his books. Or go to www.VoiceOfTheMartyrs.com .

Psalms 91:1-7 (KJV) – *1 He that dwelleth in the secret place of the most High shall abide under the shadow of the Almighty. 2 I will say of the LORD, He is my refuge and my fortress: my God; in him will I trust. 3 Surely he shall deliver thee from the snare of the fowler, and from the noisome pestilence. 4 He shall cover thee with his feathers, and under his wings shalt thou trust: his truth shall be thy shield and buckler. 5 Thou shalt not be afraid for the terror by night; nor for the arrow that flieth by day; 6 Nor for the pestilence that walketh in darkness; nor for the destruction that wasteth at noonday. 7 A thousand shall fall at thy side, and ten thousand at thy right hand; but it shall not come nigh thee.*

Psalms 119:114 (KJV) – *Thou art my hiding place and my shield: I hope in thy word.*

Psalms 17:8-9 (KJV) – *8 Keep me as the apple of the eye, hide me under the shadow of thy wings, 9 From the wicked that oppress me, from my deadly enemies, who compass me about.*

Psalms 27:4-5 (KJV) – *5 For in the time of trouble he shall hide me in his pavilion: in the secret of his tabernacle shall he hide me; he shall set me up upon a rock.*

Psalms 31:20-24 (Amplified) – *20 In the secret place of Your presence You hide them from the plots of men; You keep them secretly in Your pavilion from the strife of tongues. 21 Blessed be the Lord! For He has shown me His marvelous loving favor when I was beset as in a besieged city. 22 As for me, I said in my haste and alarm, I am cut off from before Your eyes. But You heard the voice of my supplications when I cried to You for aid. 23 O love the Lord, all you His saints! The Lord preserves the faithful, and plentifully pays back him who deals haughtily. 24 Be strong and let your heart take courage, all you who wait for and hope for and expect the Lord!*

Psalms 64:1-2 (KJV) – *1 Hear my voice, O God, in my prayer: preserve my life from fear of the enemy. 2 Hide me from the secret counsel of the wicked; from the insurrection of the workers of iniquity:*

Psalms 143:8-12 (KJV) - *Cause me to hear thy lovingkindness in the morning; for in thee do I trust: cause me to know the way wherein I should walk; for I lift up my soul unto thee. 9 Deliver me, O LORD, from mine enemies: I flee unto thee to hide me. 10 Teach me to do thy will;*

for thou art my God: thy spirit is good; lead me into the land of uprightness. 11 Quicken me, O LORD, for thy name's sake: for thy righteousness' sake bring my soul out of trouble. 12 And of thy mercy cut off mine enemies, and destroy all them that afflict my soul: for I am thy servant.

Some people see it as a regular sphere that just goes invisible. Some see the Lord or angels hiding them under giant wings. Some see a "pavilion" or tent over them that hides everything from the eyes of the enemy. Personally, I see an actual "cloak" of invisibility, because I read the Lord of the Rings as a kid (and far too many comic books – can you tell?). One of the girls read the verse about hiding a light under a bushel, so she saw the Lord putting a big basket over her to hide her. One of them would spiritually put on a jet black scuba suit. What you see in the Spirit is mostly affected by the "spin" or constraints you put on it yourself based on your conceptions or presuppositions or comfort zone. The effect in the spiritual realms is the same. A cloak hides you from the enemy when God wants it to. It's not your power or the strength of your brain. It's your faith that matters.

I can't find ANY Biblical references where the enemy makes someone blind or puts a spirit of stupor or sleep on anybody. Every time that it's referenced, it's always God that does it. His is the Power and the Glory, forever.

Exodus 4:11 (KJV) – *And the LORD said unto him, Who hath made man's mouth? or who maketh the dumb, or deaf, or the seeing, or the blind? have not I the LORD?*

Psalms 146:8 (ASV) – *Jehovah openeth the eyes of the blind; Jehovah raiseth up them that are bowed down; Jehovah loveth the righteous;*

And it doesn't matter where you hide or if the enemy tries to cloak it, God can see through it. That's why cloaks on the enemy or on witches or warlocks don't do any good at all when the God wants you to see what's going on. They have no defense against us, but our God is a great defense against them!

Jeremiah 23:24 (KJV) - *Can any hide himself in secret places that I shall not see him? saith the LORD. Do not I fill heaven and earth? saith the LORD.*

Nobody can hide from God? Where will you go that He can't see you? Where can you sin that He won't catch you? If you get under the table, can you cheat on a fast and God not notice? If you put your hand over the cookie, will He not see it? If He tells you to do something and you do 90% of it, you think that's good enough?

The opposite of "cloaked" would be to go in fully "dialed up" – 300 foot tall, flares going off, swords flashing, armor shiny. It took 15 minutes for the pastor of one congregation to physically throw me out. I was just standing there praying (but dialed up high) and he said, "I don't know who you are, but you've got to go right now." Wow!!

Empty-White-Space-Filler Personal Story

Sometimes the Lord will have me cloak up, drive somewhere, smash some stuff in the spirit, then cloak back up and go to wherever He really wanted me to be, but the enemy is still looking for my signature somewhere else. Misdirection and misinformation can be an offensive weapon. The Lord says He will have them turn their back so you can smash them to bits! :-) (Psalm 18:40)

I knew I was headed to Houston for several weeks, but He wouldn't even let me say it out loud or look at a map or contact anyone or anything. I really needed a confirmation and the Lord said I could call my young friend Elijah who hears REALLY well. I called and asked Elijah if he knew where I was going on this trip.

He said, "Yeah, but I can't tell you. He won't let me say it out loud." HA! Cute, Lord. OK, well that's sort of a confirmation right there, but now we're in a fine pickle. "So, Elijah, how am I going to get a confirmation if you can't speak it and I can't speak it?"

He says, "Well, I heard to just pray." OK, so we pray and the Holy Spirit is SCREAMING "Houston! Houston! Houston!" in my ear.

So I say to Elijah, "Brother, can you confirm that the thing being shouted at me in my ear is where I'm supposed to go?"

"Yep! I can confirm that!"

Ok, that probably sounds totally goofy to most folks and there are probably all kinds of logic problems with that, I know, but Elijah and I have been walking together for awhile now and I know He hears really good and God has confirmed it and built my trust in Elijah over and over. In fact, I'd be really hard pressed to find any time he didn't hear right. And he is very squeaky clean and Red Dragon free.

In Waco, Texas, the Lord had me tell EVERYONE I was going to College Station. I mean everybody – even people in gas stations. Then I drove to College Station making as much "noise" as possible. Smashing things, claiming the ground, praying and singing all the way. In College Station the Lord directs me directly to the Baptist Student Union at Texas A&M (which is a natural place for me to go find people to pray with). I'm sitting in front of it and He has me put a big, opaque shield around the whole building and parking lot and shockwave it and make sure it was fully cleaned out and filled full of Jesus. Then cloak the van up extra good, turn off the radio, stop praying, (even mentally!), drive to Houston in complete silence and don't call anybody until He told me to. When I got to Houston a couple of silent hours later, the enemy had no idea I was there. I pulled off the highway where the Lord told me, called a guy I knew OF in Houston. He knew I was coming and had a room ready for me – and his house was just a couple of miles from the exit where the Lord had told me to stop!

DELIVERANCE MISTAKES

First, you need to understand that I have this kind of "tough love" deliverance strategy. If you're an alcoholic but you won't admit it until you hit rock bottom and you're eating out of a dumpster and sleeping in the gutter, then let's just drive you down there <u>right</u> <u>now</u>. God says He will never let it go beyond what you can handle, so let's just load it up and see what it takes to break you. Whatever it takes to put you on your knees the soonest is fine with me. I want you begging for God and having nowhere else to go. So if I pull stuff off of you and it comes back seven times worse, if you're one of His, then He'll get you through it and it was all part of the plan. Whatever it takes to get you begging for Jesus and make you a broken and contrite vessel useful for His purposes. I've seen Christian Jesus-loving people delivered that were beating their wife and back on crack and cursing me and God <u>forty-eight hours</u> later! But it's all part of the plan. So I'm going to urge them to keep the doors shut, but if they're not ready to, then that too, was part of His big master plan. I've delivered Pride off of annoying pastors that are now completely insufferable. I don't worry about accidentally delivering someone that should be, because I'm not rebuking anything "in the name of Doug" - it's <u>His</u> authority and His Spirit in me, so if He doesn't want something off, it won't budge anyway. And I've seen that, too. He may say to leave them alone.

Sometimes the Lord has had us stand in front of the convenience store and deliver everybody coming and going of anything we saw. But maybe they'll get free long enough to make a decision for Christ, Maybe they'll just decide that was their LAST cigarette. Maybe they'll get meaner and nastier and more depraved until they end up in jail and find Jesus. Maybe they'll stop using their body to get what they want and put some decent clothes on. Maybe the broken soul tie will finally free them from that abusing boyfriend. They didn't know we did it and I don't care. It's not about me anyway. If they get worse, He'll get them through. If they get better, He'll get the glory.

Now these below are just my opinion, you understand, maybe it's just because God didn't teach it to me this way. Maybe it's because I have a point, so just in case, you might want to try to have an open mind. I don't mean to deny the good work that's being done and the people that are getting free, but truthfully, there aren't many. We don't have many deliverance ministries and a LOT of the ones we do have are totally operating from a man-made instruction manual. If you're a deliverance ministry that totally agrees with me on this stuff, I'd like to meet you! If you're a deliverance ministry that wants to try to raise the bar, if we can help, we'd be glad to, even if that means giving you everything we have. I don't care who is the most dangerous to satan, so long as SOMEBODY starts pushing back the darkness a whole lot faster than what seems to be happening now!

Questionnaires

There are lots of deliverance ministries that will have you fill out a questionnaire ahead of time so that they can tell by your own self-revelation what demons are messing with you. OK, I have a Psychology degree and anybody with any sense at all should be able to tell you that if you let someone with lying spirits SELF-DIAGNOSE you're not going to get any usable information! Give me a break! And they are ALL lying spirits! That's what they DO – all the time. I don't know who started this method of demonic identification, but I'm pretty sure some demon whispered it in somebody's ear and it took root.

I'll tell you exactly what will happen. If you haven't bound up everything on them ahead of time, they will let you get a bead on SOMETHING so that you will feel like you accomplished something – maybe a fear or a seduction or a lethargy. The lying spirits will use the "Sacrificial Lamb" strategy to give you something, but it won't be anything really big and really deep and it won't be something that is likely that they will be able to keep the doors shut well enough that the enemy will permanently lose that ground.

Are you getting this? Why would you have someone with demons tell you what demons they have – and you're just going to believe them? This is a war! The enemy is sneaky! If you're not hearing God really well – and preferrably SEEING the bad guys for yourself – then you're just going to have to take the word of the person that you KNOW needs deliverance. Can you see the problem there? If you can't walk up to a person that you've never met, never spoken with and know nothing about and immediately diagnose the things on them and start getting them off, then you're not really ready for war. Pray hard and ask the Lord for a LOT more discernment and to hear His voice a lot better. I'm not trying to be harsh and I don't mean to belittle the success and effort of all the folks that are trying hard – I'm just trying to raise the bar and tell you that Jesus NEVER had someone fill out a questionnaire! And neither should we if we want to be like Him. Ask to see through the eyes of Jesus, not through the eyes of a 50 question survey.

Demons Need To Manifest So We Know This Is Working

This is a crutch for people that don't see the demons well enough to identify them and shred them without them having to show themselves. You understand, this is basically like the questionnaire. You have to expect them to honestly self-reveal. I don't think you understand that these are MASTERS of deception and camouflage and subterfuge! Read the Demonic Strategies section again. They will flare up and then duck and you'll think you accomplished something, but they may just be ducking and giggling at you. They love a big show, they like to perform. I think they get raises or promotions based on their lying and performance ability. Which means they are LOOKING for a chance to make a big show – and maybe spread more lies or do some damage physically.

During the warm-up worship time for a missions conference, I met a young girl here in Kansas City that was a part of a big Spirit-filled ministry (that thinks they're the hottest thing going). I offered to help her get free of the stuff messing with her and clogging up her pipeline. So I started naming stuff and she agreed with it all. In fact, the folks at the ministry had already identified and diagnosed most of the same ones that I had, but they had told her that they were going to leave them there until she was strong enough to keep the doors shut. HUH?! You DO NOT play footsies with demons!! Did Jesus EVER say that to someone?! Do you trust God or don't you?!

I asked her if she wanted to be free and trusted that God would get her through, even if it got worse for awhile. She said that she did and she wanted them off. So I offered to pull them off. She said, "Don't I have to run around the room screaming or spit up or something? You can do it right here?" Sure. No biggie. So I start ripping stuff off very quietly. No waving or coughing or screaming, just praying quietly in the Spirit as I took my Sword and cleaned her off. And wouldn't you know it, it took about ONE minute for the religious spirits in the place to wig out and come try to stop me. Her "mentor" says, "You don't really believe you're doing anything do you? You're not delivering her of anything! You need to ask us before you talk to our people." Oh, OK. Well, if it ain't working, then why did it take like ONE minute for the enemy to send somebody over to stop me from doing whatever I was doing that wasn't really doing anything anyway? Well I just went ahead and finished anyway without telling him. And then ripped some stuff off of him for good measure. He's not the boss of me. ;-)

Please hear me. It doesn't have to be a big show. Sometimes they'll cough or have physical pain or shake. They will probably cry. But you don't have to yell at demons and wave your hands and shake your big King James at them. Our battle is <u>not</u> against flesh and blood and our battle is not <u>WITH</u> our <u>own</u> flesh and blood either! Get it? This war is happening in the spiritual realms. So take the battle <u>there</u> and thrash them.   Don't let them rip her clothes and make a big fuss and embarrass her and curse through her and stuff. I've never seen ANY of that stuff happen in any deliverance I've done. Why? Because I have a reputation that if you don't shut up and hop off when I tell you to then I'm going to torture you mercilessly and grin while I hear you snap and pop. I am not kidding. I've felt them squish. I've heard them scream when I snapped them in half – right before I threw them into the Abyss from which they are <u>not</u> getting out. I asked the Lord for a branding iron of the Holy Spirit that said, "LIBERTY" on it, just so everybody in the Abyss would know where they came from. I've had people get delivered of stuff just sitting next to me. They don't like me and they want to get away from me or make me go away if they can. Jesus didn't fight with them for hours. He said, "Go" – and they went. Why? Fear of the Lord.

One family's eight year old daughter wouldn't get anywhere near me when I first came in the door to stay with them. She would hide behind the sofa or behind her mom. She had always been shy, but it was unusual even to them for her to be this scared. They put her to bed and she couldn't sleep and was having terrible fears, so they brought her into the living room and prayed for her. I don't recall laying hands on her or getting anywhere near her, but I reached out with the hand of the Holy Spirit and ripped the Fear off of her and covered it in the Blood. Now she's not shy anymore. At ALL. Like not at all. Like weirdly not all. And now they realize that that Fear had just been dialed down and masquerading as a personality type, but it was really a Fear and it was entrenched and she was going to grow up with it and it would probably wreck her. Mom had been on anti-depressants and anti-anxiety meds for a long time. Mom is off all her meds now and free of her migraines.

This isn't about me. I want more than anything to see tens of thousands of people that are twenty times more scary to the bad guys than I am. This is a WAR!!! Shred them with prejudice and if you're not seeing them well enough, find somebody that does and ask them to share – or pester God until He lets you see them better. Then believe in faith that your weapons and shields are mighty and wreck them. If you can't really get into this, then God will send junkies and prostitutes and cutters and anorexics that were tortured for years by the demons and they will be MORE than happy to see them and squish them in the meanest, most painful possible ways.

If you think I'm just talking tough or bluffing, and you can't hear God well enough to ask Him if I'm lying and get a straight answer, then come see me – if the stuff on you will let you get close enough. I'm used to being in a room for a matter of minutes before somebody starts getting twitchy. I usually send folks a warning before I stay at their house because if there is anything hiding, it's going to surface and I'm going to find it and squish it.

Talking to the Demons

There have been a handful of occasions where I needed to find out who I was dealing with. Jesus did talk to the demon Legion. So I'm not saying that it's wrong to ask their name or talk to them. But I'm not going to have conversations with them! They're liars!! We have theology and methodology about how to handle demons based on what people were told by demons!

Dude!! I don't care to take names! I don't give a flying fig if they're unhappy or what they want or what they have to say. I'm here to crush them into powder and make them STOP torturing my brothers and sisters!

People say that if we have them identify themselves as they're leaving by speaking through the mouth of the person, that it builds their faith and they'll be better able to keep the doors shut. That's ASSUMING that the demon that is leaving is telling the truth about what he's doing there, and that you actually got him all the way off.

I find that it builds their faith and is a lot less traumatic if you just tell the person ahead of time what all their demons are, what they are whispering, where they are attached and what organic damage they've been doing. If you can walk up to a stranger and read them down a list of what's messing with them and what the voices (that they think are their own) have been saying, it will flatten them. They start crying and beg for you to get them off. So you slice them off in one pass, seal it over, fill their cup and teach them how to keep it full. And you're done. Piece of cake. Why do we have to wrestle with them for hours and hours and yell at stuff? Nobody told me it had to happen that way, so I just assumed it didn't and let God teach me – and He taught me the fastest, most caring, most gentle way to do it. Which is what you would expect if the Holy Spirit was in charge. But behind the scenes, there is this seething wrath of God that is doing horrific damage – which is also a component of His nature. We can't understand the limits of either – the wrath or the love of God. Just know that He's REALLY not happy with the demons that have been torturing His children for thousands of years and it's time to stock up the Abyss. And if they happen to be little bloody pieces when they get there, that's just fine.

Would you do deep deliverance on someone over coffee at Perkins or in front of the convenience store? I have. Bunches of times. Was I worried about them making a big show and her head spinning and throwing up and cursing coming out of her. Not in the least. Because I refuse to put up with that kind of showboating.

Leave Them There Until A Person Can Keep the Doors Shut

OK, if this was a war, can you explain exactly how that strategy makes sense? You have a saboteur on your nuclear submarine and you leave them there why? For what purpose? To catch them in the act? Hoping they repent and reform? As a spiritual strategy this is nonsense.

This is God Almighty we're talking about and His weapons are more than enough for any enemy. Maybe you don't believe that He is big enough to help you get through? Maybe you believe that if things aren't comfy and normal that is bad? That's just humanism. You want to be happy and content and for things to be peaceful, so it's better to leave the demons that you know instead of risking that a person might get worse. In the meantime, you've got a person that you KNOW needs deliverance in your congregation or assembly doing who knows how much damage?! When you identify the enemy and the Lord pulls the trigger, you CRUSH them! You do NOT play footsies with the enemy of your soul. What do you think "compromise" means? Pure, spotless Bride, dude.

Follow The Formula (Pray Just Like This)

Boy, when are we going to learn that man-made solutions aren't working? When are we going to get people that are led by the Holy Spirit and obey ALL the way? You can't write a "program" for handling spiritual things. I have never had two deliverance situations that were identical or that I thought I could whip out the same checklist and apply it exactly to the next person. For one thing, that takes too long. For another, it doesn't show extravagant personal attention and love to the individual. Yes, there are some things that I use, like the Cup Model diagram to show them the need to get cleaned out, but from there it's entirely personalized and on the fly. I'm sure glad that when we go to the Father for help, He doesn't run us through a 100 point checklist to identify our needs. He just KNOWS and then He custom tailors a solution to our faith, our willingness, our education level, our comfort zone and our strength at that particularly moment – all of which He knows better than we do! Please, be like Jesus. Show extravagant attention to the individual and customize to their needs – and the only way you can do that is to hear His voice really well and obey all the time.

P.S. - If you just read a standardized prayer every morning covering every possible variant and possibility of any way enemy that might come against you all you're doing is reinforcing all the ways the enemy can get you!

I Need Jesus Prayer

Almighty God, I know this stuff is real. I know they're messing with me and I know I've never been able to really keep them off. I believe that You are real and that You sent Your Son, Jesus to die for my sins. I believe that He was crucified and rose again and paid the penalty for my sins. I know that He has already taken on and beaten <u>all</u> of the demons. I don't want to fight them in my own power anymore. I want Jesus to be Lord and Master of my life. I don't want it a little bit, I want it ALL the way. Please come in and scrub me clean and take charge in every way. Please fill me so full of the Holy Spirit that nothing else can fit anymore and teach me how to stay full all the time. Please rip and tear and shred any demons that are messing with me and get them out and help me keep them out from now on. I'm sorry I tried to put You in a box. Please shield me all around and be God to me in whatever way You want to be God to me. I'm sorry it took me so long to acknowledge You. I don't want any other gods, just You. Show me people that will help me walk this out and are true to You. Thank You, Jesus. I know that I am Yours and You are mine. Help me hear Your voice real good all the time. I ask that You would cover me completely in the Blood of Jesus and set a shield all around me. In the mighty Name of Jesus Christ, my Lord. Amen.

Closing Prayer

Father, I thank You for all of those that You have given to me to minister to. Please let me be a blessing. Please equip me in every way to have all that I need so to do as much damage to the bad guys as possible. I'm sorry I haven't been as dangerous as I could have been up to now. Please help me redeem all the missed opportunities – not for my sake, but for Your glory. I want to help get Your Bride pure and spotless without blemish or wrinkle. Start with me, Lord. Scrub me down and clean me out. Then show me how to help my Brothers and Sisters. I love You, Lord. I trust You. Have Your way with me, even if it hurts. Turn up the refining fire and get this turkey finished cooking. And when I bang on the glass and ask you to turn it down, ignore me completely. Have Your way. Show me anything that stands between me and You, so that I can repent – then help me repent. I love You, Lord. In the mighty Name of Jesus Christ, my Lord. Amen.

Blessing

Dear Jesus, this book is not by me, it's by you. Please forgive me for anything here that isn't pure or directly from You. I take responsibility for it, but please let it fall harmless to the ground, if possible. For those that ventured through this book in search of Truth and Wisdom and something that would make them more dangerous to the enemy and useful for Your kingdom, I just ask that You would bless them now mightily in whatever way You think best. If there is any good thing that I have, Lord, I ask that You would facilitate the transfer and give it to them right now. That they would have more discernment of spirits, more word of wisdom and knowledge, more faith, more love, more patience, more prophecy, more boldness, and whatever authority I have. The Body is welcome to anything I have. Please get it to whoever needs it, Lord. But no stones, Lord, just bread. In the mighty Name of Jesus Christ. Amen.

I love you all and I'm not going to stop.

PARTS LEFT OVER AFTER WE PUT THE BICYCLE TOGETHER

The 2 Peter 1 Ladder and the corresponding "Ports"

Faith ←→ Witchcraft/Control

Virtue ←→ Tongue Ports – lying, cursing, gossip, dissension (James 3)

Knowledge ←→ Red Dragon (Hosea 4:6)

Self-control ←→ Lust

Perseverance ←→ Wings + Double-mindedness

Godliness ←→ Pride

Brotherly Kindness ←→ Psyphon

Love ←→ Jezebel (anti-christ)

After Jezebel replacement, then fill all ports with Godly replacement. Screw in the white light bulb. :-)

Counterfeits

Faith ←→ Witchcraft

Hope ←→ Despair / Loneliness

Love ←→ Jezebel

Please pray that God would hit this monstrosity with an asteroid!!

http://www.ourladyoftherockies.com

Bigger than the Statue of Liberty, this 90 foot tall giant graven image to a fertility goddess sits on the highest high point! On the Continental Divide in the Rocky Mountains looking down on the richest mineral deposit in America in Butte, Montana. This is horrifyingly bad thing for our country. Please ask the Lord to crush it. It is NOT the Virgin Mary and even if it were, God would still be mad! You do NOT make graven images and put them on high places!! This is very BAAAAD!! Butte needs to repent and this needs to come down. Spiritually and physically.

APPENDIX A

You Can Be Filled With GOOD Stuff:

The Lord – Psalm 16:5; 1 Cor 10:21

Fullness of God – Ephesians 3:19

Spirit of God – Exodus 31:3; Exodus 35:31; Ephesians 5:18

Glory of the Lord – Exodus 40:34-35; Numbers 14:21; 1 Kings 8:10-11; 2 Chronicles 5:14; 2 Chronicles 7:1-2; Psalm 72:19; Isaiah 6:3; Ezekiel 10:3-4; Ezekiel 43:5; Hag 2:7; Rev 15:8

Holy Ghost – Luke 1:15; 1:41; 1:67; 4:1; Acts 2:4; Acts 4:8; Acts 4:31, 6:3, 7:55, 9:17, 11:24, 13:9

Goodness of the Lord – Psalm 33:5

Blessing of the Lord – Deut 33:23

Fear of the Lord – Luke 5:26

All Knowledge – Rom 15:14

Knowledge of the Lord – Isaiah 11:9

Power by the spirit of the Lord and judgement – Micah 3:8

Knowledge of the glory of God – Habakkuk 2:14

Knowledge of His will, all wisdom & understanding – Col. 1:19

Spirit of Wisdom – Exodus 28:3; 35:35; Deut. 34:9

Wisdom & understanding – I Kings 7:14

Wisdom and grace – Luke 2:40

Wisdom and beauty – Exodus 35:35; Ezekiel 28:12

Judgement and righteousness – Isaiah 33:5

Light – Matt. 6:22 (Luke 11:34-36)

Grace and truth – John 1:14

Faith and power – Acts 6:8

Salvation – Psalm 116:13

Righteousness – Psalm 48:10; Psalm 112:4; Matthew 5:6

Fruits of Righteousness – Philippians 1:11

Comfort – 2 Corinthians 7:4

Consolation – Jeremiah 16:7

Compassion – Psalm 78:38, 86:15, 111:4, 145:8;

Joy – John 15:11; John 16:24; Acts 2:28; 2 Timothy 1:4; I Peter 1:8; 1 John 1:4; 2 John 1:12

Joy, Peace, Hope – Romans 15:13

Mercy – Psalm 119:64

Mercy and good fruits – James 3:17
   Blessing – 1 Corinthians 10:16

Good – Psalm 104:28; Psalm 107:9; Ecclesiastes 6:3

Good things – Job 22:18; Luke 1:53

Good works and almsdeeds – Acts 9:36

Goodness and all knowledge – Romans 15:14

Praise and honour – Psalm 71:8

Laughter and singing/rejoicing – Psalm 126:2; Job 8:21

Precious and pleasant riches – Proverbs 24:4

Horses, chariots, might men of war – Ezekiel 39:20

Wonder and amazement – Acts 3:10

Trembling (to enemies) – Zechariah 12:2

Full of days – Job 42:17

Children/People – Psalm 127:5; Luke 14:23

Bread (Food) – Exodus 28:3; Matthew 14:20; Matthew 15:37; Mark 6:42; Mark 8:8; Luke 9:17; John 6:26;

Need Clean Cup: Matthew 23:25; Luke 11:39; Proverbs 25:4; Isaiah 66:20; 1 Thessalonians 4:4; 2 Timothy 2:21; Hebrews 9:21

Different Size Cups: Isaiah 22:24

Need Pliable Cup: Matthew 9:17 (Mark 2:22, Luke 5:37)

Need FULL Cup: Matthew 25:4; Ruth 1:21

Chosen/Special Vessel:
Acts 9:15; Romans 9:21; I Thessalonians 4:4; 2 Tim 2:20

Hated Vessels: Romans 9:22

Things that are NEVER Full:

Hell and destruction - Proverbs 27:20

The Sea – Ecclesiastes 1:7

Appetite – Ecclesiastes 6:7

Things that can be filled: Stomach, Hearts, House of the Lord/Tabernacle, People, Tribes, Nations, God, the Earth

Or You Can Be Filled With BAD Stuff:

Sin – Job 20:11; Jeremiah 51:5; I Thess 2:16;

Evil and madness - Eccl 9:3

Satan, lies – Acts 5:3

Devils – 1 Corint 10:21

Confusion – Job 10:15; Acts 19:29

Heaviness – Psalm 69:20; Philippians 2:26

Travail and vexation of spirit – Ecclesiastes 4:6

Tossings to and fro – Job 7:4

Drunkenness and/or nakedness – Lamentations 4:21; Jeremiah 12:12

Drunkenness, Sorrow, astonishment and desolation – Ezekiel 23:33

Violence – Genesis 6:11; Genesis 6:13; Ezekiel 7:23, 8:17, 28:16

Violence, lies and deceit – Zephaniah 1:9; Micah 6:12

Lies, robbery, blood – Nahum 3:1

Abominations and filthiness – Ezra 9:11;

Abominations, filthiness of fornication – Revelation 17:4

Adultery, cannot cease from sin, beguiling, covetous practices, cursed children – 2 Peter 2:14

Bitterness – Job 9:18; Lamentations 3:15

Sorrow – John 16:6

Envy, contradicting, blaspheming – Acts 13:45

Unrighteousness, fornication, wickedness, covetousness, maliciousness, full of envy, murder debate, deceit, malignity, whisperers, backbiters, haters of God, despiteful, proud, boasters, inventors of evil things, disobedient to parents, without understanding, covenant breakers, without natural affection, implacable, unmerciful – Romans 1:29-31

Wickedness – Leviticus 19:29; Joel 3:13

Blood of innocents – 2 Kings 21:16; 2 Kings 24:4; Jeremiah 19:4

Hands full of blood – Isaiah 1:15

Bloody crimes and violence – Ezekiel 7:23

Blood and perverseness – Ezekiel 9:9

Trouble – Job 14:1; Psalm 88:3

Heaviness – Psalm 69:20; Philippians 2:26

Cursing, deceit, fraud, mischief and vanity – Psalm 10:7

Cursing and bitterness – Romans 3:14

Mischief – Proverbs 12:21; Psalm 26:10

Subtilty and mischief – Acts 13:10

Deceit – Jeremiah 5:27

Deadly Poison – James 3:8

Extortion and excess – Matthew 23:25

Hypocrisy and iniquity – Matthew 23:28

Cruelty / Strife – Psalm 74:20

Strife – Proverbs 17:1

Darkness – Matthew 6:23; Luke 11:34; Revelation 16:10

No pleasure – Hosea 8:8

Their own devices/own ways – Proverbs 1:31; Proverbs 3:10; Prov. 14:4

Dead men's bones and uncleanness – Matthew 23:27

Carcases of detestable and abominable things – Jeremiah 16:18

Wrath - Esther 3:5; Luke 4:28; Acts 19:28;

Wrath of God - Revelation 15:1; Revelation 15:7; Reve 16:19

Fury of the Lord – Isaiah 51:17; Isaiah 51:20; Jeremiah 6:11

Fury – Dan 3:19; Jeremiah 25:15

Astonishment and desolation – Ezekiel 23:33

Snare, fire and brimstone, tempest - Psalm 11:6

Trembling – Isaiah 51:17, Isaiah 51:22, Zechariah 12:2

Indignation – Esther 5:9; Isaiah 30:27; Jerem. 15:17; Acts 5:17; Rev 14:10

Judgement – Isaiah 1:21

Reproach / Shame – Lam 3:30; Habakkuk. 2:16

Scorn and derision – Psalm 123:4; Ezekiel 23:22

Contempt – Psalm 123:3

Confusion – Job 10:15

Plagues – Exodus 10:6; Rev. 21:9

Madness – Jeremiah 51:7; Luke 6:11

Disease / Pain – Psalm 38:7; Isaiah 21:3

Slain – Jeremiah 33:5; Ezekiel 9:7; Ezekiel 30:11; Ezekiel 32:5

APPENDIX B

THE RED DRAGON

The horrifying truth about why the "church" <u>cannot</u> seem to change.

from Doug Perry,

fotm@fellowshipofthemartyrs.com
www.FellowshipOfTheMartyrs.com
10/25/06 – revised 1/1/07 – revised 7/1/2011

Father God, I ask in the name of Jesus Christ that you would preserve and protect those who are reading this, that you would remove or bind up every obstacle or strategy of the enemy that would try to keep them from hearing and receiving this word. I ask that you would bind up the spirit of Jezebel in each person during the time they are reading and meditating on this so that they could hear Your voice clearly and You could minister to their spirit Yourself about this. I pray that you would bind up the Red Dragon and keep it from whispering to them during this time. I know you want us free. Please, Father! Please forgive us and show us how to make it right. Don't let the enemy steal Your words from their heart. Confirm this to their spirits and show them what to do next. Thanks, Abba. We pray in the Name of Jesus Christ, Amen.

HOW IT ALL STARTED

The Red Dragon is what I first saw sitting over the top of several charismatic ministries here in Kansas City. It looks just like a Chinese silk parade dragon - a big, scary face with the feet of people sticking out underneath. (Not the little kind that they carry up over their head on a stick, but the really big parade dragons that surround you and just your legs stick out.) At one major ministry here in town it was really trying to mess with me. I was on my knees at the altar trying to repent and stand in the gap for the sins of their people and for them going their own way. They really need somebody to repent for the damage they've done to so many people. Like Exodus 32, I was even offering to take onto myself all the guilt for what they had done. But I couldn't do it. I couldn't repent. Not because I didn't want to or was unwilling – I just couldn't even get a single tear out. Which is REALLY odd, because I cry when God lets me have a glass of water. Big chunks of most of my days are spent weeping for the state of things or for people, places or institutions. I weep at altars all the time. But at **their** altar I couldn't even get ONE tear out.

I knew something was suppressing my tears – and that's my best weapon! I started looking around trying to figure out what was messing with me and saw the Red Dragon on the roof. (It's not unusual for me to see spiritual strongholds on people or places.) I decided to rip it off and cast it down and, since I was pretty mad that it was messing with me, I decided to do some damage to it first. I went after it with the Sword of Spirit and hacked at it a few times and then the Lord said, "STOP!" I wanted to cast it down and He said, "No. I put it there and I'm not going to allow you to pull it off."

Well, that was kind of a shock. God told me to get up and leave, that it was a curse on the whole place and that HE put it there and I was not to try to deliver them of it. I stood in the parking lot for awhile and watched it on the roof and I got madder and madder. It was mocking me and telling me I had no authority and that it was in charge and I was nothing. I could see that the people in there were oblivious to it and were under all kinds of oppressions themselves, but the Red Dragon kept them from seeing the problems. This place is known internationally for it's excesses and nearly everyone I've met from there has a spirit of lust and a love of money and a big pride stronghold and is thoroughly convinced they're the hottest thing on the planet. As I stood next to my van, I was getting really hot and decided to torture it some more, but the Lord again stopped me. He said very clearly, "This is what it does, it is about pride. It makes it all about YOU. Either it convinces you to come inside and join it, or it convinces you to fight against it, but either way, it takes your eyes off of Jesus and makes you focus on IT. I told you to leave it alone! Now get in the van and go and don't come back."

Later that night, I was still having a real problem taking captive every thought as it continued to whisper and try to get pride to rise up. I was constantly thinking about what I should have done differently or how I'll show them someday and they'll see how wrong they are. I found myself scheming about all the ways I could free them or crush it or tell everyone that it was there. The Lord had to stop me again and show me that it was winning because I was making it about me and about works and about the fight with it. I had to constantly keep turning it over to God and renouncing it, but it kept coming back and sneaking in. Finally the Lord said to call a friend of mine who sees very well in spirit and has a lot of experience with deliverance. Even though I had tried to get all cleaned off, it wouldn't budge. So I called him and without prompting he saw the pride spirit right away and helped me rip it off. I'm not sure I could have done it by myself. Not because the Jesus in me isn't big enough to cast off any demon, but because THIS demon is a curse from God and is a WHOLE lot harder to get off of you. Without repentance it won't budge and it SUPPRESSES repentance! I had to beg the Lord to get it off of me and repent for having tried to attack it against His will. But without someone with a true gift of repentance helping me, I was unable to really repent and get free from it. I got it on me when I let their Dragon goad me into fighting with it when the Lord had told me to leave. I set myself above God and decided that it was OK for me to do something He had told me not to do. Just like Eve in the Garden.

Once having gained victory over any demonic power or stronghold, you gain authority over that "flavor" and have increased sensitivity. That's why people that have been sexually abused are hypersensitive to others who have been abused, for example. They can smell it on someone because they've been through it. Within a few weeks, the Lord started showing me lots of other Red Dragons. At first I thought they were just the offshoots of that one well-known ministry – as the other places where I had seen it were all connected to the first place in direct or round-about ways. But I also saw them on individuals who were only tangentially related to it.

Again I was sent to a conference of a different ministry here in town and found myself in the same situation, it was trying to either suck me in or get me to fight with it. The Lord made it clear that I was to just leave it alone, but again it required the help of another deliverance/repentance expert to get me cleaned off. After that I asked the Lord to upgrade my spiritual "shield" so that I could be in those places without it sticking to me constantly. To be placed under the curse along with them, it's enough to just be present and go along with whatever their agenda is! That was never going to work for me because I'm all over town and constantly visiting one ministry or another and can't have it messing with me constantly. The Lord honored my prayer for a tougher shield and so far it's holding.

I've seen the Red Dragon all over town. More on that below. Since the first encounter I have spent a lot of time praying and listening to the Lord about what this is, where it came from, how it got there and more importantly, how to get it off. As the Lord began to reveal more about it, I began to be horrified at what I was finding. It's not just that one ministry and it's not just an isolated outbreak. I hope you'll see as I proceed with this and that you will be equally shocked, horrified, ashamed, repentant – and have a substantial increase in your Fear of the Lord.

Some people think that this writing is about the Red Dragon and how to fight satan. It's not. This is about Fear of the Lord and what will happen when you go your own way – even a little bit. You CANNOT rebuke this off of someone. You CANNOT claim the blood of Jesus and cast this down. They HAVE to repent – and it suppresses repentance. I'm writing this to show you the mess we've made and the hopelessness of the situation without God's grace and without HIM pouring out the Gift of Repentance on His people – either directly or through the people He has raised up that already know how to weep and mourn before the altar. This writing is not about glorifying satan – he is only a tool in the hand of a fierce, jealous, living God, who at the moment is not at all happy with us.

If you don't believe that people can actually see demons (or that demons are real) or don't believe that I actually saw what I say I saw, then just consider all of this a fictional poetic allegory and see if you can get it to jive with Scripture. Whatever. I don't really care what you think of me, but ignore this message at your own risk. If I'm right, this is really, really far worse than anyone can probably get their head around and our situation is hopeless without repentance and hardly anybody can repent!

Father, I offer up everything you've ever given me toward the upbuilding and equipping of Your Body. Those who are reading this who believe in faith and can receive and are ready, please give them whatever you gave me. Whatever I have, they are welcome to drink it in right now, even if I don't get it back. I trust You, Father. Give them Discernment of Spirits, give them Wisdom, give them authority over the demons that confront them and give them Fear of the Lord. If you're willing and they're ready, let them see the Red Dragons clearly. Pour out the Gift of Repentance on them and let it be true and run strong. Give them the strength to turn and stay turned. In proportion to their faith and Your willingness and perfect will, increase all their gifts so that they can be dangerous to the enemy. Open blind eyes and let the dragon's scales fall off. Let them see the bad guys really clearly and have an unquenchable fire in their belly to free all the captives. In the name of the Lord Jesus Christ, Amen.

THE IF/THEN AXIOMS OF GOD'S WRATH

IF you are a child of God, **THEN** the requirements are higher on you than on the "world". (John 1:12, Luke 12:48)

IF you are a child of God, **THEN** you are supposed to obey God and God alone and lean not on your own understanding. (Acts 5:29, Prov. 3:5)

IF you are a child of God and you are following a Man instead (including yourself), **THEN** you are in disobedience to God. (Matt. 9:9; I Peter 2:21; John 12:25-26)

IF you are a child of God in disobedience, **THEN** the Lord would like to draw you back to Himself – by whatever means necessary. (Luke 15)

IF you repeatedly refuse correction, **THEN** God will turn you over to increasingly bad stuff until you break. (Daniel 4:28-37; Romans 1:18-32)

IF you are really, really stubborn and rebellious, **THEN** God will harden your heart and send strong delusion on you until you are utterly destroyed – or you repent, whichever comes first. (Romans 1:18-32; Rom. 9:18; John 12:40; 2 Thess. 2:11-12)

IF you are a group of people, **THEN** God may collectively turn you over to satan to teach you not to blaspheme or send oppressions upon you. (I Tim. 1:20; I Tim. 6:1, Exodus, Judges, I and II Kings, etc.)

IF you persist in your rebellion, **THEN** expect MASSIVE negative consequences both spiritually and physically. (Isaiah 31:1, Deut. 28, Lamentations, the bulk of the Bible is warnings of negative consequences for disobedience!)

IF there is a war between Good and Evil and we seem to be losing, **THEN** we are going our own way and God has blinded us and sent a strong delusion against us because we are being disobedient and rebellious. (Deut. 28, Rev. 3:14-22)

THE IF/THEN AXIOMS OF GOD'S CURSES

IF you are a child of God in disobedience, **THEN** God WILL send down curses on you until you turn. (2 Thess. 2:11-12; Acts 9:1-9; John 9:35-41, 12:40)

IF God sends down curses on you, **THEN** one of them is probably "strong delusion" or "blindness." (2 Thess. 2:11-12; Acts 9:1-9; John 9:35-41, 12:40)

IF God sends blindness or strong delusion on you, **THEN** you probably won't even know you're blind and deceived. (Rev. 3:15-17)

IF you are a prophet of God and you're in disobedience, **THEN** you will probably be VERY sure that you're hearing God really well, even though it's a lying spirit that is twisting everything up. (1 Kings 22:1-40; Matt. 15:14, 24:24; 2 Thess. 2:9-12; Rev. 3:15-17)

IF repentance is the only thing that can break the curse, **THEN** you really, really need to repent right now. (James 4:7-10; Mark 1:4; 2 Corinthians 7:9-11; Romans 2:4-5; Matt 3:1-2; Luke 13:1-5; Acts 2:36-41; Acts 17:29-31; 2 Peter 3:9; Rev. 2:5, 2:16, 2:22, 3:3; 3:19)

But, **IF** you're under a delusion and are blind or asleep, **THEN** you can't repent or don't know what to repent for. (Matt. 15:14; Rev. 3:17; John 9:40; Matt. 13:13-14)

IF you don't repent, **THEN** you are toast. (And repentance is a gift that can ONLY come from God – and He is cursing you for being disobedient and may not pour out on you the Gift of Repentance.) (Romans 2:4; 2 Tim. 2:25-26; Acts 17:30; James 4:7-10, Acts 5:31)

IF you can't or won't repent and repentance is the only hope, **THEN** you're caught in a hopeless paradox loop.

IF there is going to be any hope for you, **THEN** either God Himself or someone who already HAS a gift of repentance has to come and pour it out on you so that you can get released. And then you have to turn and **stay** turned. If you go back like a dog to its vomit, it's going to go VERY badly for you. (2 Peter 2:20-22; 2 Timothy 2:25-26; 2 Corin. 7:10)

THE IF/THEN AXIOMS OF CURRENT CHURCH CONDITIONS

IF God is for us, **THEN** nothing can stand against us. (Romans 8:31; Joshua 1:9; 1 John 4:13-18; 2 Chron. 32:7-8; 2 Kings 6:15-17)

IF God says that if you obey, nothing can stand against you, and currently things are standing against us, **THEN** we must not be obeying God.

IF there is a war between good and evil and we seem to be losing, **THEN** we must be under the curses of Deuteronomy 28, not the blessings. (Deut. 28)

IF there is hatred among brethren and adultery and envy and lust and dissension and factions and selfish ambition inside the Church and its leadership, **THEN** it CANNOT inherit the Kingdom of Heaven in its current state. (Galatians 5)

IF there is a love of money present and persistent in the Church, **THEN** the root of all evil is well entrenched in our structures and we're in big trouble. (I Timothy 6:10)

IF we are to be known as Christians by our love and we hate each other, **THEN** we might not actually be Christians. (I John 2:9,11; 3:14-24; 4:19-21; John 15:23)

IF we are not being good stewards of that which the Lord entrusted to us and we've buried our coin in the dirt, **THEN** we will be cast into outer darkness where there will be much crying and gnashing of teeth. (Luke 12:35-48; Matt. 25:25-46)

IF we can definitely show that the Church is basically doing everything exactly BACKWARDS of the way the Bible suggests we do it – and nobody seems to mind, **THEN** we have to come to the conclusion that there is a supernatural stupidity imposed on the system because nobody could intentionally design something this broken.

See http://www.fellowshipofthemartyrs.com/scary_stats.htm
See http://www.fellowshipofthemartyrs.com/pharisees.htm
See http://www.fellowshipofthemartyrs.com/humansacrifice.htm
See http://www.fellowshipofthemartyrs.com/business.htm

SAMPLE SCARY STATS –
HOW CAN WE SCRIPTURALLY JUSTIFY THIS KIND OF STUFF?

- Average cost per baptism in Cambodia - $4300

- Average cost per baptism in India - $9800

- Average cost per baptism in USA - $1,550,000

- Average cost per baptism in Germany - $2,119,000

- Less than 1% of Christian revenue is spent on evangelism to the most unreached.

- 91% of all Christian outreach/evangelism does not target non-Christians but targets other Christians.

- Out of 648 million Great Commission Christians, 70% have never been told about the world's 1.6 billion unevangelized individuals.

- Despite Christ's command to evangelize, 67% of all humans from AD 30 to the present day have never even heard of his name.

- Some 250 of the 300 largest international Christian organizations regularly mislead the Christian public by publishing demonstrably incorrect or falsified progress statistics.
- Currently there are over 41,000 "Christian" denominations and we start another one every two days.

Stats from World Christian Trends, William Carey Library, David Barrett & Todd Johnson, 2001.

The summary and analysis of the annual Christian mega-census.

WHAT IS THE RED DRAGON?

It is the enemy. It is the whore of Babylon, it is anti-christ, it is the false prophet, it is the dragon of Revelation. Not that it is the ONLY permutation or "echo" or complete manifestation of any of those things, but it is all of them as well. It is the Babylonian religious system in all it's forms and permutations. It could be Buddhism or Islam or Atheism or Catholicism or a denominational system like the Episcopalians, the Lutherans, the Methodists, etc. Everyone that has gone their own way and made up their own religion.

Don't think you made up your own religion? Well, if you've cut and pasted parts out of the Bible or added something to it that isn't really in there, then you've made a hybrid, accepted compromise and made a covenant with foreign gods of your own making. It's really obvious if you're bowing down to idols of gold or stone or wood, but it's just as much idolatry if you're bowing down to extra-Biblical documents or made up traditions or philosophies. You can worship a particular version of the Bible, you can require things of those in your fellowship that the Bible doesn't, you can refuse to associate with other people that have the Holy Spirit in them but disagree with you on some secondary issue, you can set a man up as your head instead of Jesus. Those, and thousands of other permutations, are all evidence that you are a cult and have made up your own mystery religion and are worshiping the wrong Jesus (or worshiping yourselves).

The biggest difference between the Red Dragons is whether or not God considers you part of physical or spiritual Israel. If you are NOT, then the Dragon on you (or your "church") is there because it snuck in or was invited in, but either way, it can be crushed and you can be delivered and set free. At one point the Lord had me pull one off of a Buddhist monastery and crush it and cast it down. They CAN be delivered of the Red Dragon. (That doesn't mean they won't get another one right away if they like it, but the Lord wanted to show me that it's anti-christ, but it's not there as a consequence (curse) on children of God. It's just the 'world' being the 'world.')

BUT ... if you are physical Israel (the nation/the race) or spiritual Israel (the Church), and you have a Red Dragon on the roof, then it is now firmly entrenched and GOD PUT IT THERE and it cannot be removed without repentance. It is MUCH sneakier and nastier and harder to get out from under this kind of Dragon, because God is angry and helping it along.

Hear me, if you are a "Christian" and you have gone your own way, the curses of Deuteronomy 28 have landed on you, but you are probably sure that you are just fine. This is not an "Old Testament" thing that doesn't apply anymore to Christians! For His purposes and to prove His sovereignty, God WILL harden your heart if you go your own way and WILL blind you to the true state of how bad things really are. The Church of Laodecia in Rev. 3 thought it was rich, but it was really hungry, naked, wretched and blind. That is the kind of skewed perspective that happens when you are supernaturally stupefied by this curse.

The "world" can be under a Red Dragon and really hate it and want out and be desperate for something better. They only remain trapped because they haven't heard the Truth or can't receive it yet. But the "church" under a Red Dragon actually likes it and doesn't want to change, because their ears are being tickled and their hearts are hardened. The longer it goes on, the worse it gets and subsequent generations are more and more depraved and lost. They are less and less likely to be hearing God and more and more dependent on legalism and tradition. Either way, the people die for lack of knowledge. Lack of knowledge of God's true law and lack of knowledge of what Fear of the Lord really is. And lack of knowledge about how to REALLY repent for anything.

In another effort to prove this, the Lord prompted me to do a complete study of all the times that someone in the Bible is affected by stupor, sleep, slumber, blindness or deafness. I can find NO instance in the Bible of the enemy doing this to anybody. Nearly every pastor I've ever heard preach on this believes that the Church, particularly the church in America, is, at the moment, the rich, sleepy, blind Laodecian church. If I'm right, then based on my study of scripture, GOD Himself did this to us. There is NO indication that I can find anywhere that sleep or stupor or blindness can come on God's people from ANY source other than God – and that they did it to themselves by disobeying God!! (See verses at the end of the Red Dragon section - page 146.)

Please hear me. I've spent the last two months traveling all over the country and seeing dragons large and small – on major ministries, on mega churches, on home groups, on individuals. This is FAR more dangerous than anyone wants to admit and far more deadly. You will be DEAD SURE that you are right and hearing God accurately, even while the Lord sends a lying spirit from the Throne that is intent on your destruction! He really does do that. Set your man-made theology aside for a moment and read the Bible. Read 2 Chronicles 18 and 1 Kings 22. King David is not allowed to touch the king of Israel (Saul), but God is perfectly willing to kill another anointed king (Ahab) Himself and leave His people without a shepherd.

God WILL send a deception upon you and you won't even know it. The closer you are to God, the higher His expectation that you will obey and the meaner the Red Dragon to which He will turn you over when you go your own way. I know it's really unlikely that you can hear me if you're under one of those, but please try.

WHO HAS A RED DRAGON ON THEM?

Everybody that is not fully under Christ's headship automatically defaults to the anti-christ spirit. All layers at all levels are subject to being under the "cover" of the Red Dragon. You can even be under multiple Red Dragons at the same time. That is, if someone was a part of the Body of Christ but has gone their own way (whether individually or corporately) they have created their own "mystery religion" and put themselves under a Dragon. The longer they are there, the more God will harden their hearts and blind them to the true state of their soul.

It's not as simple as being out of "church" either, or withdrawing your "letter" of membership. It is much more pervasive and sneaky. A person can have an anti-christ religious spirit on them, their family, their congregation, their city, their denomination, their country. They can be "members" of multiple layers of Dragon Teams that might even have conflicting goals and purposes – but all have set themselves against God. And probably some layers I can't even see are in play, but they must ALL be broken! You can't conform to the 'world' on ANY level!

I've found that the Red Dragon is strongest and fiercest and most active and malicious on those places that would normally hear God the best. That is, the "Spirit-filled" ministries that believe in the gifts and preach holiness and believe God speaks and seek God's face require the biggest, meanest, sneakiest Red Dragon to keep them off course. Plus, the expectations are highest for them, so the consequences of disobedience are far worse. Those are the places where it is strongest and most active and easiest to spot on the roof. A congregation that is asleep and has been for generations, and the doctrine of the denomination is fully ingrained, and they are not in any danger of hearing God and being directed by Him, doesn't hardly require a Red Dragon at all. A teeny weeny one is all that needs to be assigned to that place. Both kinds of groups are just as deceived and just as oppressed, but it's a lot less work for the enemy if you're already asleep and you like it that way. And frankly, God is a lot less mad at the sleeping ones – because they don't know what they don't know.

The good news is that it's a lot easier to repent in a place that's asleep. I have a lot of hope that the Baptists and the Brethren and the Episcopalians and the Lutherans and others will be able to receive this and repent. Their Red Dragon is not as strong and they might just sneak up on it and get free before it notices. As soon as a revival fire is lit in a Baptist congregation however, a much bigger Dragon with lots of help will show up to squash it. The element of surprise is key. Bind up what's there before it can call for help.

I'm a lot less optimistic about the charismatics. They hear God and are really proud of it and are sure that they are hearing with 100% accuracy (which is what happens when you're under a delusion from God). Their Red Dragons are VERY powerful and fierce and have a stranglehold on corporate repentance. I have seen that one up close and personal and been shocked by how much it controls the whole thing – even outside people that come in to speak at some of these places are sometimes completely, supernaturally unable to really preach corporate repentance.

Ultimately, corporate change is going to come down to the Lead Dragon Dancer. If the ministry head (pastor, apostle, prophet, bishop, priest, whatever) can throw off the Red Dragon and really repent sincerely and weep and mourn in front of his sheep, he might just free them all. But it's the longest of long shots that the ministry head will really lay it all down without picking it up again – or finding a new Red Dragon of a slightly different style. I've seen it happen, so I know it can be done, but I don't think it's going to be common. Read Ezekiel 34.

I believe that a team of people who have a true Gift of Repentance can come and turn a place around – whether or not the Lead Dragon Dancer wants it. I've seen that happen as well. I've been in a congregation and poured out what I had and seen them weeping and repenting. But it is unsustainable if the Lead Dragon Dancer won't go along with it or the people won't leave behind the institutions of Man. They will not go where you won't lead them. If the shepherds won't go, the sheep won't either. The sheep are either going to need to find a shepherd that will get them to safety – or gang up on the shepherd they have until he breaks down and becomes a broken and contrite vessel useful for God's purposes.

Without corporate change, it's just going to be up to the individuals to get out from under it. That may happen in ones and twos, or it may be a whole mass exodus that leaves the Lead Dragon Dancer standing alone. Whatever it takes, just get out from under it if you can.

HOW DID IT GET ON GOD'S PEOPLE?

They went their own way. They ate from the forbidden fruit, turned to other gods, failed to carefully and diligently follow the Lord's commands, so they opened the door. They failed to joyfully and gladly serve the Lord in time of prosperity. The farther they went, the more the Lord hardened their hearts and gave it permission to mess with them. See Deuteronomy. 28. Those curses were natural curses on natural Israel but had a spiritual component. They are also spiritual curses on spiritual Israel – which is the Church – and they have a natural component. We are currently experiencing ALL of those curses in the "church" system that we've built. It can ONLY mean that we have disobeyed God and gone our own way. (See page 223).

We brought this on ourselves. Read Lamentations. These curses DID manifest on natural Israel. And they are currently manifesting on spiritual Israel at a phenomenal rate. But since we aren't seeing in the spirit – we're judging the natural (and we're blinded by God) – we're missing it. But the sheep can feel it and they're leaving.

2 Timothy 2:19-26 (KJV) – 19 Nevertheless the foundation of God standeth sure, having this seal, The Lord knoweth them that are his. And, let every one that nameth the name of Christ depart from iniquity. 20 But in a great house there are not only vessels of gold and of silver, but also of wood and of earth; and some to honour, and some to dishonour. 21 If a man therefore purge himself from these, he shall be a vessel unto honour, sanctified, and meet for the master's use, and prepared unto every good work. 22 Flee also youthful lusts: but follow righteousness, faith, charity, peace, with them that call on the Lord out of a pure heart. 23 But foolish and unlearned questions avoid, knowing that they do gender strifes. 24 And the servant of the Lord must not strive; but be gentle unto all men, apt to teach, patient, 25 In meekness instructing **those that oppose themselves**; if God peradventure will **give them repentance** to the acknowledging of the **truth**; 26 And that they may **recover themselves out of the snare of the devil**, who are taken captive by him at his will.

If you do not depart from iniquity, if you are not purged, if you do not flee from youthful lusts, if you do not avoid foolish and unlearned questions, if you engender strifes, THEN you oppose <u>yourself</u> by getting under a Red Dragon that is designed for your own destruction. You get out from under the protecting cover of God's perfect will and open yourself up to whatever wants to come mess with you. And it will probably be something really sneaky and subtle (at least at the beginning) and it will lie to you and it will sound JUST like God. And your ONLY hope is repentance – so that you can acknowledge the Truth and maybe recover from the snare of the devil who has taken you captive at his will. And this verse says that they may not be able to do it themselves, those who are sanctified servants of the Lord may need to patiently, meekly instruct those people about how to get free. I believe that means pouring out your own Gift of Repentance on them. How did YOU get to be sanctified, gentle, meek and patient – except by repenting? Now show them how to do it! Better yet, repent in front of them so they can see how it's done.

The longer you're under the Dragon, the more blind and stupid you get. At some point you're rolling on the floor clucking like chickens or worshiping crying statues – or worse, feeding your flock poisoned fruit punch or having sex with the daughters of your fifteen wives or loading your automatic weapons while the FBI and the ATF drive tanks into your living room. And you're still ABSOLUTELY sure it was all God's idea and you're on the right track! That is, right up until you stand before God and He says, "I never knew you." THEN there will be weeping and repenting, but it will be too late. Wouldn't it be better to just do that first and maybe avoid all the other heartache?

How do you think we're going to get Him to turn without that? How about this verse? Think this is just good advice or is this a command? Is there ANY other prescription in the Bible to get Him to turn?

2 Chronicles 7:13-14 – *13 "When **I shut** up the heavens so that there is **no rain**, or **command** locusts to devour the land or **send** a plague among my people, 14 **IF my** people, who are called by **my** name, will **humble** themselves and **pray** and seek **my** face and **turn** from their wicked ways, **THEN** will I **hear** from heaven and will **forgive** their sin and will **heal** their land.*

WHAT DOES THE RED DRAGON LOOK LIKE?

The way it was shown to me, it looks just like the shell of a large Chinese dragon in a carnival or parade. It has no legs of its own and would be motionless without outside power. It has a great big, scary head with teeth and a mean look and seems very fierce and impressive – but also kind of endearing. It's covered in silk and shiny things and is designed to attract attention to itself. But it cannot do anything or get anywhere without the hands and feet of the people under its "cover" to keep it going. Just like in the parades, it is constantly chasing a "Pearl." Satan is a defeated enemy with no power of his own. He accomplishes his purposes by co-opting our own physical and spiritual energy. We are the legs that power him.

From the outside it looks very slick, the legs of the Dragon Dancers are adorned and colorful. But if you look underneath it's just a thin wood frame filled with sweaty guys in tanktops. From the inside, there's nothing really animated or special about it. All the emphasis is put on outside appearances and much work is put into making sure the "guts" are all hidden from view.

See a small Chinese parade dragon on video here - http://chcp.org/mpeg/ . And a very larger, internally lit with electric lights, fancy one here - http://www.theschoolbell.com/Links/Chinatown/dragon.mov . And lots more information and background about the Chinese dragon here - http://www.moonfestival.org/legends/dragon.htm . And more here - http://en.wikipedia.org/wiki/Chinese_dragon . If you do a Yahoo or Google search for "Chinese dragon" you might just be shocked at how much of this religious festival worshiping the dragons has been filtered down to school children as a "cultural" experience. There are pages and pages of teacher aids about how to have your class of elementary school kids do a dragon dance parade. This is a RELIGIOUS festival, this is NOT safe, fluffy fun for Christian kids! Here is an interesting writing about the Dragon throughout scripture and why we need to take this seriously – http://eifiles.cn/dp.htm .

I've seen the Red Dragons on people, too. It's a much smaller version, is mounted on their front with the tail up and the head down. That is, it's running down their front with it's tail in their face (or wrapped around their neck) and gripped on their front. Could be large or small, but it fits with the Deuteronomy 28 curse that we will be the tail and not the head. We may think we're in charge, but really we're just staring up a Red Dragon's rear end. Sometimes it will have more than one head. Sometimes it may even have a face that looks like whatever person they have knowingly or unknowingly made their god – Calvin, Luther, the Pope, their pastor, their wife – could even be themselves.

WHAT IS THE "PEARL"?

In Chinese religious mythology and in the parades, the dragons always chase a pearl. The really big red dragons chase a pearl painted blue and green like the Earth – now isn't that just straight out of the Book of Revelation!?

The Dragon dangles a shiny carrot out in front to take the attention off of itself.   It convinces everyone of a goal and uses all their energy, momentum, and physical and spiritual assets to reach that goal – which is always something **other than** the pure pursuit of Jesus. It could be a new gym or a new piece of land for a bigger sanctuary or an experience or a manifestation or to be the biggest, best prayer ministry or to run a soup kitchen or anything – just so long as they're not directly pursuing Jesus and His total headship in everything. The goal is to be constantly moving and DOING so that it is always JUST ahead and requires constant forward motion. If a goal is actually reached, another will be immediately set so that the Dragon can keep everyone constantly churning.   If a goal seems unreachable or is never met, it will be replaced by something that can affirm the Dragon Dancers and keep them urging forward. Whatever this "pearl of great price" might be, it **IS NOT** a pursuit of Fear of the Lord and a desire to be fully and completely under His headship and have constant communion with Him without any structures or systems of Man in the middle – that would destroy the Dragon. Anything but that will do. The Dragon is VERY creative. I've seen all kinds of Pearls and some of them look really honorable and noble, but the people have their eyes on the Pearl and not on Jesus. And the Pearl keeps them from seeing the Dragon that is enveloping them.

If the Pearl is ANYTHING other than what Jesus wants you to be doing at that very moment, you're going to be happily dancing OFF of the Narrow Path and out into the Broad Way that leads to destruction. There is His PERFECT will and everything else. If you aren't in His perfect will, then you're going your own way. If you can't hear His voice, then you're probably leaning on your own understanding and directing your own paths.

HOW DOES IT WORK?

The Lead Dragon Dancer is the one that is most skilled, most well-trained, most practiced and most showy. He is the one that controls the head of the Dragon (or at least he thinks he does). He is the most acclaimed, most noticed, and he dictates the direction, pace, style and movement of the Dragon. (In actuality, he's a slave to the pearl and the Dragon picked the pearl.) When the Red Dragon is over a congregation or ministry, the head of the ministry is the one closest to, most influenced by and best trained by the head of the Dragon. He is the absolute **least likely** to throw off the Red Dragon because he has the most to lose. He has worked a long time to get to be the Lead Dragon Dancer and he likes it. Plus the Red Dragon affirms him substantially and whispers to him that he is indispensable.

Just like in China, there are schools where you can go to learn how to be the "head" – how to be the Lead Dragon Dancer. (But here we call them "seminaries".) It's important that you perfect the art, and dance exactly according to the regional style and "flavor" of your particular Dragon Club. (Here we call them "denominations".) There are competitions and shows between Dragon Teams to see who is the best, who is the shiniest, who is the biggest, who is the most artistic and so on. There are all kinds of ways to stand out and make your Dragon unique and special. Everybody has some other Dragon that they want to either beat or be like. There are lots of books and conferences led by the most famous Lead Dragon Dancers about how to be more like them. We are introducing fancier and bigger Dragons all the time. In fact, we are even taking on Dragons that look just like Wall Street and Madison Avenue. We're adapting business models to our religious enterprises because their Dragons seem to be more efficient. But all we're doing it grieving God more.

The Red Dragon itself doesn't care how you dance - so long as you keep dancing and you don't get free. It wants constant motion and will constantly reinforce and draw from those who are willing to work hard to keep it going. It has no love for the individuals and it's goal is to kill, steal and destroy. It will chew people up and spit them out. It will exhaust their legs, their creativity and their resources and then discard them without a second thought because the momentum of the Dragon Team is the most important thing. It will whisper to the Lead Dancer that if people fall away not to worry because they were getting tired and useless anyway – or they were rebellious and didn't want to dance the proper way and follow along. If anyone should actually point out that the dance is getting nowhere – watch out! That will immediately get you ejected from the team!

The whole thing is rooted and based in Pride. "Look at me!" It wants to enlarge itself, improve itself, be more colorful and attractive - so that more people will watch IT and keep their eyes off of Jesus. It wants more legs, so it can dance more and grow longer. It whispers to all its Dancers, "We are the best Dragon anywhere. We're the 'hot new thing.' Everyone should be like us. In fact, anyone that doesn't dance just like us isn't even a real Dragon at all. We're the truest, best, most original, most authentic Dragon. We're the best and nobody else counts."

Just like a parade dragon, when you are inside, you can't see anything but the guts of your own Dragon. You can't see the scenery or the weather or the traffic or the other Dragons. You MUST focus on your own Dragon and follow the Dancers ahead of you. You MUST NOT take your eyes off of what you are doing or you will miss a turn or be off-beat and embarrass the whole Dragon Team. You also can't hear God because you're not looking to Him, you're watching your Dragon Team for direction and following the beat of their drums and cymbals. You might occasionally stand on the sidewalk (or at a conference) and watch a parade (or get a video) and see other Dragon Teams, but you only see them from the shiny, silky outside – not the humble underside where the sweaty, tired guys in tanktops are laboring under a Dragon held together with duct tape and bent coat hangers.

This blindness and competition keeps us compartmentalized and independent of each other so that the Body of Christ can't get unity and harmony because we all refuse to come out from under our own Dragons and yet we all insist that we're not under a Dragon, even though THOSE guys over there clearly are. We can see THEIR Dragon just fine, the thing that has twisted their denomination or congregation up into a heretical cult – but we can never see our own Dragon. Strange, isn't it? We're **so** blind and stupid and self-focused that I can only come the conclusion that it's supernaturally induced. (Which is exactly what the Bible says will happen to you when you go your own way, but I never saw it before now.) It's easier to talk about Jesus with atheists and drug dealers and kids with purple hair than with most 'church' leaders. My experience is that, with a few exceptions, church leaders seem to be SUPERNATURALLY deaf and dumb. They conveniently cut and paste out any scriptures that would upset their "system". While they are otherwise really great guys, the only conclusion I can come to is that there is a supernatural force in play – and it's not good.

ARE THE RED DRAGONS JUST OVER CHRISTIAN CHURCHES?

I've seen Red Dragons over Buddhist temples. I've seen them over a Psychic Fair. I've seen them over Mosques. It is the spirit of Antichrist and always controls those who are following any one of the millions of flavors of Antichrist religious systems. The difference is that people can be delivered out of some of those without too much effort. That is, the Red Dragon over a pagan system or individual can be bound up or cast off (by someone walking in righteousness and with enough authority). These are not a curse from God as much as they are just the "world" doing what the "world" does.

But, on the Children of God, the rules are different. Whether you are "natural" Israel (the nation/the race) or "spiritual" Israel (the Church), when you disobey, the stakes are much higher. When you are the "world" you are already under satan's headship, but when you are God's and decide you'd rather go your own way (which by default means satan's way), then really BAD things are going to happen to you and it's going to be God doing it. Just as it pleased Him to prosper you, it will please Him to crush you. We aren't really preaching that in seeker-friendly, comfy church are we?

I just bet that doesn't jive with your view of God, does it? You don't think He's mad at anybody? You don't think He's a jealous God? "But surely," you say, "the Blood of Jesus means that we are redeemed and God's wrath is turned away from us. We're redeemed and safe and that "Old Testament" God is not in play anymore!" Yeah, well, think again. To take your stand on that bit of fiction, you're going to have to deny that the Bible is true and right and still active today. But it won't surprise me if you want to leave parts of the Word out, that's how we all got under (or are still under) the Red Dragon curse in the first place. Yes, the Blood of Jesus will surely heal us, but not unless we repent and avail ourselves of it.

Let me point out that 2 Timothy 3:16 says that "ALL scripture is God-breathed and is useful for teaching, rebuking, correcting and training in righteousness, so that the man of God may be thoroughly equipped for every good work." You can't dismiss everything about God in the Old

Testament because it doesn't suit your image of Warm-Fuzzy-Loving-Shepherd-Jesus. I'm warning you now, if you ever give me that "the Old Testament is not for New Covenant believers" argument in person, I'm going to ask you to hand me your Bible. Then I'm going to quote you 2 Timothy 3:16 over and over while I start with Genesis 1:1 and tear pages out of your Bible until you make me stop. Don't think I won't do it. If you're going to insult and demean my God and His Word, I'm going to call you on it.

You can't play it both ways. You can't demand that the Ten Commandments be posted in courtrooms and schools and then deny that the Old Testament is valid. You can't pound people with Malachi 3 and insist they're stealing from God if they don't tithe and then deny that same God and covenant in the next breath. He is an awesome, fearsome, jealous God and He doesn't change! If this writing doesn't convince you, if the devastating signs and wonders that He predicted and took personal credit for and are clearly evident RIGHT NOW don't convince you, then you're in big trouble. Your heart is so hardened and your Red Dragon has so much control that I wonder if it's even possible to get you free. Please turn. Please?

Ok, let's get back to it. Would God really be pleased about crushing and obliterating His own children? Well, the Bible says that He will.

Isaiah 53:10
Yet it pleased the LORD to bruise him; he hath put [him] to grief: when thou shalt make his soul an offering for sin, he shall see [his] seed, he shall prolong [his] days, and the pleasure of the LORD shall prosper in his hand.

And that's about JESUS, His own Son!!

Deuteronomy 28:62-63 (NIV)
You who were as numerous as the stars in the sky will be left but few in number, because you did not obey the Lord your God. Just as it pleased the Lord to make you prosper and increase in number, so it will please him to ruin and destroy you. You will be uprooted from the land you are entering to possess.

Lots more examples that I don't have room for here. Read Lamentations and what He did to Jerusalem. Women were cooking their own babies. Just like Deuteronomy 28 promised would happen if they went their own way, and they did – and He did. About every 50 years Israel went their own way and God sent someone or something to oppress and/or destroy them. Then He sent some judge or warrior or king to free them when they repented. Every 50 years America has had a great sweeping revival that brought the hearts of the people back to God. Even if we aren't honoring the Year of Jubilee, God is. And we're due right now for another Awakening – but it only comes by repentance.

PERSONAL-SIZED RED DRAGONS

(as opposed to institutional/denominational ones)

People get under a Red Dragon curse from God for having taken their eyes off of Jesus and going their own way. (Deut. 28) The enemy can use just about anything to get your eyes off of Jesus. The "Object" of your attention can then become the "face" on the Red Dragon you got under. The Object can be anything – football, a pastor, a denomination, a new car, an experience or manifestation, a wife, a doctrine, etc. It should be clear that some of these are inanimate objects, so pointing a finger at the Object as the cause of the Red Dragon misses the point. It's the person that allowed it who is most responsible.

When a person goes their own way and follows something other than God – they automatically (after an indefinite grace period) get a Red Dragon with their own face on it. It may also have the face of the "Object" they were following, but ultimately it's got their own face on it, because THEY decided to follow something other than Christ. When under a Red Dragon, they will have difficulty hearing clearly from the Throne. The Father is just and He will require that those who go their own way be separated from Him. The farther it goes, the deeper the strong delusion that will turn them over to their own reprobate mind and leave them open to any forces of the enemy that want to come mess with them. The more they operate out of Self (which they inevitably will if He is not directing their paths accurately), the more doorways they open up for the enemy. They will hear all kinds of things, sometimes self-condemning things, but also grandiose things about their role as the savior of a continent or the world. They may hear that they can continue in sin in some ways and God won't mind.

There are those who are under a Red Dragon because of their willingness to follow some particular "Object" and believe in it more than they believed in (or listened to) God. It could be golf, it could be a dozen donuts, it could be Mormonism, it could be George Bush, it could be Carl Marx, it could be tattoos.

There are those who got under a Red Dragon by their violent opposition to some Object. They are not actually "in" the Dragon, but they are the flagellantes that follow along behind it whipping themselves. They are just as much in the parade and following the Dragon. It is still directing their paths because they are chasing IT instead of God. An anti-abortion protester can make that an idol and their whole life will revolve around that one issue and they will take their eyes off of Jesus. Before you know it, they'll be bombing clinics and be absolutely sure that God told them to do it. A heresy hunter can make his whole life about exposing error in the church or exposing a particular cult or leader – and they take their eyes off of Jesus, don't act in love, don't trust God to fight His own battles and get under a Red Dragon.

Both groups are under the influence of a Red Dragon, although their behavior will manifest differently.

Those under it will:

- Be obsessed with the Object, it's future, it's growth, it's support, etc.

- Show signs of deep (and annoying) Spiritual Pride

- Have a supernatural love for it that defies logic or normal experience

- Be willing to sacrifice greatly for it

- Actively evangelize on it's behalf, convincing others and defending it

- Have a lack of peace if not doing something for the Object. This is a big indicator. No peace.

- Have Garblers that confuse communication and twist it to benefit the Object. They will only hear what they want to hear.

- Polarize those around them as having to be for it or against it with no middle ground.

- Be belligerent, have anger or fits of temper or even murderous rage when the Object is insulted or assaulted.

- Exhibit unscriptural behavior justified as necessary or unavoidable – or even directed by God.

- Lack the Gift of Repentance as it relates to the Object and their involvement in it – instead of obeying Jesus.

- Show a lack of trust that God is capable of developing and increasing and growing and providing for the Object Himself.

- Refuse to fellowship or even pray with those who are not in full agreement. Encouraging division.

- One of the other good give-aways is a huge abundance of words. Many idle words that go nowhere and basically accomplish nothing.

- Show a deep spirit of competition with others to prove that their Object is the greatest.

- Will have more and more difficulty hearing God and more and more acceptance of the voice of the Object instead. When they do hear God, it may be "garbled" by going through their "Object filter".

- They will give the Object credit for any of their spiritual growth, instead of Christ.

- Groupies. Fans. Followers. Concubines. Lemmings. Whores. (That's what God calls them!)

Those violently opposed to it will:

- Be obsessed with the Object, it's destruction, it's correction, it's starvation, it's humbling, etc.

- Show signs of deep (and annoying) Spiritual Pride

- Have a supernatural hatred for it that defies logic or normal experience.

- Feel an overwhelming urgency to do something right NOW about the Object.

- Be willing to sacrifice greatly to see it destroyed, even their own relationship with God.

- May even work compulsively and violate moral or legal boundaries to destroy it.

- Actively evangelize against it and recruit ANYONE that can help them, even people that are far worse in their own way.

- Have a lack of peace if not doing something against the Object. This is a big indicator. No peace.

- Have Garblers that confuse communication and twist it to show the worst angle on the Object.

- Polarize those around them as having to be for it or against it with no middle ground.

- Be belligerent, have anger or fits of temper or even murderous rage toward the Object.

- Exhibit unscriptural behavior justified as necessary or unavoidable – or even directed by God.

- Lack the Gift of Repentance as it relates to their focus on the Object instead of Jesus.

- Show a deep spirit of competition with others to show that they are better (smarter, holier, stronger, faster, wiser) than the Object.

- Show a lack of trust that God is capable of dealing with the Object Himself – or believe that God has appointed this person to be His agent to chasten or destroy the Object.

- Refuse to fellowship or even pray with those who are not in full agreement. Encouraging division.

- One of the other good give-aways is a huge abundance of words. Many idle words that go nowhere and basically accomplish nothing.

- Will have more and more difficulty hearing God and more and more hatred of the voice of the Object instead. When they do hear God, it may be "garbled" by going through their "Object filter".

- They will hate it when the Object speaks at all and will take nearly everything they hear in the worst possible way. They will be constantly expecting to catch the Object in an error to justify their position against it. There is no grace for a mis-spoken or misunderstood word, Everything is a heresy and ANY comment that seems to be ANYTHING less than pure, absolute truth is evidence that the Object is a tool of satan. Unreasonably high standards. Especially considering their own words and actions!

- They will blame the Object for any fallen state of their own instead of accepting their own responsibility for having taken their eyes off of Jesus. Anything bad that happens to them they will attribute to warfare or curses from the Object to get them to stop what they believe is effective warfare of their own.

- Persecutors. Haters. Murderers. Hunters. Lemmings. Whores. (Again, according to God.)

In all cases, they may hear something they are VERY sure is God, but it will inevitably offer some clues that there is a problem. The sacrifice of Jesus meant that He was seated with God so as to send the Gift of Repentance to men. (Acts 5:31) Despite the strong delusion from the Throne, the Holy Spirit works with the Son to find a way to leave clues that there is a problem so that those who have ears to hear and eyes to see will turn and be healed. But the blind will head into a ditch. Only those who have eyes and ears and an expectation of their unworthiness and the danger of this will see the problem early and stop it before it goes too far. A constant state of repentance and fear before God is the best defense.

The Father requires justice, but the Son wants that none should perish. So He will tell the Holy Spirit to speak in such as way as to discomfort slightly or leave some hint that there is problem. There will always be signs that, although subtle, will probably be clearly visible later when the fog is gone. The Spirit may also speak to those around to show them that the person is off track. He will always leave a trail of bread crumbs back to the original incident so that the person can find their way back to the root and repent. Follow the trail, if you can.

Acts 5:31 (ASV) - *Him did God exalt with his right hand to be a Prince and a Saviour, to give repentance to Israel, and remission of sins.*

2 Tim 2:25-26 (KJV) – *25 In meekness instructing those that oppose themselves; if God peradventure will give them repentance to the acknowledging of the truth; 26 And that they may recover themselves out of the snare of the devil, who are taken captive by him at his will.*

Matt 3:7-8 (ASV) – *7 But when he saw many of the Pharisees and Sadducees coming to his baptism, he said unto them, Ye offspring of vipers, who warned you to flee from the wrath to come? 8 Bring forth therefore fruit worthy of repentance:*

INVERTED RED DRAGONS – FLAGGELANTS

"Flaggelants" are those who go about whipping themselves. This is the visual image that the Lord showed of what is really going on when someone is obsessed with an Object (ministry, person, etc) in a negative way and becomes intent on their destruction. They have been hurt and they keep opening up the wounds themselves to prove what martyrs they are. And along the way, grieve God and become what they hate.

> 2 Timothy 2:24-26 – *And the servant of the Lord must not strive; but be gentle unto all [men], apt to teach, patient, In meekness instructing those that **oppose themselves**; if God peradventure will give them **repentance** to the acknowledging of the truth; And [that] they may recover themselves out of the **snare of the devil**, who are **taken captive** by him at his will.*

This is important enough that we wanted to expand substantially on this in Version 4 of this book. I expect that this will get MUCH more common as more Christians actually start acting like Jesus. They need to know what to expect. The similarities between warfare because you are being effective for the Lord and a crushing because you are disobeying God can sometimes be terrifying. Ultimately you have to hear the Lord, know that YOU aren't exhibiting symptoms of the Red Dragon yourself.

It's important to understand the continuum here. That the enemy can get your eyes to the left or to the right and either way, he's got you. For example, you can make food an idol by gluttony or by anorexia. You can make sexuality an idol by an insatiable desire or a terrifying fear of it. You can make a ministry an idol by getting under it and giving them full reign over your life – or by chasing it everywhere, intent on "exposing" it and destroying it. You make a spouse an idol and look to them more than God – then divorce and turn all the love into bitter hatred. It's a radical supernatural swing from one extreme to the other. Either way, you get your eyes off of the Cross of Christ and the devil has still got you right where he wants you.

What is the Goal of the inverted Anti- Red Dragon?

To bring division, kill, steal and destroy – ministries, relationships, momentum for the kingdom of God. Create paralysis and victimization mentality in you. Block rejoicing in affliction by creating an obsessive quest to "expose" or "save others".

How it works:

It beats on a person by whatever means, usually physical, financial, emotional, relational stress that weakens them, then it starts inserting lies – "this is HIS fault, this is all because of HIM, if He hadn't done this everything would be OK, I'm suffering because of HIM, I'm scared and hurting because of HIM." Always getting the focus on a person/ministry/ construct instead of JESUS, always failing to rejoice in affliction, failing to see the big picture, failing to trust the Lord, hope all things, believe all things, endure all things, keep no record of wrongs (I Corin. 13). Love is lost. Gossip and backbiting increases and as the demon gets them to hearken to some voice OTHER THAN the voice of God and obey the commands of God, then the accuser of the brethren is justified to claim Leviticus 26 and Deuteronomy 28 (etc) over them.

How it gets permission to jump on a person:

Because they stop listening to and obeying God and instead listen to the person or the demon that is whispering to them things that go against God. It can be very subtle, and the closer you are to God, the more the risk. If you need further clarification, read "Pilgrim's Progress" and see a REAL account of how hard the Christian life is likely to be – and all the trickeries the enemy can throw at you.

What this does:

It begin to throw up walls and convince you to become more distant from the person in question. Hardens your heart. Locked doors. Secret conversation about them. Refusal to face the person or reason together. Seeing them as spiritual dangerous to even converse with or convincing that it's pointless to try.
It tries to get them to do some or all of the things God hates:

> 16 These six things doth the Lord hate: yea, seven are an abomination unto him: 17 A proud look, a lying tongue, and hands that shed innocent blood, 18 An heart that deviseth wicked imaginations, feet that be swift in running to mischief, 19 A false witness that speaketh lies, and he that soweth discord among brethren. Prov 6:16-19 (KJV)

Why:

This evil spirit does NOT want to be ejected. It does not want the miscommunication or lie cleared up, does not want people to repent and reconcile. It will do all it can to take them away and block phone numbers, change emails, whatever so that it can cement the damage done. Leviticus 26 says that if the demon can get them to hearken to a voice other than Gods and go against His commands (1. Love the Lord, 2. Love neighbor as yourself, etc.) then it can get legal authority to terrorize them into running away as fast as they can with unrealistic and imagined fears. The goal is to prevent any forgiveness or reconciliation and to destroy the work of the Lord. The Lord may allow it to humble someone or refine another, but it's still going to have to require serious repentance to get out of it.

What are some of the symptoms that you have an ANTI- Red Dragon:

- Stop loving – even while you insist all along that it's loving for you to do what you're doing. (Matt 5:44 "But I say to you, love your enemies, and pray for those who persecute you.")
- Forget everything good that was ever done for you by them. Just flat scrubbed out of remembrance – or unable to speak it. This is one of the scariest of all. Especially between husband and wife or close brethren. (Psalm 55:12-14, Luke 21:16, etc.)
- Hyperinflate anything bad. Make mountains out of molehills. Or create them. (Prov. 6:16-19)
- Make anything that was just annoying or questionable into something horrible.
- Generate lies based on anything "suspicious" even if there is no real evidence to support it.
- Raise secondary doctrinal disagreements to the level of salvation issues to justify the labels used ("They're not a Brother and never were – because of their stance on _____.").
- Refuse to reason together or be gentle. Slam doors of communication shut. What we call "drive-by rebuking." (I was actually staying with a man who wrote me a letter that started with, "I'm writing this rebuke, I'm going to print it, delete it from my computer and I never want to discuss this

with you." Then had his wife give it to me with no opportunity for rebuttal or discussion. And he was absolutely sure he was righteous in all of it. Many times I've seen people flee in the night, refusing any communication for fear – raw terror – of being talked out of their position.)

- Refuse proper Biblical instructions for problem resolution (Matt. 18) or use them to rally troops and accuse, but not to resolve, reconcile or seek Truth and peace.

- Use "terminal" words for emotional effect and to do maximum harm with no grace or mercy - "false teacher," "apostate," "heretic," "cult leader," "heathen," "unbeliever," "warlock/witch," "jezebel" and worse. They forget the Biblical imperatives (commands) to try to live at peace, to not devour one another, to avoid useless quarrels about secondary issues, if you don't love the brethren the love of God is not in you – and so they themselves become apostate (unforgiving, unloving, not rejoicing, etc.), all in the name of "defending the faith".

- Determining that it is one's personal mission in life now to rescue the other "captives" and tell as many people as possible all that they "know" - or all the dirt they can gather from ANY source whatsoever, no matter the credibility or veracity. Gets their eyes off the Cross and become obsessed with the object of this.

- If someone that was previously VERY close to them and very respected as a man/woman of God tells them they are doing wrong, that person is now "part of the cult" or "under the delusion" and is dismissed with prejudice – no matter how close they were before. They will block, ban, eject, defriend, sue or get restraining orders on anyone that tries to talk them out of it.

-

- They begin to have a harder and harder time hearing the Spirit of God so they tend to get back under Law. They become Judaizers that default to the written code, dietary laws, black and white reading of scripture without any willingness to reason about the deep things of God or the spiritual application and understanding behind the Law – which was a shadow of things to come. They can't be led by the Holy Spirit anymore because they're not hearing God, so they're back under Law. (Gal. 5:18) Like the Judaizers that chased Paul, they make it their quest to chase, persecute and tear down those who are walking in the freedom of Christ through the Spirit – even if previously THEY were one of them!

- Be unable to truly forgive and move on. Constantly obsessing and dwelling on the past. (Matt. 6:14-15, Mark 11:26, Luke 6:37, etc.)
- They may also experience physically or spiritually some of the curses in Lev. 26 or Deut. 28 – wasting diseases with no cure, madness, blindness, terror, unreasonable fear, etc.
- The closer they were walking with God, the greater their rebellion – thus the the more likely that the Lord will afflict them with some or all of the serious curses in Leviticus 26 and Deuteronomy 28. You may say that, "as believers we are not under the law and the old covenant," but if you are rebelling against God then you are NOT believing Him and you are NOT being led by the Holy Spirit, so you ARE under Law (inverse of Galatians 5:18). You can't say that because you once obeyed Him that you have permanent access to the New Covenant. That is, if you are stiff-necked and won't obey and won't hearken to His voice, then you're going to wander in the desert until you die. If your heart is uncircumcised then you are not a True Jew under the Blood. (Romans 2:28-29)
- Worst of all, they begin to tear down everything they truly heard from the Lord, chalk it up to being "under the influence" or "trapped in the delusion with them" and systematically unravel every good thing that God ever spoke to them or did for them during that time. This is the devil's way to get you to grieve the Holy Spirit and attribute the works of God to the devil himself. This is the devil's way to take back ground and victories previously won.

One of the strangest manifestations of this that we have seen is the occasional person that is overwhelmed with a spirit of fear – or rather raw naked panic – and leaves the ministry in utter terror and fear for their lives. Please don't think I'm kidding. We've seen breathless, shaking, panic-stricken people that could not name their fear, had no real evidence for it, but just HAD to leave RIGHT NOW in the middle of the night without saying goodbye to anyone, sometimes leaving many personal things behind - as if the house were on fire! It doesn't happen all the time, but when it does, it's shockingly supernatural. There is no other explanation. There have never been allegations of physical violence or threats or anything, yet people flee, literally in fear for their lives. And all the while insisting that God told them to do it and that they have peace. They claim that they do not have a spirit of fear, but of love and of power and of a sound mind (2 Timothy 1:7). But any psychiatrist looking in from the outside would say that it was a paranoid delusional psychotic episode and offer to medicate or institutionalize them. If they had power, they would just rebuke the enemy and be victorious, but they cannot. And the love is completely gone – totally scrubbed out and replaced with inflated memories of the bad and no memories of the good. The object is demonized, no matter how close they were before – even spouses or family members.

God never tells the righteous to panic. God may tell them to dust their feet off, or move on to another place, or even flee urgently to the mountains when the antichrist shows up – but not in a panic. I know that I can take a nap in the middle of a warlock convention and be safe. I know that I can stand in front of the devil himself and be safe. I will NOT panic before ANY man or demon of hell. Because God is on my side and if I am righteous, then I can have the confidence to operate in love and peace and patience and forgiveness – but never panic.

I've been asked, "People keep leaving your ministry in the middle of the night, in terror and fear for their lives, how can this be OK? How can this be God? There must be something wrong with you." That's a reasonable question, so I sought the Lord on that. The time that it happened most recently, the very next day the Lord gave me Leviticus 26. I've read through the Bible many times, but I never saw this in this context before. Truly it answers how this could happen. Proverbs 28:1 says, "The wicked flee when no man pursueth, but the righteous are bold as a lion." Leviticus 26 goes much farther. It's truly scary. Stay right with God, hearken to His voice. If you listen to another, if you despise His instructions and commands, it's ALL bad! Let's take a look:

More evidence that this is from GOD: *{comments added}*

Leviticus 26:14-46 (BBE)
14 But if you do not give ear to me, and do not keep all these my laws; 15 And if you go against my rules and if

you have hate in your souls for my decisions *{not just behavior is enough, your heart has to be right!}* **and you do not do all my orders, but go against my agreement** *{refuse to fulfill your vows, do what you know He told you to do}*; **16 This will I do to you: I will put fear in your hearts** *{spiritual/mental, panic, terror}*, **even wasting disease and burning pain** *{could be spiritual or physical wasting – or both}*, **drying up the eyes** *{spiritual or physical, can't see the enemy, no spirit of repentance, no hope, can't rejoice in affliction}* **and making the soul feeble** *{definitely spiritual, defenseless, shields down}*, **and you will get no profit from your seed** *{business, ministry, testimony, children, efforts}*, **for your haters will take it for food.** *{Enemies, demons will feed on it}* **17 And my face will be turned from you** *{Won't hear}*, **and you will be broken before those who are against you** *{enemies/demons}*, **and your haters will become your rulers** *{oppressed/possessed/afflicted/ruled over}*, **and you will go in flight when no man comes after you.** *{Flee in a panic for NO reason. This is a big one. A true sign that something is wrong. God never has the RIGHTEOUS flee in fear. Proverbs 28:1 says "The unrighteous flee when no man pursueth, but the righteous are bold as a lion." There is a BIG difference between dusting your feet off and moving on because you're not received – and fleeing in utter terror of an IMAGINARY threat.}*

If that doesn't do it, then it gets seven times WORSE:

18 And if, even after these things, you will not give ear to me, then I will send you punishment seven times more for your sins. 19 And the pride of your strength will be broken *{humbled, crushed, best thing taken away – could be physical or spiritual or mental}*, **and I will make your heaven as iron** *{prayers bounce - spiritual}* **and your earth as brass;** *{toil and sweat with little result – spiritual or physical}* **20 And your strength will be used up without profit** *{spiritual or physical}*; **for your land will not give her increase and the trees of the field will not give their fruit.** *{Whatever your land, it will not produce fruit – spiritual or physical. You will be void of the fruit the Lord is looking for.}*

If that doesn't do it, then it gets 49 times WORSE:

21 And if you still go against me and will not give ear to me, I will put seven times more punishments on you because of your sins. 22 I will let loose the beasts of the field among you *{wild animals, could be treacherous people, could be demons that are now free to devour you – could be spiritual or physical}*, **and they will take away your children** *{spiritual or physical offspring lost, people you "parented" stripped from you}* **and send destruction on your cattle** *{wealth, provision, pride, savings, all gone – spiritual or physical}*, **so that your numbers will become small and your roads become waste.** *{You will be very few, fell outnumbered, feel alone and be unable to upkeep your land – spiritual or physical}*

If that doesn't do it, then it gets 343 times WORSE:

23 And if by these things you will not be turned to me *{the point of all this is medicinal}*, **but still go against me; 24 Then I will go against you, and I will give you punishment, I myself, seven times for all your sins. 25 And I will send a sword on you to give effect to the punishment of my agreement** *{no telling what this could mean – spiritual or physical}*; **and when you come together into your towns I will send disease among you** *{when you gather with the others who rebelled against God, wherever that might be, whatever is the safe place you ran to, even a chat room on the internet – this could be spiritual disease, lies, corruption, false gifts, false anointings, delusion, fear – or physical diseases like cancer clusters or wasting diseases}* **and you will be given up into the hands of your haters** *{people or demons will take you over, you will be HANDED to them – physical or spiritual slavery}*. **26 When I take away your bread of life, ten women will be cooking bread in one oven** *{in the siege, there is so little wood and grain, bread will be so scarce that there are 9 people standing around, lots of people to do a little work}*, **and your bread** *{physical or the spiritual bread of Truth}* **will be measured out by weight** *{Siege/starvation rations}*; **you will have food but never enough.** *{You will not be able to get enough of the bread to be satisfied. Truth will escape you. You may have a little Truth, but it's only a tiny bit and won't it satisfy.}*

If that STILL doesn't do it, then it gets 2,401 times WORSE:

27 And if, after all this, you do not give ear to me, but go against me still, 28 Then my wrath will be burning against you {can't believe it would go this far!}, **and I will give you punishment, I myself, seven times for your sins. 29 Then you will take the flesh of your sons and the flesh of your daughters for food;** {This happened PHYSICALLY to Jerusalem in Lamentations. Most likely spiritual sons and daughters that you will devour/suck dry/destroy, just to satisfy the burning inside you or to feel like you're getting somewhere.} **30 And I will send destruction on your high places** {Physical or spiritual, places of idolatry, or the high place of the MIND}, **overturning your perfume altars** {Physical or spiritual altars you have built, thinking God likes the smell, but He doesn't}, **and will put your dead bodies on your broken images** {He considers you dead inside already if it's gone this far, but He will destroy the idols/images and leave you on them}, **and my soul will be turned from you in disgust.** {God will look away and turn His back on you in DISGUST. That's HARSH!} **31 And I will make your towns waste** {Whatever walled city you trusted, whatever place of safety you ran to, will be pulled down} **and send destruction on your holy places** {whatever you made sacred in your idolatry}; **I will take no pleasure in the smell of your sweet perfumes** {He will ignore your offerings and sacrifices – spiritually or physically}; **32 And I will make your land a waste, a wonder to your haters living in it.** {Your haters may be people or demons or both – but even they will be impressed with how thoroughly the Lord is against you.} **33 And I will send you out in all directions among the nations** {the disobedient will be scattered even from one another, geographically/physically or spiritually or mentally}, **and my sword will be uncovered against you, and your land will be without any living thing, and your towns will be made waste.** {The places of safety you ran to will be uninhabited by those who truly follow the Lord, judgement will pour on everyone there because of you.} **34 Then will the land take pleasure in its Sabbaths while it is waste and you are living in the land of your haters** {In captivity – spiritually or physically. In a strange place.}; **then will the land have rest. 35 All the days while it is waste will the land have rest, such rest as it never had in your Sabbaths, when you were living in it.** {He will *have justice and give rest to the Land because of your failure to observe the Sabbath, to be dedicated to Him and His commands.}*

At His discretion, some of them will get the treatment above, some will get this – or some combination thereof:

36 And as for the rest of you, I will make their hearts feeble in the land of their haters *{weak hearts,no strength, no defenses, full of fear and panic, whether the "haters" are real or not – could be physical or spiritual, demons or people}*, **and the sound of a leaf moved by the wind will send them in flight** *{the slightest sound will sound to them like a mighty army, they will flee over <u>NOTHING</u> in absolute panic, convinced to their core that it's justified – that is an <u>extreme</u> DELUSION!}*, **and they will go in flight as from the sword, falling down when no one comes after them;** *{They will believe that a sword is imminent, destruction, death, worst case scenario – physically or spiritually – in terror, but NO ONE is chasing them. In fact, the enemy of their souls has them right where he wants them.}* **37 Falling on one another** *{tripping over each other to run so fast}*, **as before the sword, when no one comes after them** *{repeated again – NO ONE is chasing them}*; **you will give way before your haters** *{Part of the delusion is that you BELIEVE they are your haters and you're running from them, but NO ONE is chasing you. It's a delusion that creates an enemy that is NOT there and makes him GIGANTIC – when whatever it was, it was as dangerous as a LEAF falling from a tree. But the demons will drive you before them and they will rule over you}*. **38 And death will overtake you** *{spiritually or physically}* **among strange nations** *{not on the land you are supposed to be, surrounded by people that don't follow the Lord}*, **and the land of your haters will be your destruction** *{and you will eventually be destroyed there}*. **39 And those of you who are still living will be wasting away in their sins in the land of your haters; in the sins of their fathers they will be wasting away.** *{And if they don't die, they will waste away, spiritually or physically or both.}*

But ... Here's the good news! Eventually they break!

40 And they will have grief for their sins and for the sins of their fathers, when their hearts were untrue to me, and they went against me; 41 So that I went against them and sent them away into the land of their haters *{turned them over to demons}*: **if then the pride of their hearts is broken and they take the punishment of their sins,** *{If they confess their sins and turn}* **42 Then I will keep in mind the agreement which I made with Jacob and with Isaac and with Abraham, and I will keep in mind the land. 43 And the land, while she is without them, will keep her Sabbaths; and they will undergo the punishment of their sins** *{there IS punishment due – until the Blood of the Lamb is applied to this}*, **because they were turned away from my decisions and in their souls was hate for my laws.** *{their hearts rebelled against what they KNEW to be true and right}* **44 But for all that, when they are in the land of their haters I will not let them go, or be turned away from them, or give them up completely; my agreement with them will not be broken, for I am the Lord their God.** *{Despite ALL of this, He will not utterly forsake them. He will still try to break them, but will not let them go! What a God!!}* **45 And because of them I will keep in mind the agreement which I made with their fathers, whom I took out of the land of Egypt before the eyes of the nations, to be their God: I am the Lord. 46 These are the rules, decisions, and laws, which the Lord made between himself and the children of Israel in Mount Sinai, by the hand of Moses.**

WHAT ABOUT LOVE?

An inverted Red Dragon, an Anti- Red Dragon, will almost immediately suck all the love out. It doesn't matter if it was your best friend, ministry partner, a family member, even a loving wife or husband – it will suck all the love out. And it can do it <u>SO</u> fast and <u>SO</u> completely that it will shock you. The ONLY explanation is that it has to be supernatural. Whatever the thing that has become the idol – the Object of the obsession – it keeps their eyes off the Cross and they are trapped in the delusion. They are obsessed with the object instead of the Cross. Only God can release them.

1 Corinthians 13 – *1 If I speak in the tongues of men and of angels, but have not love, I am only a resounding gong or a clanging cymbal.*

Though you speak in tongues or speak much about love – if it's not in you, then it's all noise. The delusion will cause you to speak about everything other than love. But you will SAY that whatever you are doing to destroy the object is done because of your "love" for them.

2 If I have the gift of prophecy and can fathom all mysteries and all knowledge, and if I have a faith that can move mountains, but have not love, I am nothing.

Though you may still have gifts, even a calling as a prophet or apostle, though you have a mighty faith, if you don't have love, then you are NOTHING. Your faith is misplaced, you're under a delusion. Whatever you know or think you know is wasted and useless.

3 If I give all I possess to the poor and surrender my body to the flames, but have not love, I gain nothing.

No matter how sacrificial you THINK you are being, though you are martyred, if it was not done for the sake of true LOVE, then it was in vain.

4 Love is patient, love is kind. It does not envy, it does not boast, it is not proud.

An obsession, an Anti- Red Dragon, is the very OPPOSITE of unconditional agape love. It is NEVER patient, NEVER kind, it envies the success or blessing of the object, it paces about hoping to see destruction and be justified, it boasts about all that it knows, it is SUPREMELY proud in it's absolute certainty of being right – even while manufacturing "facts" and operating out of fear, anger, and unforgiveness. It will not hear anyone that says that it's wrong. It does all the things it accuses the object of doing – and more. It is entirely self-focused and self-justifying and will not hear any rebuttal.

5 It is not rude, it is not self-seeking, it is not easily angered, it keeps no record of wrongs.

It is extremely rude, even to the point of violating what ANYONE – even heathen - would call common decency. Willing to say anything to anyone, just to win its point. It is entirely about holding itself up as an "expert witness" and building up its own authority. It is furious continually, a constant boiling cauldron of anger just below the surface and will scream and fly off the handle at any moment when its buttons are pushed. It will block, ban, defriend, sue, or get restraining orders against anyone that disagrees. It generates a HUGE LIST of wrongs - some real, some imagined, usually all twisted for maximum effect - and will recite them to anyone that will listen. There is NO forgiveness – and no repentance by the Object would be sufficient to satisfy them. It WILL NOT let go until God releases them from this delusion and pours out repentance on them. Keeping a record of wrongs is the EXACT OPPOSITE of the commands to rejoice in affliction, to believe that all things work to the good for them that love the Lord, to turn the other cheek, forgive seventy times seven, love your enemies, leave vengeance to the Lord, etc. It's total rebellion against the HEART of the Gospel, all justified as necessary and right in order to "expose" the object.

6 Love does not delight in evil but rejoices with the truth.

The very opposite is true, evil flourishes and is fed and grown. Truth, and truly being willing to seek the truth, dies. The voices that support the anger and unforgiveness are lifted up, no matter how bad their credibility previously. "The enemy of my enemy is my friend." The voices that might actually speak reason, faith, love, truth, peace, patience – are dismissed instantly. Even a person that was previously beautiful and godly in heart, mind, speech and demeanor will become a sarcastic, gossiping, backbiting, lying, fearful, hate-filled, unforgiving, shriveled up husk of what they were.

7 It always protects, always trusts, always hopes, always perseveres.

The dragon seeks to kill, steal and destroy. To self-fulfill prophecies of doom and destruction and judgment made over the object. It doesn't trust God to do the work, but sets its own hand to help God. It doesn't trust any voice that defends the object, no matter how trustworthy they were before. It doesn't hope, it makes itself a victim and makes the object responsible for ALL bad things that ever happened to them. It runs into the night rather than persevering. It escapes as quickly as possible, cuts off communication and WILL NOT offer to endure patiently as God does a work with whatever is wrong. (IF anything is even truly wrong.) It does not truly hope for restoration of relationships or the unity of the Body, it is repulsed by the idea. It may give lip service to the object being restored and their soul saved, but all the actions taken are toward destruction, embarrassment, humiliation, or worse – not toward restoration in love.

8 Love never fails. But where there are prophecies, they will cease; where there are tongues, they will be stilled; where there is knowledge, it will pass away.

Love dies. No matter how great, how pure, how beautiful – it inverts into a spirit of hatred, murder, lying, faction, division and ugliness. Prophecies that were received, positive words about the Object that they KNEW were from the Lord previously, are all dismissed. Any good thing that the Lord told them about the Object is chalked up to "being under their spell" and couldn't have been God. It is attributed to flesh or the devil – dangerously flirting with blasphemy of the Holy Spirit. Their tongue NEVER ceases to run to anyone that will listen, but speaking good or blessing over the Object will be stopped. Knowledge of right, remembrance of any good thing that was done for them, will be scrubbed out of their mind. They will be practically unable to even THINK of any way the Object has ever blessed them, much less admit it.

9 For we know in part and we prophesy in part, 10 but when perfection comes, the imperfect disappears.

This IS the imperfect coming. This may even be perfect delusion that takes over and does all of the opposite of what the coming of Jesus would do. This is like the Lord taking someone as FAR away from LOVE as is possible. Yet, they will insist they have love and that all they are doing is motivated by love. They will insist they have peace like never before, even while they scramble endlessly to self-justify their behavior and feelings and obsess about the Object. People looking in from the outside don't see peace or hope or love or grace or gentleness or any of the fruits of the Spirit – where the Object is concerned.

11 When I was a child, I talked like a child, I thought like a child, I reasoned like a child. When I became a man, I put childish ways behind me.

Other people will look in and be SHOCKED by how childishly they are acting, how much like a scared little kid that is just terrified and fighting back with whatever they can. How immature the reasoning, how unwilling to discuss or reason together, how not led by the Spirit of God, how much their brain just doesn't seem to work right and process the higher, deeper things. They only see Law – and even that misapplied. They only see the letter of the Law, and can no longer see the deeper things of the Spirit – as it applies to the Object. Because they are not being led by the Spirit of God, but by the delusion. No childish thing is put behind. Even the written Law that would condemn this kind of behavior is completely ignored (John 15; Proverbs 6:16-19; Leviticus 19:16; Proverbs 16:28; Proverbs 18:8; Proverbs 20:19; Leviticus 26; I Corinthians 13; Galatians 5; Romans 12; 2 Corinthians 12:20; I John 4:18; I Peter 3:14; Prov. 10:12; etc.)

12 Now we see but a poor reflection as in a mirror; then we shall see face to face. Now I know in part; then I shall know fully, even as I am fully known.

Even in the BEST of times, with someone being truly obedient to the Lord and NOT under a delusion, we're still going to see darkly. But this is like a total veil over their mind and heart and eyes that blocks ALL truth and love (at least as it relates to the Object). There is no doubt that God fully knows the person under this delusion, but THEY don't seem to fully know anything other than their own hurt, bitterness, anger, self-righteousness and pride. And they will insist that they DO NOT see through a glass darkly as it relates to the Object, but have perfect, reliable, pure revelation.

13 And now these three remain: faith, hope and love. But the greatest of these is love.

All three are at risk, but love dies first. The total lack of real love in someone that previously HAD real love is one of the first signs that something is desperately wrong. And this "love" in Greek is "agape" meaning pure, unconditional, unstoppable, self-sacrificing, Godly LOVE. That is God's love, something HE has to put in us. When you make an idol and chase it – for good or bad – it is agape that dies first. The Lord Himself withdraws and the first thing to go with Him is His love.

How does a person avoid being an Object?
Those who speak lies and promote themselves will accumulate behind them those who will make them the Object of their worship or adoration. Those who actively and effectively promote themselves will always draw unto themselves those who are susceptible to that kind of thing. But speaking things that aren't "Truth" isn't required. The Apostle

Paul healed and preached truth and in Athens they tried to worship him as a God. He did right in rejecting that instantly and being unwilling to be used as the face on their Red Dragon. He saw that the Corinthians were doing that by saying, "I'm for Paul. I'm for Cephas. I'm for Apollos." He rejected it and tried to make them stop and look to Christ alone. Even being purely like Jesus is not guarantee someone won't make you an idol and stop looking toward the Father and the Cross.

Also, a person that is speaking Truth from the Throne of God cannot avoid being an Object for those who will persecute them. The enemy will always whisper to someone and try to raise up <u>anyone</u> who will obsessively devote their lives to the destruction of that Object that is being effective for the Gospel. In Athens, when Paul wouldn't allow them to adore and worship him, they instantly decided to kill him! He was STILL the Object of their Red Dragon, but now they're intent on Paul's destruction!

There is ONE Truth in the Universe. All else is lies of the enemy. The One Truth is that we are to be under Christ and follow His face. Anything else is destined for our destruction. Everything but His face is a counterfeit of the enemy. You can't be <u>under</u> a Jesus Red Dragon, there's no such thing. That's where you are SUPPOSED to be! Everything BUT that is a Red Dragon. Even just being <u>partially</u> under His

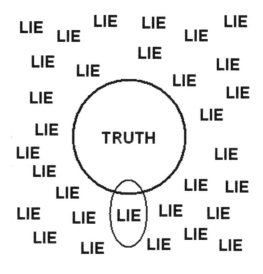

headship is still a lie. There are all kinds of flavors. Anything that exists can be made an idol. Theoretical constructs, like Evolution, can become the object of a Red Dragon. No matter how much Truth it may contain, unless it is 100% pure, it's mixture and a lie. And there is no source of Perfect Purity except by staying IN Christ.

Even though Jesus Christ <u>was</u> <u>NOT</u> Himself a Red Dragon, He was the Object of of MANY flaggelants and continues to be. He was the object of hatred and persecution and murderous rage of many obsessed people. He was (and is) the face on many people's man-made mystery religions that justified murder and hate. Not because He is the object of their worship and obedience, but because He the desire to see Him stopped is the still the consuming object of their lives.

Saul made it his mission in life to go and find and kill Christians. He put everything else in his life on hold so as to persecute Jesus. And Jesus said that it would be the same for all of those that were like Him. He even said that those of your own house would kill you and think they were doing God a favor. The more you are like Jesus, the more people are going to get under murderous Red Dragons with your face on it. Particularly those susceptible to a spirit of competition.

You can eliminate (or at least minimize) the number of people that are trying to idolize and adore you, but you can't do anything about those that want to kill you – unless you preach soft and fluffy and never speak Truth.

The more you are like Jesus, the more murderous Red Dragons there will be focused on you as their Object and the fewer idolatrous ones. (But understand, they've both made you an idol in a different way.)

It's OK for people to idolize God - that's the idea. He wants no other idols BEFORE Him. HE is supposed to be the sole object of your worship and idolatry. Anything else is going to bring judgement upon you for violation of the First Commandment. Even making the Bible an idol is wrong. That's not the fullness of God. The book itself is His word, but it's not <u>Him</u>. We can't have relationship with a book, even a beautiful, glorious, living Word – we're ultimately supposed to worship Him, not His Word.

You can make heaven an idol. You can make your own salvation the end-all-be-all of your walk with Christ. That denies that relationship with Him and His glorification by our daily lives must be the ultimate goal, not the avoidance of hell.

So Jesus gets a pass if people made Him an idol when He was here. That was the idea. But did people make Paul an idol? Yes. Peter? Yes. Speaking in tongues? Yes. Signs and wonders? Yes. Are those automatically bad things? No, not unless you get your eyes on them instead of Jesus. They are tools and side effects and men - but they must NOT be the main point!

Paul said, "Be like me, because I was like Christ." Did never opening his mouth except to speak Truth keep him from being an idol to someone? Nope. Did speaking something from his flesh MAKE them get under a Red Dragon? Nope. Did speaking Truth keep him from being persecuted? No, in fact, the more he became known for that, the worse it got.

How do we keep people from making us an idol?

We can't. If we spend all of our time trying to keep them from doing that, then we are in danger of getting our OWN eyes off of Jesus and making it about US! All we can do is point them to Jesus and speak what He tells us to speak and rest, knowing that He will work it out. We can just speak Truth and let the Lord work it all out.

There WILL be those that try to worship you. Most of them that you will never even know about. They'll just read something or hear something and seek to be like you and watch you instead of Jesus. Those that DO come into contact with you should be discouraged from doing so. You can accomplish that to a degree by being human and transparent and always pointing them toward Jesus. Do not allow any illegal soul-ties by accepting connectivity or obligations that shouldn't be there. Don't take responsibility to protect or provide or direct or any other thing that they should be getting straight from the Throne. It's an illusion that you can do any of that stuff anyway.

If you listen and obey, the Lord will tell you if someone is doing it to you and looking to YOU as their Source when they shouldn't. Do as He directs. Don't feed it. Point them to the Cross and get out of the way. We can't be someone's "crystal ball". We HAVE to help them hear God so that HE can direct all of their paths. None of us are capable of righteously directing our OWN paths, much less someone else's.

Paul could sincerely say that the blood of no man was on his head because he didn't make it about HIM. He didn't draw men unto him – he stood behind them and shoved them toward Jesus. If we maintain and feed a "priest" class where some people are more holy than others and you need to do as they tell you, then we are putting obstacles before men – and it's US!

Please, hear me. Point them toward Jesus and get out of their way. And rejoice in affliction when people persecute and hate you. Jesus said it would be like that if you were like Him. Praise God! You must be getting more like Him! This is a WAR – if nobody is shooting at you, then maybe you're not dangerous. Or worse, maybe the enemy already co-opted you and you've created a mystery religion that grieves God and sets YOU as people's head – and you're under a Red Dragon and don't even know it.

WHO DOES NOT HAVE A RED DRAGON ON THEM?

A few weeks ago the Lord led me to Ezekiel 9 again (this passage comes up regularly lately). If you don't know it right off, please go read it right now (and the chapters right before it to see what they were doing wrong). Basically, the Lord gives Ezekiel this vision of how really horrible the spiritual state of Jerusalem had become and all of the pagan practices that have been integrated with the worship of God (or replaced it). The elders and priests are fully sold out to all kinds of badness and compromise. Then the glory of God leaves the Temple and the Lord sends an angel to put a mark on the foreheads of those who are repenting and weeping and mourning for the sad spiritual state of Jerusalem. Then He sends death angels to mercilessly slaughter everyone else – men, women & children – and instructs them to start with the elders who are in front of the Temple! Then to take all the dead bodies and defile the Temple. Now remember, these are God's people in God's city used to defile God's Temple. He is perfectly willing to do it and there's ample Biblical proof that He's done it before. The ONLY people that survive, the only remnant that remains are those who are repentant for the sins of Jerusalem and were marked by the angel.

Out of the blue, I'm reading that chapter and the Lord says to me, "You know, I already did that. Your temples are all full of dead bodies."

OUCH!! I can't argue with Him. I've been to dozens of congregations in the last two years and they are pretty universally oppressed, deceived and/or dead. There are bright lights in there, to be sure, but mostly they're dead. There is even one charismatic ministry here in Kansas City where several of us have been in a particular room in their building and all seen (in the spirit) massive piles of rotting dead bodies and demons feeding on them like vultures. There is a very strong, very palpable oppression on the whole place, but they are just SURE that they are God's chosen and that they are inside His perfect will.

How do you know that you are truly Red Dragon-free? If you have been given the Gift of Repentance for the sad state of things and grieve and mourn and weep over all the detestable things done in the name of God. If you're only repenting for "those other people," that doesn't count. If you're repenting for just a specific thing, like abortion, you may have a selective repentance or you may just be sad about the babies. But Ezekiel 9 is clear that the only ones who escaped were those repenting for the spiritual state of their city and their own part in it. If you need a little more help getting up to speed, read Ezekiel 16 and see if that's not a really good picture of the church in America. Also read Hosea with an eye toward whether we are doing all of those things as well and what God says will happen to those who do. You might also read Matthew 23 and the seven woes that Jesus pronounces on the Pharisees who were the religious conservatives of the day. We're doing all of those things as well. And in MUCH greater measure. We're in big trouble and as many people as possible need to start repenting until God turns.

Surely judgement will start with the elders before the temple. Hear me, we don't need to worry about some future "falling away" and great deception in the church. It's here right now and we're fully fallen. There is no other way to explain such blatant, unrepentant disobedience like having 37,000 "Christian" denominations when we are commanded to be ONE BODY. The word says that if you hold anything against a brother and you take Communion unworthily you will get sick and die. At least in part, we are all sick and dying (spiritually and physically) because we are taking Communion unworthily. By definition, there is no way to split a church and restrict fellowship between believers without holding something against a brother! Deuteronomy 28 says we will have wasting diseases that have no cure and no one will come to our aid – until we repent.

If there is anyone in the temples amongst the piles of dead bodies that is still breathing somehow, then they need to "come out of her" as fast as they can. If you're spiritually dead and being consumed by demons and you didn't know it, then (if you can) start weeping and repenting and maybe He'll turn. If you're not sure how dead you are, just ask yourself when was the last time you felt like your spiritual "cup" was really all the way full and you had peace and joy and victory? Maybe you could pray this prayer:

Lord Jesus, I'm not sure how spiritually dead I really am, but I don't think I'm as full of Your Spirit as I should be. Please forgive me for whatever I've done that got in Your way and kept me from walking in the fullness of all that You have for me. I'm sorry I leaned on my own understanding and made compromises with the world. Please show me anything that stands between You and me and give me the ability to repent. I want peace and joy and victory. I don't want anything of the enemy to gain any ground in me. Please show me how to keep my cup so full of Jesus that nothing else will fit. I'm sorry for my part in anything that disgraced You or brought harm to Your Body. Please forgive me. And teach me more fear of the Lord. That would be good. That way I'll obey You more and have more wisdom. Thanks. I love You, Lord. I pray this in the Name of Jesus Christ, Amen.

HOW DO YOU KNOW IF YOU'RE UNDER THE RED DRAGON CURSE?

- Pride, haughty eyes (Prov. 6:16-19, 2 Timothy 2:15)
- Lying tongue – blatantly leaving stuff out of the Word or adding to it
- Hands that shed innocent blood – lack of proper respect and care for the sheep
- A heart that devises wicked plans – and wicked plans are any plans that aren't HIS plans

- Feet swift in running to evil – alliances with the "world" and rampant oppressions on your sheep

- False witness speaking lies – false assurance to others that you are telling the Truth and know all the answers

- Sowing discord among brethren – being sectarian and denominational, allowing factions and splits, ejecting brethren from your fellowship over doctrinal or personality issues

- Lack of Fear of the Lord – which is the BEGINNING of wisdom (Ps. 111:10, Prov. 3:5-6, James 4:16)

- Institutional, hierarchical system instead of truly Spirit-led in EVERY way – someone other than God setting your goals and guidelines.

- Lack of Love for the WHOLE Body (I John 3:10-23)

- Sexual immorality, impurity and debauchery; idolatry and witchcraft; hatred, discord, jealousy, fits of rage, selfish ambition, dissensions, factions and envy; drunkenness, orgies and the like – WILL NOT inherit the Kingdom of Heaven (Gal. 5:19-21)

- Worshiping the wrong Jesus (or worshiping the Holy Spirit)

- Evidence of Deuteronomy 28 curses in physical and/or spiritual realms

- Inability to repent - or inability to even figure out what to repent for

- God's glory has departed from the temple, you can't feel the Holy Spirit – or the promises of the Bible for healing or deliverance don't come as they should.

- Can't hear the voice of God and/or not letting Him direct all your paths (Prov. 3:5-6)

- Constant seeking for the new best thing, anxious mind, eyes weary from longing and despairing heart. Always hoping for something different and better. (Deut. 28:65-67) No peace.

- The loss of your children to the demonic structures and systems of your enemies. (Deut. 28)

- and the like...

I have been in over 300 congregations or ministries in the last few years. I have seen every single one of these in play. Usually all of them. I have been physically ejected from a congregation for praying (silently). I have been banned from worshiping with some congregations for no apparent reason. Even by people that have acknowledged that I love Jesus with all my heart and that the Holy Spirit is at work in me. Even people that have declared me a prophet and a healer and a man of God, have later turned completely around. There is one "Spirit-filled" holiness pastor that describes me as a "thing" now and not even as a man. Another that refuses to even pray with me and others that insist I'm full of demons – but can't tell me what they are and won't help deliver me. Pastors that hate me – seriously HATE me – and have said they <u>cannot</u> love me because they don't know what "spirit" I am of – even though Jesus COMMANDED us to love our enemies. (Matt. 10:22, John 15:18-25, Mark 3:22, Luke 7:33-34, Matt. 12:22-30, Prov. 6:16-19)

But I generally seem to get along fine with Baptists, Lutherans, Presbyterians, Methodists and others. It's the "Spirit-filled" Lead Dragon Dancers (that should be hearing God the best) that are the most supernaturally unable to hear anything I have to say – and are the most willing to divide the Body and the most afraid of losing control. To those whom much has been given, much is expected. If God speaks to you, gives you dreams and visions, gives you gifts, gives you a big job to do and THEN you go and make it about <u>you</u> and your conferences and DVD's and new book deal, God is going to turn you over to your own depraved mind and whatever demonic forces want to come mess with you – and you won't even see it coming. At some point you might end up on national news for having sex with your gay massage therapist or hiring a stripper or abusing little boys – and everybody under YOUR particular Red Dragon will say they never even saw it coming. That's just supernatural stupidity and a complete lack of discernment of spirits – cause everybody outside of YOUR dragon totally saw it coming.

Part of what I do is flush out the strongholds that are in play. Just like Jesus and the Apostles (and thousands of other people with a big cup of Jesus), pretty much anywhere I go, the demons that are hiding start surfacing and manifesting. Which is great! That's what I prayed for (even though it really hurts sometimes). Better to flush them out then let them stay camouflaged and hidden. But I have been constantly astounded at how hard-hearted so many "men of God" could be and oblivious to their own sinfulness and obvious heresy while they INSIST they are holy and sanctified. I can come to no other conclusion than that they are supernaturally blind and deaf and dumb and under a strong delusion from

God. Satan couldn't do this to them if they were righteous. It had to come from God. And I have been banging my head for two years trying to break them free of a curse that GOD HIMSELF put on them and won't lift! But it was all part of the plan so that I would see the truth of what is behind all of this mess.

Now I know not to come at them with anger or frustration or bitterness. They are trapped and yoked and under the oppression of a curse. And worst of all, it's from God. And the only solution is repentance, but the curse keeps them from repenting!! In fact, many of them HATE repentance! It creeps them out to see people crying and they just want to focus on the "love" of God and not make people feel bad. Many of them have canceled intercessory prayer meetings and squelched the handful of people in their congregation that were actually willing to cry out to God and weep. True repentance is the most rare thing to be found in the "church" today – and yet, the ONLY thing that is going to turn this mess around. In all my years growing up, I can't remember EVER seeing anyone on their knees crying in a Baptist church! Even many charismatic ministries that know what it's like to feel the presence of God seem to think that if you "declare a holy fast, call a sacred assembly, lay around and giggle on the floor, then He will turn." (Joel 1:13-14 – sort of) But that's just not in there. Not even close! That's just NEVER going to work to turn this ride around. But that's as close to repentance as they can seem to get. Lots of talk about the problems "out there", but no actual crying for their own part in it. Oh, people can repent for personal, individual issues, but not for corporate, system-wide apostasy like division in the Body or selective use of the Bible. Or they can repent for all the parts of the Body that are in darkness and apostate and backslidden, but not for their own part in not stopping it sooner.

I don't know how many of them we can get free, but I know that they're in a really horrible place and I desperately want them all to be free. It's going to come down to whether or not the Lord will pour out the Gift of Repentance on them (or send someone with one) and they will receive it. If not, they're probably toast – and their sheep with them.

> **Acts 5:31** (KJV) – *Him hath God exalted with his right hand to be a Prince and a Saviour, for to **give** repentance to Israel, and forgiveness of sins.*

That's the order in which this works. First, God gives repentance and then you get forgiveness. Jesus came so that He could have right hand access so as to give us the Gift of Repentance. God exalted Jesus so that Jesus could be the mediator and request on our behalf that the Father would give us repentance, even when we don't know to ask for it because we are deaf and blind and stupid. Only THEN can we get forgiveness for our sins individually and corporately. When you lose the Gift of Repentance, you should start worrying that you might be back under a Red Dragon.

> **2 Timothy 2:25 (KJV)** – *In meekness instructing those that oppose themselves; if God peradventure will **give** them repentance to the acknowledging of the truth;*

> **Acts 11:18** (KJV) – *When they heard these things, they held their peace, and glorified God, saying, Then hath God also to the Gentiles **granted** repentance unto life.*

> **Romans 2:4** (KJV) – *Or despisest thou the riches of his goodness and forbearance and longsuffering; not knowing that the goodness of God **leadeth** thee to repentance?*

> **2 Peter 3:9** (KJV) – *The Lord is not slack concerning his promise, as some men count slackness; but is longsuffering to us-ward, not willing that any should perish, but that all should come to repentance.*

> **Hebrews 12:25-29** (KJV) – *25 See that ye refuse not him that speaketh. For if they escaped not who refused him that spake on earth, much more shall not we escape, if we turn away from him that speaketh from heaven: 26 Whose voice then shook the earth: but now he hath promised, saying, Yet once more I shake not the earth only, but also heaven. 27 And this word, Yet once more, signifieth the removing of those things that are shaken, as of things that are made, that those things which cannot be shaken may remain. 28 Wherefore we receiving a kingdom which cannot be moved, let us have grace, whereby we may serve God acceptably with reverence and godly fear: 29 For our God is a consuming fire.*

Please hear me. Please! See the justice and severity of God. Repent and keep repenting until this thing gets turned around. Give your eyes no rest until Jerusalem is free – and all the other cities. Shout this from the watchtowers. There is NO other solution. There is NO other way to turn this around. Weep and mourn and grieve for all the detestable things that are done in the name of Jehovah and Jesus. If you can't repent for your part in this mess, start worrying about whether you're under a Red Dragon of your own. ONLY the Ezekiel 9 remnant will escape. If this could have been turned around sooner, then you should have tried. Don't blame anybody else, this is on YOUR head. If one man, determined and willing, under the anointing of the Holy Spirit, can change the world, then you should have changed it. Stop pointing fingers and repent for not having acted sooner.

> **Isaiah 62:6-7** – *6 I have set watchmen on your walls, O Jerusalem; They shall never hold their peace day or night. You who make mention of the LORD, do not keep silent, 7 And give Him no rest till He establishes And till He makes Jerusalem a praise in the earth.*

Just because you're sure you're hearing God and He seems to be saying you're OK, that's no proof. If you ARE under a Dragon, you'll hear God and be sure it's God and every way you know how to test the spirits, it checks out as God, but it can still be a lying spirit from the Throne intent on your destruction. Repentance is the only safe place. Believe me, it's REALLY easy to get back under a Red Dragon. All you have to do is go your own way – even a little. Then you've basically made up your own religion that says you don't have to obey God ALL the time, you can pick and choose which of His commands are important. If you get very far out from under His perfect will, you may not be able to find your way back. Some folks have never even BEEN in His perfect will, so they don't even know what it would be like to have Him direct every step! Or worse, they don't believe that God is interested in or willing to or capable of directing their every step – which flies in the face of the Bible. We are NOT to lean on our own understanding and direct our own paths – not even a little bit.

The time is over to argue about who is the bigger heretic. We're all cults. Every denomination is a cult. There is no Biblical justification for any division inside the Body over secondary issues. We are clearly commanded not to add to or take away from the Bible and yet every denomination has choice traditions they add to it or portions of scripture they've conveniently explained away or ignore altogether. Stop arguing about who is the most off track! So long as we're willing to hack the Body of Christ up into little pieces or not speak out against it, we're all guilty. We're beating Jesus' Body with a cat-of-nine-tails and leaving little pieces all over while His precious Blood is spilled and nobody seems to care. We have to knock it off before it's too late.

DID THE BIBLE PREDICT THIS?

Yep.

> **2 Thessalonians 2:3-12 (NIV)** – *Don't let anyone deceive you in any way, for that day will not come until the rebellion [falling away NKJV] occurs and the man of lawlessness is revealed at the proper time. For the secret power of lawlessness is already at work; but the one who now holds it back will continue to do so until he is taken out of the way. And then the lawless one will be revealed, whom the Lord Jesus will overthrow with the breath of his mouth and destroy by the splendor of his coming. The coming of the lawless one will be in accordance with the work of Satan displayed in all kinds of counterfeit miracles, signs and wonders, and in every sort of evil that deceives those who are perishing. They perish because they refused to love the truth and so be saved. For this reason **God** sends them a powerful delusion so that they will believe the lie and so that all will be condemned who have not believed the truth but have delighted in wickedness.*

If I'm right, then the falling away is not some future event. We are already so fallen that I don't believe there is any hope for most of the systems and structures we've built. There are millions dying by our hand every week that this 'Ponzi' scheme that we call a "church" continues as it is. (And I can prove it factually and statistically beyond any room for debate. There can be no interpretation except that we are massively and supernaturally backwards.)

So the rebellion has to happen first, right? Could that be like 37,000+ denominations when Jesus said to be One Body? You would sure think that would qualify as rebellion, wouldn't you?

So who is this man of lawlessness that is to be revealed? Could that be the guy that doesn't believe the Old Testament is for today and Jesus didn't come to fulfill the Law, but to abolish it and that once we're under the Blood and have accepted Him as our personal savior we can do whatever we want because we're safe? That sounds pretty lawless to me. (I know that's not the only application for this verse, but it sure seems like one of the "spirals" to me.)

And who was the one that restrained the secret power of lawlessness? I'm pretty sure that would be the Holy Spirit. So who restrained Him and took Him out of the way? I'm pretty sure we did. We denied that the Holy Spirit talks to people, we denied that the Gifts of the Spirit are real and for today, we denied that He should be directing ALL our paths. We turned our back on the Holy Spirit and went our own way and hired consultants and marketing experts and pop-psychology speakers and professional hired shepherds to lead us to whatever THEY think is green pasture. I'm just pretty sure that we picked the Holy Spirit up and set Him off to the side. And when we did, He stopped restraining the secret power of lawlessness and it took us over. And we didn't even notice – because it's SECRET. Kind of goes without saying, doesn't it? If God turns you over to a powerful delusion, you won't know, or else it's not a very good delusion. See?

And what kind of lying signs and wonders should we be expecting? Well, one of the really obvious ones is that the world starts liking you. You live at peace with those who should be persecuting you and you think that means you're reaching them, when really you're just a friend to the world and an enemy to God. (James 4:4) What are the lying signs and wonders at the end of the age? For my dollar, I'm betting that they include all the people preaching "peace and safety" and singing and dancing and being given in marriage right up until the very end of all things. That's pretty miraculous to me, that they would say they love Jesus, but would be friends with the world and completely oblivious to how bad things really are. Pope John Paul II was said to be the most popular and respected and loved man on the planet. But Jesus said that if you were like Him you would be persecuted and hated.

How is the lawless one going to be overthrown? By "the breath from the mouth of Jesus" and he will be destroyed by the splendor of His coming. Now, I'm not saying this doesn't have Apocalyptic application, but I happen to have personally experienced the lawless one in me being overthrown by the breath from the mouth of Jesus and the splendor of His coming, so I know this has other meanings. When Jesus shows up in force, the lawless one gets burned up. Read Jeremiah 4:11-12 - *"At that time this people and Jerusalem will be told, 'A scorching wind blows toward my people, but not to winnow or to cleanse; a wind too strong for that comes from me. Now I pronounce my judgements against them."* (Read the rest of the chapter and see if it doesn't describe the state of the "church". Weep if you can.)

It DOES NOT say that Satan is in charge of all this. It says the coming of the lawless one will be in accordance with the workings of Satan. That doesn't mean Satan does it or has power. It means that it will be like him and in harmony with his goals and plans and style. If the "church" is having the effect of killing, stealing and destroying people spiritually, emotionally or materially, then it is accomplishing the work of Satan for him and is in accordance with the normal workings of the darkness.

It says that there will be counterfeit signs and miracles, and all sorts of evil that deceives those who are perishing. Let me be frank (for a change), the greatest miracles that I have seen are that people spouting clearly heretical, extra-Biblical and dangerous NONSENSE are constantly tolerated and even promoted within the Church! What kind of a miracle is required to make a multi-millionaire lady with pink hair that is constantly crying and begging for money for a multi-Billion dollar TV network seem like a normal, acceptable part of the Church of Jesus Christ? What can be more miraculous than that people who have advanced degrees in "Bible" absolutely REFUSE to acknowledge that certain passages are even IN there?! How miraculous is it that we are the most divided, factious, sectarian religion on the planet and WE are the ones whose Founder said not to EVER break up into pieces?! How many are perishing because they are worshiping the wrong Jesus, but are just sure that they are fine? How many have been deceived? Where do I even start to point out all the heresies preached in the "church" that will send you straight to Hell, but have millions – or billions – convinced that they're safe?!

Why are all these people perishing? Why are they deceived? Why are they walking in accordance with the workings of Satan? BECAUSE they refused to love the Truth.

"WAIT!" you say. "I thought it was because the Antichrist came and Satan is in charge and the Holy Spirit is withdrawn after the Rapture and that's when everyone falls away?" Fine. Believe what you want. But I'm convinced that we've already fallen away and that we've already taken the Holy Spirit out of the way and set Him off to the side by grieving and blaspheming Him for the gazillionth time and that we're under a powerful delusion and we're corporately working for Satan because we refused to love the Truth and so be saved.

Does Satan send the powerful delusion? Nope. Read it again, **God** did it Himself. He said He would and He has. We're in it and hardly anybody can see through it. How strong a delusion do you think it is? If we're covered in the Blood of Jesus and Satan sends a delusion, we should be able to see through it. That's my experience anyway. We should be able to take every thought captive and bring it into obedience with Christ. After all, our weapons of war are mighty and no power of darkness can stand against us.

But do you really think you're big enough to see through a strong delusion that came from God? How does the Blood of Jesus protect us from a delusion from God? Didn't we invite the delusion by not really loving Truth and maybe not being under the Blood of Jesus in the first place?

"All will be condemned that believed not the truth but delighted in wickedness." Period. That's the Bible and it's final. Our denominations and sects and ministries are delighting in wickedness. Every single day that we continue to believe that we are just fine and things are peachy, we continue to go the way of the Laodecian Church in Revelation 3 and we get more blind and more naked and more wretched – and more people die because of us.

We better get back to Truth – and pure, unadulterated, untouched by Man, nothing-but, Truth – before it's too late. And I have no idea what that looks like, but I know you can NEVER find it so long as you're under a Red Dragon and you can't get out from under a Red Dragon without repentance and "coming out of her" and getting her out of you. And the Red Dragon will try to keep you from repenting at ALL costs. See the problem?

I'm not taking away from that this passage in Thessalonians that it has application to some future anti-christ person that afflicts the world, but as with all of the Bible it has multiple applications and in the context of the Church, I think this man of sin, this son of perdition is **us**. I think the Lord is making it very clear that the falling away will get worse and worse until we realize that we have exalted ourselves above all that is called God, have sat ourselves (or the men we anointed and appointed) as the idols in our temples and have declared ourselves to be God. We have hired consultants to teach us how to be more like the world. We have gotten in bed with government and business and marketing and fund-raising and in all sorts of other ways have intermarried with the nations we were supposed to displace and destroy. We have taken on their gods and worshiped them and by so doing have declared ourselves God. **We** are the sons of perdition. (John 17:6-26)

What are the workings of Satan that come with all power and signs and lying wonders?

That we're just fine and everything is just as it should be. "Peace and Safety. Peace and Safety. All is well. Go back to sleep." He has bamboozled the "church." Nearly all of the "elect" have **ALREADY** gone astray.

What is the true sign and wonder of this age that proves the sovereignty of God?

> **Deuteronomy 28:45-48 (NIV)** – *All these curses will come upon you. They will pursue you and overtake you until you are destroyed, because you did not obey the Lord your God and observe the commands and decrees he gave you.* ***They will be a sign and wonder to you and your descendants forever.*** *Because you did not serve the Lord your God joyfully and gladly in the time of prosperity, therefore in hunger and thirst, in nakedness and dire poverty, you will serve the enemies the Lord sends against you. He will put an iron yoke on your neck until he has destroyed you.*

> **Deuteronomy 28:62-63 (NIV)** – *You who were as numerous as the stars in the sky will be left but few in number, because you did not obey the Lord your God. Just as it pleased the Lord to make you prosper and increase in number, so it will please him to ruin and destroy you. You will be uprooted from the land you are entering to possess.*

DID JESUS PREDICT THIS?

Yep.

Matthew 24:4-25 – *Jesus answered: "Watch out that no one deceives you. For many will come in my name, claiming, 'I am the Christ,' and will deceive many. You will hear of wars and rumors of wars, but see to it that you are not alarmed. Such things must happen, but the end is still to come. Nation will rise against nation, and kingdom against kingdom. There will be famines and earthquakes in various places. All these things are the beginning of the birth pains.*

Then you will be handed over to be persecuted and put to death and you will be hated by all nations because of me. At that time many will turn away from the faith and will betray and hate each other, and many false prophets will appear and deceive many people. Because of the increase of wickedness, the love of most will grow cold, but he who stands firm to the end will be saved. And this gospel of the kingdom will be preached in the whole world as a testimony to all nations, and then the end will come.

So when you see standing in the holy place the abomination that causes desolation, spoken of through the prophet Daniel – let the reader understand then let those who are in Judea flee to the mountains. Let no one on the roof of his house go down to take anything out of the house. Let no one in the field go back to get his cloak. How dreadful it will be in those days for pregnant women and nursing mothers. Pray that your flight will not take place in winter or on the Sabbath. For then there will be great distress, unequaled from the beginning of the world until now – and never to be equaled again.

If those days had not been cut short, no one would survive, but for the sake of the elect those days will be shortened. At that time if anyone says to you, 'Look, here is the Christ!' or, 'There he is!' do not believe it. For false Christs and false prophets will appear and perform great signs and miracles to deceive even the elect – it that were possible. See I have told you ahead of time.

Again, this passage has global, apocalyptic applications, but it is like a repeating, increasing spiral. Before it applies to the world, it applies to the Church. The spiritual goes first, then is manifested in the natural. If we look at the implications of this to the Church, I think you can see that we are already full on with all of these things and that Jesus predicted this. And that it had to happen to spiritual Israel before it can happen to natural Israel and the World.

We were to watch out that no one deceive us. We didn't. There will be wars between nations and kingdoms – which is how Christians killed so many other Christians through the Dark Ages and the Reformation and which is how we now have 37,000+ denomiNATIONS and start a new one every other day. Can you really split a denomination without hatred in your heart? And if you have hatred for a brother in your heart, that's the same as murder. There are spiritual famines among God's people and the occasional earthquake shaking that seems like something might break loose, but is soon over. All these are the beginning of the birth pains.

THEN we will be handed over to be persecuted. By who? By the enemy, by the Red Dragon. And many have been put to death by the Red Dragon. We are hated by each other and hated by the world. Many have turned away from the faith and betray and hate each other. Many false prophets have appeared and deceive many. Every man that says we don't need to be one body and we don't need to obey the Bible and love our brothers unconditionally is a false prophet – and they are legion. The love of most has grown cold and it's because of the wickedness that we allowed to enter by going our own way and following after false prophets. But ONLY he who stands until the end will be saved. ONLY those who are not under a Red Dragon will be saved. ONLY those can preach the true gospel of the kingdom to all nations.

The abomination that causes desolation is the antichrist and when we see the Spirit of Antichrist in our holy places, on our congregations and ministries or in our own hearts – we are to RUN FOR THE HILLS and not look back. Take nothing, go back for nothing. Say goodbye to no one. Run and don't look back. If you go back, you will get back under the Red Dragon. And if you're not careful, at home alone you'll get under one of your own making!

The Lord makes it clear that so many will be deceived and so many will die that NO ONE would survive if it weren't cut short. The Red Dragon has devoured nearly everything. The days were cut short for the sake of those who were standing firm until the end. Otherwise even the last of the elect would be deceived and no one would be left.

I'm begging you, come out of her. Run! Get away! Get out from under the Red Dragon and get the Red Dragon out of you! And the only way is to repent. Someone with the Gift of Repentance has to pour it out on you. Now I understand better than ever why the Lord had me write the "Apology to the World." The Lord said that if I pray with someone and repent sincerely in front of them for the things that I have done and they so much as nod their head in agreement that they have done the same things and need forgiveness, then He will turn from His fierce anger on them and will heal them and restore their land. He really, really wants to lift this curse, but He is just and His rules are clear. Without repentance there is no remission of sins. And a strong delusion will keep you from repenting at all. So you will die. Period. Unless the Lord finds a way to release you. Unless the Lord sends someone to show you the way, you are toast. I was under it and I know now how badly deceived I was. And if I get back under it again, I know it will be even worse because the stakes are getting higher and higher all the time.

OK, not only that, but you have to see that Jesus recruited as disciples people that were NOT under the Red Dragon curse at the time. The Pharisees and Sadducees were supernaturally stubborn and blind and Jesus said they were sons of hell and would not enter heaven (Matt. 23). Even though they were in the synagogue praying at least three times a DAY! (That's sure more pious than just Sundays and Wednesday nights!)

Clearly, Israel had gone it's own way at the time and were worshiping all kinds of things other than the one true God. I think the argument could be made pretty effectively that Jesus was aware of the Red Dragon religious spirits and the Deuteronomy 28 curse and was wise enough to recruit as disciples those who were not already under it. Even though they had less scripture knowledge, they had an easier time seeing their Messiah and embracing His message, because they weren't under a curse from God. Why else would He constantly be hanging around tax collectors and fishermen and prostitutes – that is, all the people the "religious establishment" thought were unclean? Perhaps it's their very "uncleanness" that kept them safe from the Red Dragon curse! If I'm right, that really changes the whole approach to who we need to reach doesn't it? Instead of getting people to transfer from one Red Dragon to another, let's go find the people that ARE NOT under a curse from God because they were never in the institutional "church" in the first place!

I'm just pretty sure Jesus understood this really well and it was what colored His style and focus of ministry. Go get the little children, the ones with faith like a child, the ones uncorrupted by the antichrist religious systems and structures and "wisdom" of the day. And if you put a stumbling block in their way and put them under a Red Dragon, it would be better for you to have a millstone tied around your neck and thrown in the ocean. (Matt. 18:6)

HOW DO YOU GET OUT FROM UNDER IT?

Ezekiel 9 is still the solution. Repentance individually and corporately is ALWAYS the right answer. Have I mentioned that already? It can't be overstated. Repentance is the key that opens every door.

All you have to do is say you're sorry and mean it. He's not unreasonable, he's just waiting for you to see what you did wrong and admit it! Do you treat your children any differently? Will YOU let them have their toy truck back without them saying they're sorry for hitting their brother with it? Heck, NO! They're in a time out until they've had time to think about what they did and say they're sorry! What kind of parent overlooks one kid bashing another over the head? Isn't that what we're doing all the time in "church"? You don't get out of the time out until you say you're sorry!

> **James 4:7-10** – *You adulterous people, don't you know that friendship with the world is hatred toward God? Anyone who chooses to be a friend of the world becomes an enemy of God. Or do you think Scripture says without reason that the spirit he caused to live in us envies intensely? But he give us more grace. That is why Scripture says: "God opposes the proud but gives grace to the humble." Submit yourselves, then, to God. Resist the devil, and he will flee from you. Come near to God and he will come near to you. Wash your hands, you sinners, and purify your hearts, you double-minded.* **Grieve, mourn and wail.** *Change your laughter to mourning and your joy to gloom. Humble yourselves before the Lord, and he will lift you up.*

> **2 Chronicles 7:14** – **If** *my people, which are called by my name, shall humble themselves, and pray, and seek my face, and turn from their wicked ways;* **then** *will I hear from heaven, and will forgive their sin, and will heal their land.*

Jeremiah 3:12-13 – "'Return, faithless Israel,' declares the Lord, 'I will frown on you no longer for I am merciful,' declares the Lord, 'I will not be angry forever, **only acknowledge your guilt** - you have rebelled against the Lord your God, you have scattered your favors to foreign gods under every spreading tree, and have not obeyed me,'" declares the Lord "Return, faithless people," declares the Lord, "for I am your husband. I will choose you - one from a town and two from a clan - and bring you to Zion. Then I will give you shepherds after my own heart, who will lead you with knowledge and understanding."

Jeremiah 26:13
Therefore now amend your ways and your doings, and obey the voice of the LORD your God; and the LORD will repent him of the evil that he hath pronounced against you.

Ezekiel 18:21-32 – (Go read it.)

LOTS more like this. (See Page 234.)

Joel 1:13 – "Put on sackcloth, O priests, and mourn; wail, you who minister before the altar. Come, spend the night in sackcloth, you who minister before my God; for the grain offerings and drink offerings are withheld from the house of your God. Declare a holy fast, call a sacred assembly. Summon the elders who live in the land to the house of the Lord your God, and cry out to the Lord." (And again in Joel 2:15-17)

Then the Lord responds in **Joel 2:18-19**

"**THEN** the Lord will be jealous for his land and take pity on his people. The Lord will reply to them, "I am sending you grain, new wine and oil, enough to satisfy you fully; never again will I make you an object of scorn to the nations."

And AFTER they say they're sorry, AND He takes pity on them and turns, <u>THEN</u>:

Joel 2:28-32 – "And AFTERWARD, I will pour out my Spirit on all people, your sons and daughters will prophecy, your old men will dream dreams, your young men will see visions. Even on my servants, both men and women, I will pour out my Spirit in those days. I will show wonders in the heavens and on the earth, blood and fire and billows of *smoke. The sun will be turned to darkness and the moon to blood before the coming of the great and terrible day of the Lord. And everyone who calls on the name of the Lord will be saved; for on Mount Zion and in Jerusalem there will be deliverance, as the Lord has said, among the survivors whom the Lord calls."*

People really misuse that chunk of that last verse, "Everyone who calls on the name of the Lord will be saved." That doesn't say to call on the name of "Jesus the Savior," it says to call on the name of the LORD – master, king, commander, ruler, monarch – that means daily, instant, radical obedience, not calling one time like the lifeguard at the local pool. But that doesn't end there, those saved are not "everyone," but those who call on the name of the Lord AND are among the survivors whom the LORD calls. Who are the survivors? The Ezekiel 9 remnant that are weeping and repenting and mourning for the state of things. Not EVERYONE that calls on the name of the Lord will be saved. It's clear from Matt. 25:31-46 that many will say "Lord, Lord" and He may still say, "Get away from me, I never knew you." Remember, He tells the death angels in Ezekiel 9 to slaughter everyone and to start with the elders that were before the Temple! Don't get too comfy, you better be REALLY sure that you know you're on the right team. Even being an elder in the temple is no guarantee that you're safe! Repentance is the key.

In short, if you can't repent or don't think you need to repent, you're probably under the curse. Find someone that CAN repent and have them show you how or pour their gift out on you. My entire focus is on raising up people that are Dragon-free and can stay that way. If you need me to come and pray for/with you and/or your ministry, I'd love to do that (if the Lord allows).

There are others out there as well, I'm not saying it's just me, but not as many as you would think. Even a lot of people that are outside of the "institutional church" system are still under their own Red Dragon. There is a "house church" Red Dragon, too. There is a "lone wolf, wandering prophet" Red Dragon. (I've met a bunch of those.) And a thousand other flavors.

If you're reading this and you're a pastor, priest, bishop, apostle, pope, lay leader, parent or otherwise have a flock of any size that depends on you, please pray this with all your heart – if you can:

Dear Jesus, I don't really have any idea how much of the stuff that I'm supporting is man-made, but I'm sure some of it is. I'm really sorry. I want pure Truth and nothing but. I want Your Spirit to be fully and completely in charge of me in every way. If there is anything in me or my ministry that isn't pleasing to You, please kill it. Whatever it takes, rip it, burn it, shred it, shake it – if I can't lay it down then just tear it out of my grasp. If I can't see it, please remove the scales from my eyes by whatever means necessary. Just cleanse your temple and start with me. Don't let me be complacent and settle for what used to be. I want Your full presence right now. Please, Lord, pour out the Gift of Repentance on me and my sheep in full measure. Let me see through Your eyes, even if it hurts. I mean it. Whatever it takes. Please just hold my hand when it hurts. I love You, Jesus. I trust You. I'm sorry I ever went my own way, even in the littlest detail. Please, Father, in the Name of Jesus, please fix it. Amen.

WHAT WOULD IT LOOK LIKE TO BE COMPLETELY FREE OF THE RED DRAGON?

Well, when Israel was completely obedient and following God's commands, no nation could stand against them. The Bible says that He will lift you above nations and no weapon formed against you will prosper. So, the way I see it, the people who are fully free of every yoke, are out from under every curse, have been transformed by the renewing of their minds, and are dead and it's Christ in them that lives – are the manifest sons of God that the earth is groaning for. (Romans 8:19) We've seen little glimmers of it before in Elijah and Elisha and Moses and Abraham and Enoch and others who were counted as righteous. But the Bible says the greatest of all the prophets was John the Baptist and that the least among US that has the Holy Spirit is greater than him! So how come we're not seeing it in every Christian everywhere? Because they're not manifesting their Sonship – because they're going their own way.

Consider this, people often discuss all the possible reasons why God seems to heal people more often (and more dramatically) in Africa and India and Asia. I have friends that I trust that have seen with their own eyes as people regrew limbs or spines straightened or giant tumors just fall off or even miraculous weight loss while in a prayer line. By the power of God through me I have seen people healed of autism, hearing problems, heart problems, joint problems, migraines, chronic or urgent pain of all kinds, spinal and head injuries - as well as demonic oppressions like schizophrenia, agoraphobia, depression, fear, lust, and addictions of all kinds instantly lifted. I know it's real and I know God moves that way today.

I've heard all kinds of theories about why we don't see more of that in America, from lack of faith, to not being child-like enough, to those that say it's all fake or satanic and not really from God anyway. (And I dare you to find ANYWHERE in the Word where it says satan heals people.) Anyway, none of those arguments satisfy me. People are getting healed there, even raised from the dead. Something else is behind this.

The best answer I've found is this, Deuteronomy 28 says you will have wasting diseases that cannot be cured, that you will be afflicted and there will be no one to help, that the sky over you will be brass, that you will suffer until you are destroyed. If a nation or a people or a village don't know God and never did, when someone righteous and sent by God shows up and prays for healing for them, it's likely that they will get healed so that God can show His glory and prove Himself to them. But when a country or a people or a village already knew God and have intentionally and rebelliously gone their own way, they should not expect any supernatural healing to show up on any kind of a regular basis. And if it shows up at all, it's just God's mercy on an individual here and there.

So the best explanation I can find of why people get healed in Africa and Asia and not in America (or the West, for that matter) is that the West is already evangelized and has turned their back on God by creating their own blended mystery religions and calling them "Christian" and He has put upon them the curses of Deuteronomy 28. The prayer of a "righteous" man availeth much. The prayer of a "denominational" man may not avail much at all.

Warm and fluffy and "seeker-friendly" isn't going to cut it. Want to know what your "purpose" is? You don't need forty days to figure out what YOU can do for God. Just weep and repent and mourn before the altar for the fact that you haven't known **all along** what God's purpose for you is – and been walking in it. There's no telling how much blood is on your head for the missed opportunities and outright rebellion of going your own way this whole time. **You don't get revived until you say you're sorry for being the kind of person that needs reviving!** If you cry out to Him, He will open the doors and explain everything and the Holy Spirit will be your teacher. No MAN can tell you who you are in Christ - not even you. You need to hear God directly and walk in it.

So what might it look like to be fully Dragon-free? For one thing, the diseases of the Egyptians wouldn't stick to you anymore and your prayers for deliverance would have real power. Maybe people in America might actually start getting healed and delivered on a large scale. In combination with keeping your cup full of Jesus and being a part of a Lampstand city, probably nothing could stand against you. (Read more about that on the website.)

WHAT WOULD IT BE LIKE TO BE COMPLETELY UNDER CHRIST'S HEADSHIP?

Not that I have fully attained the goal, but I strive toward the prize and I die daily so that Christ in me can live. To His glory, He has allowed me to hear His voice very clearly. Not just in dreams and visions, but all day every day. He directs my paths in every way. I would recommend that you read "The Practice of the Presence of God" by Brother Lawrence. It was formative for me and I sought after that kind of intimacy with God. And He says that if you seek Him, you will find Him. And I did.

He wakes me up in the morning. I have no alarm clock. I don't wear a watch. He tells me what Scripture to read and what it means and how it will apply to my day. He tells me what to wear, what to eat, where to go, what to say (or not say), what job to take and how to do it. He tells me what to pray. He prays through me or speaks through me to those in need. He crushes the demons that come against me every day. He is my shield and my provider. He is my Head and I am His bond-servant. I fear no man and follow no man. I am not under anyone's "cover" because Christ is my head. There is no man that stands between me and God and tells me what to do. Though there are many brethren around me that advise and counsel and teach and reprove and rebuke, ultimately I have to get a confirmation from the Throne on everything. I make no plans, I spend no money, I go nowhere, I eat nothing without an assurance that it's what He wants me to do. And I have more joy and peace than I ever knew possible – even in the face of astounding amounts of opposition and affliction.

Do I make mistakes? Yes. Sometimes I hear wrong, sometimes I pester Him into allowing something He'd rather not allow, but He humors me to teach me a lesson. Sometimes I ask "Can I" instead of "Should I". (That one got me into a lot of trouble until He explained the difference and wrote it on my heart!) At times I have been under a Red Dragon of my own making and heard what I was sure was God, but it was a lying spirit from the Throne intent on my destruction for having gone my own way. Sometimes the people around me hear wrong and I don't double-check with Him. Sometimes I just pop off before asking what I should say. Sometimes I've spoken out revelation that was just for me personally and not for any other ears. But it's getting better all the time and I don't ever ask Him to turn down the refining fire.

The ministry that He has called me to is under His headship. He dictates the pace, the scope, the impact, the focus, the budget, the method, the timing – everything. There are no committee meetings. There are no votes, there are no paid consultants. There is just Christ as the Head and me as the hands and feet. When I need a confirmation, He provides one. When I need a rebuke, He does it Himself or sends someone.

In a worship or prayer meeting, He sets the time and place, He invites the people, He directs the prayers, He moves through us as He wills. He identifies the needs in the people present and makes sure they get met in order of priority. Nobody goes home unchanged. He consistently shows up in a powerful way because we get out of His way. I have never been anywhere and experienced the kind of presence and power of God that I did in God's little furniture store in Liberty, Missouri. And even though that season is past, He continues to show up every time we get out of His way and sincerely invite Him to be fully in charge and we take Him out of whatever box we might have tried to cram Him into.

What would it do to "church" to really, truly get out of His way? Do we even see how much we're getting in His way? Because of the blindness of our hearts, I doubt that hardly any leaders of the church really see how much they are grieving the Holy Spirit. I would love to tell them – and I have tried at times – but it never seems to do any good. In fact, it supernaturally never seems to do any good! The most hardened secularist or atheist or businessman would listen more politely – just in case I might actually have a point about something and it would improve what they were doing. Most any restaurant or service business will have a Customer Comments box and carefully review feedback – but that seems like the VERY last thing a pastor wants to spend time doing. How a man that says he loves God and fears Him could so callously and obliviously ignore anyone that comes in the name of the Lord and shows them their error is beyond me. It HAS to be supernatural. I can't find any other explanation for how normally loving, caring, sweet, 'Christian' people can stone prophets – except that God has hardened their hearts, blinded their eyes, shut up their ears and doesn't want them free yet.

Matthew 13:14-15

14 And in them the prophecy of Isaiah is fulfilled, which says: '*Hearing you will hear and shall not understand, And seeing you will see and not perceive; 15 For the hearts of this people have grown dull. Their ears are hard of hearing, And their eyes they have closed, Lest they*

should see with their eyes and hear with their ears, Lest they should understand with their hearts and turn, So that I should heal them.'

All of the things that He has taught me in the last two years (and before) somehow integrate with this message about the Red Dragon. I know that if we were under His headship, the model of the church would be the city church – one body in one town, under His headship and working as He directed. How that would manifest and look in real practice in each particular town, I have no idea. In some towns you could all gather in one building. In some it will mean house churches all over town, in some it will mean stadiums full of people. In some it might not look that different than what we have right now. I have no idea. Happily, it's not my job to direct your town. It's my job to get you free of the Red Dragon so you can hear God and HE can direct all your paths.

I know that if we were under His headship, the way we handle money would be vastly different. The way we relate institutionally to the government would be vastly different. The way we relate to other Christians would be vastly different. Music would be different. Church "services" would be different. Leadership would be different. Healing would be different. I think we can't even get our heads around how creative He can be to customize each situation to the exact needs of the people present at that moment. Nothing would be repetitive or even predictable. People we never expected would be the mightiest evangelists and prophets and teachers and musicians. The Holy Spirit blows like the wind and no one knows where He goes or where He came from. We would be much like that. But we would be effective for the Gospel and we would be pushing back the darkness instead of being co-opted by it.

As soon as the Red Dragon can stop using our legs and our spiritual authority and our assets to accomplish his purposes, then we can gain the upper hand and begin to crush Him under our heel.

Wouldn't that be nice?

There is still that little issue of the Great Commission, the final charge of Jesus to spread the TRUE Gospel to all the world. (Matt. 28:18-20, Mark 16:14-20) Is there anything more important than this? How exactly are we going to do that while we're fighting and fussing with each other and all going our own way? Whose Gospel do we preach anyway? Jesus did NOT say to go into all the world and preach the Baptist Gospel or the

217

Pentecostal Gospel or the Lutheran Gospel. We are to preach Christ and Him crucified. We are to be One Body and we are to love each other. If they will know us by our love and we are full of hatred and wrath and dissension and factions – maybe we should stop preaching ANYTHING until we knock it off and the LORD HIMSELF opens our mouths. Maybe we should hit our faces and admit that we are ALL men of unclean lips and from a people of unclean lips and beg for Him to burn it out of us by whatever means necessary. (Isaiah 6) We need to stop traveling over land and sea to make a single convert and then make him twice as much the sons of hell that we are. (Matt. 23:15) Yeah, that would be nice.

We can't spread the true Gospel until we are true Christians. And we can't be true Christians until we are fully under Christ's headship and no other. We have to repent and throw off all the Red Dragons. All of them. Of the seven letters to the churches in Revelation 2-3, two of them were not criticized – Smyrna and Philadelphia, both of them poor. No matter what the other five were criticized for, the prescription is always the same – REPENT!

There is NO other solution offered by Jesus. There is no other hope. There is no amount of good worship music and really excellent child-care facilities and great expository teaching that is going to turn this around. The ONLY solution, the only prescription, the only thing that is going to get His attention is repentance.

Start with this – Appendix G. Maybe you've already seen it. Read the "Apology to the World" letter and if you feel that you've been a part of helping build – or not having personally tried harder to stop sooner – a system that is not what God wanted, then repent for your sins and the sins of your forefathers. **And mean it, and don't go back.** Run for the hills right now and don't even go back to get your coat. Come out of her my people – and get HER out of YOU, too! (Rev. 18:4-8)

> **Lord, pour out the Gift of Repentance on Your Body and on this nation. Please forgive us for going our own way. Please have mercy on us and turn from Your righteous anger. You are just and true and your judgement is righteous. We deserve far worse than what You have done. Please, Father, please for the sake of Your Holy Name remember Your people and turn from Your wrath. Please send out the remnant that can teach us how to pray and how to repent in spirit and in truth. Please turn this around, Abba.**

Please fix it. I'm sorry we broke it. I'm sorry we didn't follow the instructions. It doesn't work and there are parts left over. Please fix it, Dad. In the name of Jesus Christ, our Lord, Amen.

If that still doesn't do it for you and you don't feel that you've repented enough to get out from under your Red Dragon, contact me. (fotm@fellowshipofthemartyrs.com) I have a special anointing for gently telling people (and groups) what they overlooked that they still need to repent for. And repenting in front of them so they can see how it's done.

If that takes care of it and the Lord pours out on you a true and deep gift of repentance, then please, PLEASE, I'm begging you – please go find somebody to pour it out on. Go weep in front of them until they see how bad it is and how desperate we really are. I spent two days weeping on the sidewalk in the middle of town last summer (June 2006). Do whatever it takes. Pour out your gift of repentance on those around you who are trapped under the Red Dragon. Pour it on the Lead Dragon Dancers if you can, but know that they have the hardest time receiving it.

Please, Brethren, if you have ears to hear, please hear. Then GO into all the world and show them how to repent.

COMMON SYMPTOMS / SIDE EFFECTS OF THE RED DRAGON:

Cut-and-paste Demon - Anything not related to what YOU are doing is of no importance. Scriptures that disagree with your position don't exist. Baptists ignore or marginalize or explain away the Book of Acts. Pentecostals ignore "decent and in order". 'Oneness' groups ignore Father, Son, and Spirit references. Seventh Day Adventists ignore that JESUS is Lord of the Sabbath and EVERY day should be dedicated to Him. Catholics ignore "don't call any man Father." Mormons ignore "don't add anything to this book." ALL of them ignore "factions will not inherit the kingdom." Anything that disagrees is supernaturally blocked out of their field of vision. Like that section of their Bible is just missing or has a fuzzy block over it. Just like when you are inside the Dragon, you can't see the scenery, just the inside of your own Dragon and all the dancers that are with you.

Deaf-and-Dumb Demon - Can't see, can't hear where you are going except by following the others in front. You can see where you've been, but you have no idea what is ahead of you. You are following the Lead Dancer and assuming that he knows where he is going. And he thinks he's in charge, but the Dragon is really the one telling him how to dance and where. When criticism comes, it's ignored because it comes from outside the Dragon. If criticism comes from inside the Dragon, the messenger is ejected as unloyal and unable to properly dance and represent the Dragon team. The Dragon will NOT tolerate disunity under it's own cover.

Spirit of Competition - Closely attached to the Pride, this encourages the Dragon team to be the VERY best and ignore weaknesses. They should be an EXCELLENT Dragon, particularly since they are doing everything they do to bring glory and honor to God. They need EXCELLENT silk and sequins and only the best costumes and dancers will do. They need consultants and personal trainers and professional choreographers. If possible, upgraded sound systems and lighting and videography so they can properly record how well they are dancing and tell the world. After a couple of generations of highlighting strengths and ignoring weaknesses, they become totally inbred and have developed their own languages and idiosyncrasies and style. In the Body of Christ, they become a barn full of toes and they like it that way and clone new toes as fast as they can. They have no balance, but they are the best bunch of toes anywhere.

Spirit of Bondage - The Dragon works hard to whisper to all involved that they are critically important to the welfare of the team and that they MUST remain under the Dragon. They CANNOT venture out on their own or go to some competing Dragon. They MUST remain under the "cover" of the Dragon or the Lead Dancer or else they will be rejected and alone and the enemy will get them. What enemy? The same enemy they're already under, but it will never admit that.

Spirit of Hurry (Time Focus) - This artificially inserts all kinds of deadlines and forces urgency. It keeps everyone busy all the time. Twice on Sundays and Wednesday and visitation and softball leagues and potlucks and summer camp and committee meetings and Christmas Pageant and more and more. Always taxing those already over-taxed and seeking fresh "legs" for the Dragon. It HAS to keep dancing. It has to keep everyone in motion. It keeps their eyes off of Jesus if it can keep them focused on the structure, style, timing, programs, staff, improvement, growth of the Dragon.

Spirits of Envy, Jealousy and Hatred - Gal. 5:19-21 are rampant in the congregations and denominations of America. There is a constant finger-pointing and one trying to pull down another. The Dragon is always whispering that YOUR Dragon is prettier and smarter and older and better and longer and shinier and faster than all those other Dragons. It's critically important that the people in the Dragon KNOW what all the other Dragons are doing wrong and why THEIR Dragon is the best one of them all. They will even persecute each other or refuse to even participate in events together. Even though we are supposed to be ONE BODY (John 17), the enemy broke us up into competing teams so we can never go anywhere together.

Spirit of Empty (Idle) Words - Eph. 5:5-7, Job 35:13, Isaiah 58:13, This is disguised as "fellowshipping" but is really just wasted time while people are dying. It's far better to bond together in the heat of common battle (or boot camp), than to casually greet each other as tourists on the same beach. This one may be disguised as telling stories about what God has done, which is nice, but it fills the time and keeps us from watching Him do something RIGHT NOW in our midst. It's not obedience to tell a story about the greatness and majesty of God – unless He tells you to tell that story at that moment. It might be a great story, but you're out of order if you tell it at the wrong time. It won't be anointed and it won't have the effect He wants it to have. This is VERY, VERY common in the "church" and is slowly sucking the life out of millions because of the missed opportunities to see Him move because we won't shut up.

Spirits of Lust and Greed - Almost ALL under the Red Dragon have a spirit of lust and a constant desire for more. It's no wonder that we have rampant obesity, porn, divorce, greed, adultery and other things inside the "church". There is a constant "arms race" to keep up with or exceed other Dragon Teams. And it spills over into the personal lives of all the members, even outside of the Dragon dance. The Red Dragon is all about accumulation and growth and gathering unto itself for self-gratification. That spirit is rampant and there is no one to stop it because it's an essential element of the nature of the Dragon.

Spirit of Fear - The Dragon GREATLY discourages individuality and presents a constant stream of reasons why the individual is incapable of defending themselves, standing alone or being effective without the Team. Despite constantly saying that God is sufficient and "greater is He who is in us than He who is in the world," the Dragon insists that anyone who is not under "cover" and actively and regularly doing the Dragon Dance will be eaten for lunch by the darkness. All kinds of fears are encouraged and this, too, spills over into the personal lives of the Dancers. We have rampant depression, anxiety attacks, agoraphobia, even suicidal thoughts because of the constant pounding on the Dancers by this spirit. (And that is NOT from God!)

Spirit of Gloating - Rejoices in the downfall of other brethren. It is anti- I Corinthians 13. Doesn't rejoice in it's OWN affliction, but sure enjoys watching others be afflicted and brought down - or taken out of the Dragon Dance competition altogether.

Charismania – A desire for some manifestation above relationship – drunk in the spirit, barking, gold teeth, slain in the spirit, a prophetic word, a word of knowledge, an impartation, whatever. Might be perfectly reasonable, perfectly Biblical, perfectly decent and in order, but NOT if it becomes the OBJECT of desire. It becomes the pearl to chase, rather than relationship with Christ and full obedience. That will open them up to a spirit of lust that will do all kinds of other damage. If you seek a gift to be better equipped for God's war, that's one thing, but if you seek it so as to show off or be like everybody else or have a bigger, flashier ministry and make a name for yourself – that is not good at all and will surely result in your destruction (unless you repent).

Hardening of Hearts - Eph 4:17-19, Continual lust for more, given over to sensuality. This is one of the scariest of all. This one doesn't just come from the Red Dragon, this one is from God Himself. As we began to go our own way, the Lord turned us over more and more to the Dragon and hardened our hearts. The VERY WORST side effect of this monstrosity is that it is practically IMPOSSIBLE to repent. By far the least seen, least preached, least practiced expression of faith in the "churches" is real, true repentance. Even more rare is repentance for having been a part of a system that wasn't what God wanted and has been adulterous and left the true path. Anyone under a Dragon that repents for having been a part of the Dragon at all is almost instantly ejected with prejudice. Which makes it very difficult to get any more people out from under the Dragon.

Let me repeat that. This is a CURSE FROM GOD for having gone our own way and the curse carries with it hardening of the hearts. The only way to get out from under the curse is to repent, but the curse keeps you from repenting. In fact, it keeps you from listening to anybody that even TALKS about repenting. If you're even reading this and you got this far, that's a really good sign that either you're free or the grip on you is breaking.

This is by NO means complete. Pretty much ANY other kind of oppression or demonic influence in Satan's arsenal is available and in use for this task. God will pretty much turn you over to whatever wants to come mess with you and you may not be able to be delivered of it at all unless you repent for having gone your own way!

Wait, there's more.

DEUTERONOMY 28
from the NIV with commentary and application

Blessings for Obedience

1 **If** you **fully** obey the LORD your God and **carefully** follow **all** his commands I give you today, the LORD your God will set you high above all the nations on earth. 2 **All** these blessings will come upon you and accompany you **if** you obey the LORD your God:

3 You **will** be blessed in the **city** and blessed in the **country**. 4 The **fruit of your womb will** be blessed, and the **crops** of your land and the young of your **livestock**—the **calves** of your **herds** and the **lambs** of your **flocks**. 5 Your **basket** and your **kneading trough will** be blessed. 6 You **will** be blessed when you **come in** and blessed when you **go out**.

7 The LORD **will** grant that the enemies who rise up against you will be **defeated** before you. They will come at you from one direction but **flee** from you in seven.

8 The LORD **will** send a blessing on your **barns** and on **everything** you put your hand to. The LORD your God **will** bless you in the **land** he is giving you.

9 The LORD **will** establish you as his **holy** people, as he promised you on **oath**, if you **keep the commands** of the LORD your God and **walk in his ways**. 10 **Then all** the peoples on earth **will** see that you are called by the name of the LORD, and they **will** fear you. 11 The LORD **will** grant you **abundant prosperity**—in the fruit of your **womb**, the young of your livestock and the crops of your ground—in the **land** he swore to your forefathers to give you.

12 The LORD **will open the heavens**, the storehouse of his bounty, to send **rain** on your land in season and to bless all the **work** of your **hands**. You will **lend** to many nations but will **borrow** from **none**. 13 The LORD **will** make you the **head**, not the **tail**. If you pay attention to the **commands** of the LORD your God that I give you this day and **carefully follow them**, you **will** always be at the **top**, never at the **bottom**. 14 **Do not** turn aside from **any** of the commands I give you today, to the **right** or to the **left**, following other gods and serving them.

By the testimony of two witnesses is a thing established. Here God repeats THREE TIMES that IF you do certain things, THEN He will respond a certain way. It is a GUARANTEE. If you are fully obeying then you WILL BE benefiting from these blessings. It is not optional for God. It is an automatic and universal law, like gravity. If you are His children and come under the covering of His promises and you are being obedient, then these things WILL come to pass. However, the better you know Him, the higher the tightrope. Nobody was closer to God than Moses and all He had to do to keep from inheriting the promise was tap the rock instead of talking to it. God isn't kidding around here. He expects OBEDIENCE. Especially from those of His children who know Him the best. The stakes are highest for those that have been drawn closest to God.

This should be pretty clear. IF you obey, THEN God will keep you from any harm and lift you above nations and you will be the head and not the tail. He WILL do it. I don't see anything vague about this. It might not manifest the way you think, but He WILL do it.

But here comes the scary part:

Curses for Disobedience

15 *However, if* you *do not* obey the LORD your God and *do not carefully* follow *all* his commands and decrees I am giving you today, *all* these curses *will* come upon you and overtake you:

These are described as natural consequences on natural Israel, but they have spiritual ramifications as well. On spiritual Israel (the Church), they are primarily spiritual consequences, but have natural ramifications as well.. Let's take a little more detailed look.

16 You *will* be cursed in the *city* and cursed in the *country*.

17 Your *basket* and your kneading *trough will* be cursed.

Your congregations will be cursed whether in the city or in the country. Your spiritual bread will be scarce. You will have nothing but day-old stale manna. Jesus, the Bread of Life, will be distant.

18 The *fruit* of your *womb will* be cursed, and the *crops* of your land, and the *calves* of your herds and the *lambs* of your flocks.

Your offspring will be even more distant from God than you are. The young of your flocks will be cursed. Are we not seeing a massive loss of the young people from the church? Are we not seeing massive movement away from God in our youth groups and among our children? Are they not being won over by culture?

*19 You **will** be cursed when you **come in** and cursed when you **go out**.*

You will be cursed when you go in and when you go out. No matter where you go, home missions or foreign missions, inside the walls or outside the walls, your efforts will have very little spiritual results.

*20 The LORD will send on you **curses, confusion** and **rebuke** in everything you put your hand to, **until you are destroyed** and come to **sudden ruin** because of the evil you have done in **forsaking him**.*

The Lord will put on you curses, confusion and rebuke in everything until you are destroyed. Can you find any denomination that isn't filled with confusion and rebuke? Any that hasn't found itself arguing about secondary issues and become factious? Are we not filled with constant confusion about this or that new doctrine or teaching?

*21 The LORD **will plague** you with **diseases** until he has **destroyed** you from the land you are entering to possess. 22 The LORD **will** strike you with **wasting disease**, with **fever** and **inflammation**, with scorching **heat** and **drought**, with **blight** and **mildew**, which will **plague** you **until you perish**.*

Are our churches not full of people plagued with spiritual diseases that don't seem to have a cure? Are they not inflamed by their passions and addictions and the fevers of their lusts? Do we not have 50% of pastors using pornography? (According to Barna.) Do we not have clergy sexually abusing little kids? Do we not have more divorce in the church than in the general population? Are we not starving to death for the real meat of the Word? Are we not dying of thirst for the Living Water? Are our people not bloated with the world and starving for God? We are losing $16 BILLION a year to fraud inside our own church organizations. We are losing untold billions to waste and abuse. Millions of Christians are dying everyday because of our neglect.

*23 The **sky** over your head **will** be **bronze**, the **ground** beneath you **iron**.*

Your prayers will not be answered, they will bounce. The ground that you toil will be hard and barren.

*24 The LORD **will** turn the rain of your country into **dust** and **powder**; it will come down from the skies **until** you are **destroyed**.*

The Lord says that He will send the early and latter rains, but not until you repent. Instead you will get dust and powder that will make your work even harder and choke whatever you do get to grow.

*25 The LORD **will** cause you to be **defeated** before your enemies. **You** will come at them from one direction but flee from them in **seven**, and **you** will become a thing of horror to **all** the kingdoms on earth.*

Are we not already a thing of horror? Are we not a laughingstock to the world? Why would anyone want to join this mess? So they can give up 10% of their income for a concert and motivational speech once a week? We bring in $250 BILLION a year and spend 95% of it on our own comforts. Our spiritual enemies are trouncing us. We have rampant addiction and lust and fear and anger and hatred inside our own walls and no sign on the horizon that we have any plan to deal with them effectively. Our enemies chase us and we flee. We have no victory.

*26 **Your carcasses** will be food for all the **birds** of the air and the **beasts** of the earth, and there will be no one to frighten them away.*

This is a reference to demons and the spiritual powers of darkness that will eat us like carrion. I have seen this (in the spirit) at a local congregation. A giant room full of dead bodies being devoured by dark demonic birds and beasts. And there is no one to drive them away. We have very, VERY few deliverance ministries – and even fewer that have any real authority and effectiveness. And I'm aware of even fewer that are capable of city-wide or regional spiritual warfare against strongholds.

*27 The LORD **will** afflict you with the **boils** of Egypt and with **tumors**, **festering sores** and the **itch**, from which you **cannot be cured**.*

When they were in the wilderness, under the protection of God, the children of Israel did not get sick. In the book of Acts, the apostles healed any that were sick. The only medical advice given for Christians in the New Testament is to call the elders and the prayer of faith WILL heal them. But our churches are FULL of people with every imaginable condition and syndrome and disease and our prayers seem to have little effect. Many incurable diseases are rampant in the churches. Why isn't God listening? If we're being obedient, why do we have sick people?

*28 The LORD **will** afflict you with **madness, blindness** and **confusion of mind**.*

Are we not the most confused, dysfunctional, schizophrenic religion on the planet? (With the possible exception of the Jews.) Are our pews not full of people with spiritual dyslexia and mixture of all sorts? Are we not full of people with depression, anxiety, panic attacks, Alzheimers, Parkinsons, and all sorts of dementia? How is that possible if we're being obedient to God?

*29 At midday you will grope about like a **blind** man in the dark. You will be **unsuccessful** in **everything** you do; day after day you will be **oppressed** and **robbed**, with **no one** to rescue you.*

Are we not groping around in the dark for any possible new program or curriculum or system that will save our ailing churches? If it's not Purpose Driven, it's Mars/Venus, or Shepherding, or Toronto, or Brownsville, or Word of Faith, or any of thousands of fads and fashions that kept us occupied for a moment and hopeful that we'd finally found the way to revival. Even though the lights are on at full brightness, we can't see the obvious in front of our faces – that REPENTANCE is the ONLY Biblical prescription that works for this disease. Statistically, we are unsuccessful in everything that we do. We are a giant money loser and are daily oppressed and robbed to the tune of $16 BILLION a year – at LEAST. And no one seems to be coming to rescue us.

*30 You **will** be **pledged** to be married to a woman, but **another** will take her and **ravish** her. You **will** build a house, but you **will not** live in it. You **will** plant a vineyard, but you **will not** even begin to enjoy its fruit. 31 Your ox **will** be slaughtered before your eyes, but **you will** eat none of it. Your donkey **will** be forcibly taken from you and **will not** be returned. Your sheep **will** be given to your enemies, and **no one will** rescue them.*

Despite what you think you were promised, you will not get it. Though you worked for years to build something, you will not really live in it. You will not enjoy the fruits of your labors because they were in vain. Your enemies own your houses and your livestock. The powers of darkness are currently fully entrenched in the churches in America and show no sign of doing anything other than getting stronger. All that you have worked for is being spent on air.

*32 Your **sons** and **daughters will** be given to another **nation**, and you **will wear out your eyes** watching for them day after day, **powerless** to lift a hand.*

The church is not raising up spiritual warriors, it's raising up youth that are mostly coming because of the pizza parties and ski trips and movie nights. They don't hear the voice of God and we don't know how to teach them how to – or don't believe it's possible. But they're fascinated with the supernatural stories told by their Wicca and New Age friends. They hunger for the power and truth of God, but can't find it, because it got buried under "Religion". We have rampant sexually transmitted diseases in the church youth. We are losing a whole generation. Their parents were more distant from God than their Grandparents – and these kids are even farther away. The culture and the media and the music and the public schools (and satan) are devouring them.

*33 A people that you do not know **will** eat what your **land** and **labor produce**, and you **will** have **nothing** but **cruel oppression all** your days. 34 The sights you see **will** drive you **mad**.*

The institutions that we have built are being gobbled up by do-gooders and social scientists and pop-psychologists. The culture is crushing in on us and the "church" is not defending anyone in any real measure. My kids can watch practically nothing on television and all that is on the news is depressing and violent and scary. We have tsunamis and earthquakes and hurricanes and wars and terrorists and we have no peace. How can that be if we're being obedient to God? Aren't we supposed to be the head? How come we feel like the tail so much?

*35 The LORD **will** afflict your **knees** and **legs** with painful **boils** that cannot be cured, **spreading** from the **soles** of your **feet** to the **top** of your **head**.*

Your walk will be severely affected. At first it will just be your feet, but the more your spiritual walk is affected, the more it spreads until it even takes over your head. Then you will be covered in painful boils and sores that will not heal. Spiritually, most "Christians" I meet seem to be covered in spiritual boils and nobody seems to notice or care.

*36 The LORD **will drive you** and the king you set over you to a nation unknown to you or your fathers. There you **will** worship **other gods**, gods of wood and stone. 37 You **will** become a thing of **horror** and an object of **scorn** and **ridicule** to **all** the nations where the LORD **will** drive you.*

How many nations have we been driven out of? Are we not now captive in a nation we don't recognize any longer? Is America not bowing down to gods unknown to our fathers and their fathers? Would the founders even recognize it? Are we not worshipping our structures and buildings and cathedrals of wood and stone? Are we not a thing of horror and scorn and ridicule? Maybe not all the way, but sure a whole lot more than we used to be and it's getting worse every day. And were we really supposed to set a king over us? Isn't Christ the King?

*38 You **will sow much seed** in the field but you **will harvest little**, because **locusts will devour** it. 39 You **will** plant vineyards and cultivate them but you **will not** drink the wine or gather the grapes, because **worms will eat them**. 40 You **will** have olive trees throughout your country but you **will not** use the oil, because the olives **will drop off**. 41 You **will** have **sons** and **daughters** but you **will not keep them**, because they **will go into captivity**. 42 Swarms of locusts **will take over all** your trees and the crops of your land.*

We spent tens of Billions of dollars on plans to evangelize the whole world by the year 2000 and didn't even keep up with population growth. The average baptism in the United States costs $1,550,000. We are building and planting and growing – and demons are taking it all over. We our losing our country and our institutions more and more every day. Can this be victory?

*43 The alien who lives among you **will rise above you** higher and higher, but **you will sink lower** and lower. 44 **He will lend to you**, but **you will not lend to him**. **He will be the head**, but **you will be the tail**.*

Every foreign religion, every Eastern guru, every New Age weirdness, every alternative lifestyle is now embraced and mainstreamed. America is converting to Islam and Wicca and a thousand other lies faster and faster every day.

> 45 **All** these curses **will** come upon you. They **will pursue** you and **overtake** you **until** you are destroyed, because you **did not obey** the LORD your God and **observe** the **commands** and **decrees** he gave you. 46 **They will be a sign and a wonder to you and your descendants forever.** 47 **Because you did not serve the LORD your God joyfully and gladly in the time of prosperity,** 48 **therefore in hunger and thirst, in nakedness and dire poverty, you will serve the enemies the LORD sends against you. He will put an iron yoke on your neck until he has destroyed you.**

Please understand, this is fatal. Unless you do the ONLY thing that will stop it, the guaranteed result of this course is complete destruction. There is NO OTHER way out. Repentance is the only way to fix this.

> 49 The LORD **will** bring a nation **against you** from far away, from the ends of the earth, like an eagle swooping down, a nation whose language you will not understand, 50 a fierce-looking nation without respect for the old or pity for the young. 51 They **will** devour the young of your livestock and the crops of your land until you are destroyed. They **will** leave you **no grain, new wine or oil,** nor any calves of your herds or lambs of your flocks **until** you are **ruined.** 52 They **will** lay siege to **all** the cities throughout your land **until** the **high fortified walls** in which you trust **fall down.** They **will** besiege **all** the **cities** throughout the land the LORD your God is giving you.

I believe that at least one of the interpretations and applications to these verses is that demons will take over and swarm down upon us. And they have. The "churches" are riddled with them. They are devouring everything and leaving none of the three aspects of God behind – the bread, the wine and the oil. They have laid siege to every city. There were no city churches – no place in America where the Body of Christ in one town was united and under His headship. The high fortified walls of the "church" in which we have trusted are all caving in. We are besieged on every side by culture and media and witchcraft and all the other forces of darkness aligned against us.

> 53 Because of the **suffering** that your enemy **will** inflict on you during the siege, you **will** eat the **fruit** of the **womb,** the **flesh** of the **sons** and

daughters the LORD your God has given you. 54 Even the most gentle and sensitive man among you **will** have no compassion on his own brother or the wife he loves or his surviving children, 55 and he **will** not give to one of them any of the flesh of his children that he is eating. It **will** be all he has left because of the **suffering** your enemy **will** inflict on you during the siege of **all** your **cities**. 56 The most gentle and sensitive woman among you—so sensitive and gentle that she would not venture to touch the ground with the sole of her foot—**will** begrudge the husband she loves and her own son or daughter 57 the **afterbirth** from her **womb** and the **children** she **bears**. For she intends to **eat them secretly** during the siege and in the distress that your enemy **will** inflict on you in your cities.

Are we not devouring our own children? Are we not raising up spiritual children, plugging them into service jobs in the "churches" until they are used up and then spitting them out? Are we not forceably milking them for a tithe until they go bankrupt? Have you ever seen a pastor tear into another pastor for "stealing sheep"? I have. Why? Because they NEED those sheep to keep this whole thing going. It's too hard to go find another one. Even people that say they are "men of God" will devour each other and split churches and feud and fight and hate rather than give up the child of their womb that they intend to eat during the siege. If we were growing exponentially and nothing could stand against us and people were not falling away in droves and having their lives destroyed by demonic forces, we wouldn't so jealously guard and control each little sheep. Can't you see? Please see.

58 If you do not **carefully follow all** the words of this law, which are written in this book, and **do not revere** this glorious and awesome name—the LORD your God- 59 the LORD **will** send **fearful plagues** on you and your **descendants, harsh** and **prolonged disasters**, and **severe** and **lingering illnesses**. 60 He **will** bring upon you **all** the diseases of Egypt that you dreaded, and they **will** cling to you. 61 The LORD **will** also bring on you **every kind of sickness and disaster not** recorded in this Book of the Law, **until** you are **destroyed**. 62 You who were as numerous as the stars in the sky **will** be left but **few** in number, because you **did not obey the LORD your God**. 63 **Just as it pleased the LORD to make you prosper and increase in number, so it will please him to ruin and destroy you.** You **will** be **uprooted** from the land you are entering to possess.

Again, the Lord repeats the whole thing. We must CAREFULLY FOLLOW ALL His words and instructions. Yes, we are New Covenant believers. That doesn't mean we don't follow the Ten Commandments, that means we have the Holy Spirit in us to talk to us and guide us and to write His words on our hearts. But if we shun His voice, then we are left to lean on our own understanding – and we're fodder for the Red Dragons.

Can He be any more clear? Can He be any more definitive? This WILL happen to you and God WILL do it. And God has already done it to us! We have plagues and disasters and severe and lingering illnesses in the natural and in the spiritual. We are no different than the Egypt we were told to leave. He's even inventing new diseases and oppressions that aren't mentioned in the Book. He says that He will creatively come up with all kinds of NEW tortures if you don't obey! Like flesh-eating viruses and HIV/AIDS and new strains of smallpox and new kinds of demonic oppressions like anorexia and trans-sexualism and who knows what. If you hear Him really well, ask Him! If we don't repent, when He is done with us there will surely be only a few in number. If He doesn't cut the days short, there will be no one left!

And just as it pleased Him to prosper America and the Church, it will please Him to crush it. But He would sure rather that we repent and start obeying. He WILL turn, if WE turn. That's a guarantee, too.

> 64 Then the LORD **will** scatter you among **all** nations, from one end of the earth to the other. There you **will** worship other gods—gods of wood and stone, which neither you nor your fathers have known. 65 Among those nations you **will** find **no repose, no resting place** for the sole of your foot. There the LORD **will** give you an **anxious mind, eyes weary with longing**, and a **despairing heart**. 66 You **will** live in **constant suspense**, filled with **dread** both night and day, **never** sure of your life. 67 In the morning you **will** say, "If only it were evening!" and in the evening, "If only it were morning!"-because of the **terror** that **will fill your hearts** and the **sights that your eyes will see**. 68 The LORD **will** send you back in ships to **Egypt** on a journey I said you should never make again. There you **will** offer yourselves for sale to your enemies as male and female slaves, **but no one will buy you**.

Are we not constantly in search of whatever new program or curriculum will turn this around? Are our eyes not weary of longing and despairing for something that will reach the people in spirit and in truth? How can we be this lukewarm and asleep and nothing seems to shake it off of us? Because it's a curse from God.

The only growth in the "church" in America is the mega-churches. And it's not new growth, it's transfer growth from little churches that are being killed by the large monoliths that are just warehousing people – but they have really great music and childcare! Everyone is looking for greener pastures. If only it were evening. If only it were morning. But nothing satisfies. Why?

Because we're under a curse from God.

If it were from satan, we could cover it in the Blood and bind it up and cast it down. But no amount of praying against the forces of darkness has made a difference in the state of the Church. Because they have legal ground. Because we aren't diligently and carefully following God and He has put these things upon us until we are totally consumed and destroyed – or we repent, whichever comes first.

In the end, if we don't turn, we will offer ourselves to Egypt, to the One World Government and One World Church, but they won't even buy us. They will take us for slaves and give us nothing in return.

And that is the Word of the Lord.

Red Dragon-related VERSES

Repent, Curse, Slumber, Sleep, Stupor, Blind, Hardened, Destroyed, Lying Spirit

REPENT

1Ki 8:47 [Yet] if they shall bethink themselves in the land whither they were carried captives, and **repent**, and make supplication unto thee in the land of them that carried them captives, saying, We have sinned, and have done perversely, we have committed wickedness;

Jer 18:8 If that nation, against whom I have pronounced, turn from their evil, I will repent of the evil that I thought to do unto them.

Jer 18:10 If it do evil in my sight, that it obey not my voice, then I will repent of the good, wherewith I said I would benefit them.

Jer 26:3 If so be they will hearken, and turn every man from his evil way, that I may **repent** me of the evil, which I purpose to do unto them because of the evil of their doings.

Jer 26:13 Therefore now **amend** your ways and your doings, and **obey** the voice of the LORD your God; and the LORD will **repent** him of the evil that he hath pronounced against you.

Eze 14:6 Therefore say unto the house of Israel, Thus saith the Lord GOD; **Repent**, and turn [yourselves] from your idols; and turn away your faces from all your abominations.

Eze 18:30 Therefore I will judge you, O house of Israel, every one according to his ways, saith the Lord GOD. Repent, and turn [yourselves] from all your transgressions; so iniquity shall not be your ruin.

Eze 24:14 I the LORD have spoken [it]: it shall come to pass, and I will do [it]; I will not go back, neither will I spare, neither will I **repent**; according to thy ways, and according to thy doings, shall they judge thee, saith the Lord GOD.

Jon 3:9 Who can tell [if] God will turn and **repent**, and turn away from his fierce anger, that we perish not?

Mat 3:2 And saying, Repent ye: for the kingdom of heaven is at hand.

Mat 4:17 From that time Jesus began to preach, and to say, Repent: for the kingdom of heaven is at hand.

Mar 1:15 And saying, The time is fulfilled, and the kingdom of God is at hand: repent ye, and believe the gospel.

Mar 6:12 And they went out, and preached that men should repent.

Luk 13:3 I tell you, Nay: but, except ye repent, ye shall all likewise perish.

Luk 17:3 Take heed to yourselves: If thy brother trespass against thee, rebuke him; and if he **repent**, forgive him. Luk 17:4 And if he trespass against thee seven times in a day, and seven times in a day turn again to thee, saying, I **repent**; thou shalt forgive him.

Act 2:38 Then Peter said unto them, **Repent**, and be baptized every one of you in the name of Jesus Christ for the remission of sins, and ye shall receive the gift of the Holy Ghost.

Act 3:19 **Repent** ye therefore, and be converted, that your sins may be blotted out, when the times of refreshing shall come from the presence of the Lord;

Act 8:22 **Repent** therefore of this thy wickedness, and pray God, if perhaps the thought of thine heart may be forgiven thee.

Act 17:30 And the times of this ignorance God winked at; but now commandeth all men every where to repent:

Act 26:20 But shewed first unto them of Damascus, and at Jerusalem, and throughout all the coasts of Judaea, and [then] to the Gentiles, that they should **repent and turn to God**, and do works meet for repentance.

Rev 2:5 Remember therefore from whence thou art fallen, and **repent**, and do the first works; or else I **will** come unto thee quickly, and **will** remove thy candlestick out of his place, except thou **repent**. *(Church of Ephesus)*

Rev 2:16 **Repent**; or else I **will** come unto thee quickly, and **will** fight against them with the sword of my mouth. *(Church of Pergamum)*

Rev 2:21 And I gave her space to **repent** of her fornication; and she repented not.
Rev 2:22 Behold, I **will** cast her into a bed, and them that commit adultery with her into **great tribulation**, except they **repent** of their deeds. *(Church of Thyatira)*

Rev 3:3 Remember therefore how thou hast received and heard, and hold fast, and **repent**. If therefore thou shalt not watch, I **will** come on thee as a thief, and thou shalt not know what hour I **will** come upon thee. *(Church of Sardis)*

Rev 3:19 As many as I love, I rebuke and chasten: be zealous therefore, and **repent**. *(Church of Laodecia)*

CURSE

Gen 12:3 And I will bless them that bless thee, and **curse** him that curseth thee: and in thee shall all families of the earth be blessed.

Deu 11:26 Behold, I set before you this day a blessing and a curse;
Deu 11:27 The blessing if you obey the commands of the Lord your God that I am giving you today;
Deu 11:28 And a curse, if ye will not obey the commandments of the LORD your God, but turn aside out of the way which I command you this day, to go after other gods, which ye have not known.

Deuteronomy 28 – covered previously in this writing

Deu 30:1 And it shall come to pass, when all these things are come upon thee, the blessing and the **curse**, which I have set before thee, and thou shalt call [them] to mind among all the nations, whither the LORD thy God hath driven thee,

2Ki 22:19 Because thine heart was tender, and thou hast humbled thyself before the LORD, when thou heardest what I spake against this place, and against the inhabitants thereof, that they should become a desolation and a **curse**, and hast rent thy clothes, and wept before me; I also have heard [thee], saith the LORD.

Neh 10:29 They clave to their brethren, their nobles, and entered into a curse, and into an oath, to walk in God's law, which was given by Moses the servant of God, and to observe and do all the commandments of the LORD our Lord, and his judgments and his statutes;

Pro 24:24 He that saith unto the wicked, Thou [art] righteous; him shall the people curse, nations shall abhor him:

Pro 28:27 He that giveth unto the poor shall not lack: but he that hideth his eyes shall have many a curse.

Pro 30:10 Accuse not a servant unto his master, lest he curse thee, and thou be found guilty.

Isa 24:6 Therefore hath the curse devoured the earth, and they that dwell therein are desolate: therefore the inhabitants of the earth are burned, and few men left.

Isa 43:28 Therefore I have profaned the princes of the sanctuary, and have given Jacob to the curse, and Israel to reproaches.

Isa 65:15 And ye shall leave your name for a curse unto my chosen: for the Lord GOD shall slay thee, and call his servants by another name:

Jer 24:9 And I will deliver them to be removed into all the kingdoms of the earth for [their] hurt, [to be] a reproach and a proverb, a taunt and a curse, in all places whither I shall drive them.

Jer 25:18 [To wit], Jerusalem, and the cities of Judah, and the kings thereof, and the princes thereof, to make them a desolation, an astonishment, an hissing, and a curse; as [it is] this day;

Jer 26:6 Then will I make this house like Shiloh, and will make this city a curse to all the nations of the earth.

Jer 29:18 And I will persecute them with the sword, with the famine, and with the pestilence, and will deliver them to be removed to all the kingdoms of the earth, to be a curse, and an astonishment, and an hissing, and a reproach, among all the nations whither I have driven them:

Jer 42:18 For thus saith the LORD of hosts, the God of Israel; As mine anger and my fury hath been poured forth upon the inhabitants of Jerusalem; so shall my fury be poured forth upon you, when ye shall enter into Egypt: and ye shall be an execration, and an astonishment, and a curse, and a reproach; and ye shall see this place no more.

Jer 44:8 In that ye provoke me unto wrath with the works of your hands, burning incense unto other gods in the land of Egypt, whither ye be gone to dwell, that ye might cut yourselves off, and that ye might be a curse and a reproach among all the nations of the earth?

Jer 44:12 And I will take the remnant of Judah, that have set their faces to go into the land of Egypt to sojourn there, and they shall all be consumed, [and] fall in the land of Egypt; they shall [even] be consumed by the sword [and] by the famine: they shall die, from the least even unto the greatest, by the sword and by the famine: and they shall be an execration, [and] an astonishment, and a curse, and a reproach.

Jer 44:22 So that the LORD could no longer bear, because of the evil of your doings, [and] because of the abominations which ye have committed; therefore is your land a desolation, and an astonishment, and a curse, without an inhabitant, as at this day.

Dan 9:11 Yea, all Israel have transgressed thy law, even by departing, that they might not obey thy voice; therefore the curse is poured upon us, and the oath that [is] written in the law of Moses the servant of God, because we have sinned against him.

Zec 8:13 And it shall come to pass, [that] as ye were a curse among the heathen, O house of Judah, and house of Israel; so will I save you, and ye shall be a blessing: fear not, [but] let your hands be strong.

Mal 2:2 If ye will not hear, and if ye will not lay [it] to heart, to give glory unto my name, saith the LORD of hosts, I will even send a curse upon you, and I will curse your blessings: yea, I have cursed them already, because ye do not lay [it] to heart.

Mal 3:9 Ye [are] cursed with a curse: for ye have robbed me, [even] this whole nation.

Mal 4:6 And he shall turn the heart of the fathers to the children, and the heart of the children to their fathers, lest I come and smite the earth with a curse.

Gal 3:10 For as many as are of the works of the law are under the curse: for it is written, Cursed [is] every one that continueth not in all things which are written in the book of the law to do them.

Gal 3:13 Christ hath redeemed us from the curse of the law, being made a curse for us: for it is written, Cursed [is] every one that hangeth on a tree:

(Yeah, but... If you make up your own law and get back under it, you invoke it on yourself again and deny the work of Christ.)

Rev 22:3 And there shall be no more **curse**: but the throne of God and of the Lamb shall be in it; and his servants shall serve him:

SLUMBER, SLEEP, STUPOR

Isa 56:10 His watchmen [are] blind: they are all ignorant, they [are] all dumb dogs, they cannot bark; sleeping, lying down, loving to **slumber**.

Rom 11:8 (According as it is written, **God hath given them** the **spirit** of **slumber (stupor, NIV)**, eyes that they should not see, and ears that they should not hear;) unto this day.

Gen 2:21 And the LORD God caused a deep **sleep** to fall upon Adam, and he slept: and he took one of his ribs, and closed up the flesh instead thereof;

1Sa 26:12 So David took the spear and the cruse of water from Saul's bolster; and they gat them away, and no man saw [it], nor knew [it], neither awaked: for they [were] all asleep; because **a deep sleep from the LORD** was fallen upon them.

Psa 76:6 At thy rebuke, O God of Jacob, both the chariot and horse are cast into a dead **sleep**.

Psa 127:2 [It is] vain for you to rise up early, to sit up late, to eat the bread of sorrows: [for] so **he** giveth his beloved **sleep**.

Isa 5:27 None shall be weary nor stumble among them; none shall slumber nor **sleep**; neither shall the girdle of their loins be loosed, nor the latchet of their shoes be broken:

Isa 29:10 For the **LORD hath poured out upon** you the **spirit** of **deep sleep**, and hath closed your eyes: the prophets and your rulers, the seers hath he covered.

Jer 51:39 In their heat I will make their feasts, and **I will make them drunken**, that they may rejoice, and **sleep** a **perpetual sleep**, and not wake, saith the LORD.

Jer 51:57 And **I will make** drunk her princes, and her wise [men], her captains, and her rulers, and her mighty men: and they shall **sleep** a **perpetual sleep**, and not wake, saith the King, whose name [is] the LORD of hosts.

Jhn 11:11 These things said he: and after that he saith unto them, Our friend Lazarus sleepeth; but I go, that **I may awake** him out of **sleep**.

Rom 13:11 And that, knowing the time, that now [it is] high time to **awake** out of **sleep**: for now [is] our salvation nearer than when we believed.

1Cr 11:28 But let a man examine himself, and so let him eat of [that] bread, and drink of [that] cup.
1Cr 11:29 For he that eateth and drinketh unworthily, eateth and drinketh damnation to himself, not discerning the Lord's body.
1Cr 11:30 For this cause many [are] weak and sickly among you, and many sleep.

(If I'm right about the Red Dragon and divison and faction – then we ARE holding something against our Brothers and need to repent and if we don't, then we're taking communion unworthily and people in our congregations will get sick and die. Which they are. Hmmm.)

1Th 5:6 Therefore let us not **sleep**, as [do] others; but let us watch and be sober.

BLIND

Exd 4:11 And the LORD said unto him, Who hath made man's mouth? or who maketh the dumb, or deaf, or the seeing, or the blind? have not I the LORD?

Deu 16:19 Thou shalt not wrest judgment; thou shalt not respect persons, neither take a gift: for a gift doth **blind** the eyes of the wise, and pervert the words of the righteous.

Deu 27:18 Cursed [be] he that maketh the **blind** to wander out of the way. And all the people shall say, Amen.

Deu 28:29 And thou shalt grope at noonday, as the **blind** gropeth in darkness, and thou shalt not prosper in thy ways: and thou shalt be only oppressed and spoiled evermore, and no man shall save [thee].

Psa 146:8 The **LORD openeth [the eyes of] the blind**: the LORD raiseth them that are bowed down: the LORD loveth the righteous:

Isa 29:18 And in that day shall the **deaf** hear the words of the book, and the eyes of the **blind** shall see out of obscurity, and out of darkness. **(GO READ THIS CHAPTER!!)**

Isa 35:5 Then the eyes of the **blind** shall be opened, and the ears of the deaf shall be unstopped. **(GO READ THIS CHAPTER!)**

Isa 42:7 To open the **blind** eyes, to bring out the prisoners from the prison, [and] them that sit in darkness out of the prison house.

Isa 42:16 And **I will** bring the **blind** by a way [that] they knew not; I will lead them in paths [that] they have not known: I will make darkness light before them, and crooked things straight. These things will I do unto them, and not forsake them.

Isa 42:18 Hear, ye **deaf**; and look, ye **blind**, that ye may see.

Isa 56:10 His watchmen [are] **blind**: they are all ignorant, they [are] all dumb dogs, they cannot bark; sleeping, lying down, loving to slumber.

Lam 4:14 They have wandered [as] **blind** [men] in the streets, they have polluted themselves with blood, so that men could not touch their garments. **(GO READ THIS IN CONTEXT!!)**

Zep 1:17 And I will bring distress upon men, that they shall walk like blind men, because they have sinned against the LORD: and their blood shall be poured out as dust, and their flesh as the dung.

HARDENED

(Either you did it to yourself or God does it to you. There is NO indication that Satan can do it to.)

Exd 7:13 And he hardened Pharaoh's heart, that he hearkened not unto them; as the LORD had said.

Exd 7:14 And the LORD said unto Moses, Pharaoh's heart [is] hardened, he refuseth to let the people go.

Exd 7:22 And the magicians of Egypt did so with their enchantments: and Pharaoh's heart was hardened, neither did he hearken unto them; as the LORD had said.

Exd 8:15 But when Pharaoh saw that there was respite, he hardened his heart, and hearkened not unto them; as the LORD had said.

Exd 8:19 Then the magicians said unto Pharaoh, This [is] the finger of God: and Pharaoh's heart was hardened, and he hearkened not unto them; as the LORD had said.

Exd 8:32 And Pharaoh hardened his heart at this time also, neither would he let the people go.

Exd 9:7 And Pharaoh sent, and, behold, there was not one of the cattle of the Israelites dead. And the heart of Pharaoh was hardened, and he did not let the people go.

Exd 9:12 And the LORD hardened the heart of Pharaoh, and he hearkened not unto them; as the LORD had spoken unto Moses.

Exd 9:34 And when Pharaoh saw that the rain and the hail and the thunders were ceased, he sinned yet more, and hardened his heart, he and his servants.

Exd 9:35 And the heart of Pharaoh was hardened, neither would he let the children of Israel go; as the LORD had spoken by Moses.

Exd 10:1 And the LORD said unto Moses, Go in unto Pharaoh: for I have hardened his heart, and the heart of his servants, that I might shew these my signs before him:

Exd 10:20 But the LORD hardened Pharaoh's heart, so that he would not let the children of Israel go.

Exd 10:27 But the LORD hardened Pharaoh's heart, and he would not let them go.

Exd 11:10 And Moses and Aaron did all these wonders before Pharaoh: and the LORD hardened Pharaoh's heart, so that he would not let the children of Israel go out of his land.

Exd 14:8 And the LORD hardened the heart of Pharaoh king of Egypt, and he pursued after the children of Israel: and the children of Israel went out with an high hand.

Deu 2:30 But Sihon king of Heshbon would not let us pass by him: for the LORD thy God hardened his spirit, and made his heart obstinate, that he might deliver him into thy hand, as [appeareth] this day.

1Sa 6:6 Wherefore then do ye harden your hearts, as the Egyptians and Pharaoh hardened their hearts? when he had wrought wonderfully among them, did they not let the people go, and they departed?

2Ki 17:14 Notwithstanding they would not hear, but hardened their necks, like to the neck of their fathers, that did not believe in the LORD their God.

2Ch 36:13 And he also rebelled against king Nebuchadnezzar, who had made him swear by God: but he stiffened his neck, and hardened his heart from turning unto the LORD God of Israel.

Neh 9:16 But they and our fathers dealt proudly, and hardened their necks, and hearkened not to thy commandments,

Neh 9:17 And refused to obey, neither were mindful of thy wonders that thou didst among them; but hardened their necks, and in their rebellion appointed a captain to return to their bondage: but thou [art] a God ready to pardon, gracious and merciful, slow to anger, and of great kindness, and forsookest them not.

Neh 9:29 And testifiedst against them, that thou mightest bring them again unto thy law: yet they dealt proudly, and hearkened not unto thy commandments, but sinned against thy judgments, (which if a man do, he shall live in them;) and withdrew the shoulder, and hardened their neck, and would not hear.

Job 9:4 [He is] wise in heart, and mighty in strength: who hath hardened [himself] against him, and hath prospered?

Isa 63:17 O LORD, why hast thou made us to err from thy ways, [and] hardened our heart from thy fear? Return for thy servants' sake, the tribes of thine inheritance.

Jer 7:26 Yet they hearkened not unto me, nor inclined their ear, but hardened their neck: they did worse than their fathers.

Jer 19:15 Thus saith the LORD of hosts, the God of Israel; Behold, I will bring upon this city and upon all her towns all the evil that I have pronounced against it, because they have hardened their necks, that they might not hear my words.

Dan 5:20 But when his heart was lifted up, and his mind hardened in pride, he was deposed from his kingly throne, and they took his glory from him:

Mar 6:52 For they considered not [the miracle] of the loaves: for their heart was hardened.

Mar 8:17 And when Jesus knew [it], he saith unto them, Why reason ye, because ye have no bread? perceive ye not yet, neither understand? have ye your heart yet hardened?

Jhn 12:40 He hath blinded their eyes, and hardened their heart; that they should not see with [their] eyes, nor understand with [their] heart, and be converted, and I should heal them.

Act 19:9 But when divers were hardened, and believed not, but spake evil of that way before the multitude, he departed from them, and separated the disciples, disputing daily in the school of one Tyrannus.

Hbr 3:13 But exhort one another daily, while it is called Today; lest any of you be hardened through the deceitfulness of sin.

DESTROYED

Exd 22:20 He that sacrificeth unto [any] god, save unto the LORD only, he shall be utterly destroyed.

Deu 2:21 A people great, and many, and tall, as the Anakims; but the LORD **destroyed** them before them; and they succeeded them, and dwelt in their stead:

Deu 4:26 I call heaven and earth to witness against you this day, that ye shall soon utterly perish from off the land whereunto ye go over Jordan to possess it; ye shall not prolong [your] days upon it, but shall utterly be **destroyed**.

Deu 7:24 And he shall deliver their kings into thine hand, and thou shalt destroy their name from under heaven: there shall no man be able to stand before thee, until thou have **destroyed** them.

Deu 9:8 Also in Horeb ye provoked the LORD to wrath, so that the LORD was angry with you to have **destroyed** you.

Deu 9:20 And the LORD was very angry with Aaron to have **destroyed** him: and I prayed for Aaron also the same time.

Deu 12:30 Take heed to thyself that thou be not snared by following them, after that they be destroyed from before thee; and that thou enquire not after their gods, saying, How did these nations serve their gods? even so will I do likewise.

Deu 28:20 The LORD shall send upon thee cursing, vexation, and rebuke, in all that thou settest thine hand unto for to do, until thou be destroyed, and until thou perish quickly; because of the wickedness of thy doings, whereby thou hast forsaken me.

Deu 28:24 The LORD shall make the rain of thy land powder and dust: from heaven shall it come down upon thee, until thou be destroyed.

Deu 28:45 Moreover all these curses shall come upon thee, and shall pursue thee, and overtake thee, till thou be destroyed; because thou hearkenedst not unto the voice of the LORD thy God, to keep his commandments and his statutes which he commanded thee:

Deu 28:48 Therefore shalt thou serve thine enemies which the LORD shall send against thee, in hunger, and in thirst, and in nakedness, and in want of all [things]: and he shall put a yoke of iron upon thy neck, until he have destroyed thee.

Deu 28:51 And he shall eat the fruit of thy cattle, and the fruit of thy land, until thou be destroyed: which [also] shall not leave thee [either] corn, wine, or oil, [or] the increase of thy kine, or flocks of thy sheep, until he have destroyed thee.

Deu 28:61 Also every sickness, and every plague, which [is] not written in the book of this law, them will the LORD bring upon thee, until thou be destroyed.

Jos 23:15 Therefore it shall come to pass, [that] as all good things are come upon you, which the LORD your God promised you; so shall the LORD bring upon you all evil things, until he have destroyed you from off this good land which the LORD your God hath given you.

2Sa 24:16 And when the angel stretched out his hand upon Jerusalem to destroy it, the LORD repented him of the evil, and said to the angel that destroyed the people, It is enough: stay now thine hand. And the angel of the LORD was by the threshingplace of Araunah the Jebusite.

1Ch 5:25 And they transgressed against the God of their fathers, and went a whoring after the gods of the people of the land, whom God destroyed before them.

1Ch 21:15 And God sent an angel unto Jerusalem to destroy it: and as he was destroying, the LORD beheld, and he repented him of the evil, and said to the angel that destroyed, It is enough, stay now thine hand. And the angel of the LORD stood by the threshing floor of Ornan the Jebusite.

Ezr 4:15 That search may be made in the book of the records of thy fathers: so shalt thou find in the book of the records, and know that this city [is] a rebellious city, and hurtful unto kings and provinces, and that they have moved sedition within the same of old time: for which cause was this city destroyed.

Psa 11:3 If the foundations be destroyed, what can the righteous do?

Psa 37:38 But the transgressors shall be destroyed together: the end of the wicked shall be cut off.

Psa 73:27 For, lo, they that are far from thee shall perish: thou hast destroyed all them that go a whoring from thee.

Psa 78:38 But he, [being] full of compassion, forgave [their] iniquity, and destroyed [them] not: yea, many a time turned he his anger away, and did not stir up all his wrath.

Psa 78:45 He sent divers sorts of flies among them, which devoured them; and frogs, which destroyed them.

Psa 92:7 When the wicked spring as the grass, and when all the workers of iniquity do flourish; [it is] that they shall be destroyed for ever:

Pro 13:13 Whoso despiseth the word shall be destroyed: but he that feareth the commandment shall be rewarded.

Pro 13:20 He that walketh with wise [men] shall be wise: but a companion of fools shall be destroyed.

Pro 29:1 He, that being often reproved hardeneth [his] neck, shall suddenly be destroyed, and that without remedy.

Isa 9:16 For the leaders of this people cause [them] to err; and [they that are] led of them [are] destroyed.

Isa 34:2 For the indignation of the LORD [is] upon all nations, and [his] fury upon all their armies: he hath utterly destroyed them, he hath delivered them to the slaughter.

Jer 12:10 Many pastors have destroyed my vineyard, they have trodden my portion under foot, they have made my pleasant portion a desolate wilderness.

Jer 48:8 And the spoiler shall come upon every city, and no city shall escape: the valley also shall perish, and the plain shall be destroyed, as the LORD hath spoken.

Jer 51:8 Babylon is suddenly fallen and destroyed: howl for her; take balm for her pain, if so be she may be healed.

Jer 51:55 Because the LORD hath spoiled Babylon, and destroyed out of her the great voice; when her waves do roar like great waters, a noise of their voice is uttered:

Lam 2:5 The Lord was as an enemy: he hath swallowed up Israel, he hath swallowed up all her palaces: he hath **destroyed** his strong holds, and hath increased in the daughter of Judah mourning and lamentation.

Lam 2:6 And he hath violently taken away his tabernacle, as [if it were of] a garden: he hath destroyed his places of the assembly: the LORD hath caused the solemn feasts and sabbaths to be forgotten in Zion, and hath despised in the indignation of his anger the king and the priest.

Lam 2:9 Her gates are sunk into the ground; he hath destroyed and broken her bars: her king and her princes [are] among the Gentiles: the law [is] no [more]; her prophets also find no vision from the LORD.

Hsa 4:6 My people are destroyed for lack of knowledge: because thou hast rejected knowledge, I will also reject thee, that thou shalt be no priest to me: seeing thou hast forgotten the law of thy God, I will also forget thy children.

Hsa 13:9 O Israel, thou hast destroyed thyself; but in me [is] thine help.

Act 3:23 And it shall come to pass, [that] every soul, which will not hear that prophet, shall be destroyed from among the people.

1Cr 10:10 Neither murmur ye, as some of them also murmured, and were destroyed of the destroyer.

2Pe 2:12 But these, as natural brute beasts, made to be taken and **destroyed**, speak evil of the things that they understand not; and shall utterly perish in their own corruption;

Jud 1:5 I will therefore put you in remembrance, though ye once knew this, how that the Lord, having saved the people out of the land of Egypt, afterward **destroyed** them that believed not.

LYING SPIRIT

1Ki 22:22 And the LORD said unto him, Wherewith? And he said, I will go forth, and I will be a **lying spirit** in the mouth of all his prophets. And he said, Thou shalt persuade [him], and prevail also: go forth, and do so.
1Ki 22:23 Now therefore, behold, the LORD hath put a **lying spirit** in the mouth of all these thy prophets, and the LORD hath spoken evil concerning thee.

2Ch 18:21 And he said, I will go out, and be a **lying spirit** in the mouth of all his prophets. And [the LORD] said, Thou shalt entice [him], and thou shalt also prevail: go out, and do [even] so.
2Ch 18:22 Now therefore, behold, the LORD hath put a **lying spirit** in the mouth of these thy prophets, and the LORD hath spoken evil against thee.

APPENDIX C

The Jezebel Spirit

What It Is, Who's Got One and Why.

from Doug Perry
www.FellowshipOfTheMartyrs.com
September 25, 2006
Revised March 15, 2007

Father God, I ask in the name of Jesus Christ that you would preserve and protect those who are reading this, that you would remove every obstacle or strategy of the enemy that would try to keep them from hearing and receiving this word. I ask that you would bind up the spirit of Jezebel in each person during the time they are reading and meditating on this so that they could hear Your voice clearly and You could minister to their spirit Yourself about this. Don't let the enemy steal Your words from their heart. Thanks, Abba. You're the greatest! In the name of Jesus Christ our Lord, Amen.

First let me start by saying that I've never read any book about the spirit of Jezebel. I've never been taught by any man about this stuff. Whatever I've learned, God taught me Himself through the Holy Spirit and the experiences He ran me through. I'm not trying to disagree with anything the Lord showed somebody else.

I was instructed to write this down, so I am, but it's not a rebuttal of anybody else or a defense of anything. This is what I see because this is the way God showed it to me. I know that He shows things to other people differently and sometimes even in ways that might seem to conflict. His ways are NOT our ways and He reserves the right to do things that our brains cannot comprehend. So I'm not arguing that my understanding of the Jezebel spirit is the only and right one. I'm just saying this is what I learned. For what it's worth, take it or leave it. If you disagree with me, fine, I love you anyway.

Please don't try and talk me into seeing it your way because God taught me this and you can't unteach me. If you believe that I am Biblically in error, please show me and if you're right I'll repent. Please don't pester me with stuff about how God doesn't talk to people and the Gifts of the Spirit aren't for today or Christians can't be oppressed by demons. You're arguing with theory instead of observation and it's undefendable (and a waste of everybody's time). If a Christian has a lust or a fear or an addiction or a bitterness, then they have allowed the enemy entrance and they are oppressed. (Some say possessed, but I don't care to argue about the difference. Either way you have rulers jerking you around.)

I'm not saying I'm right. I'm saying this is what He showed ME personally. I'm perfectly willing to believe that He showed it to you some other way. Or maybe you just reasoned it out and you're guessing (in which case you might want to ask God to help you hear Him better so you don't have to lean on your own understanding anymore.) Just because I sound sure of myself and authoritative, doesn't mean I'm imposing it on you. I'm just REAL sure about what He showed ME. I don't want you to listen to me or take my word for anything, I want you to pray and ask God to show you these things in this or some other way.

I just want you ready for war and the Jezebel spirit is the covert operative behind enemy lines that is the hardest to find and root out. I'm just trying to offer back to the Body of Christ what He taught me. If He confirms it in you, great. Otherwise, ask Him to explain it some other way that you'll understand. But DO NOT go into battle without knowing about the Jezebel spirit – because it's really, really bad. If you deliver someone of everything BUT that, you almost might as well have not bothered at all. And if you don't know where to look for it, you're going to miss it. It's a very elusive target and far more subtle and far more pervasive than I ever realized before. I don't think it's enough to just name it, rebuke it and expect that it will be gone. In the pages that follow you'll see why.

As always, I give all glory and honor to God Almighty who is above all. There is no good thing in me except Jesus Christ. Anything I have, anything I gain, anything that heals or restores or teaches is from Him and not from me. Anything that is True is from Him. Anything that is confused or wrong or in error is because I let some Doug get in the way of what He was trying to say. I take full responsibility for the blood of any man that results from mistakes I made in communicating this, either in tone or style or content. Don't blame Jesus just because I'm flawed. He's perfect and He's your only hope. Don't look to me, I didn't get on the Cross for anybody. Just get so full of Jesus that nothing else can fit and you'll be alright.

I just pray this helps someone get stronger and ready for war.

Doug Perry - servant of God
fotm@fellowshipofthemartyrs.com

THE BEGINNING

During an amazingly intense "boot camp" experience in 2005 and 2006, the Lord taught me a lot about demonic oppressions and deliverance of all kinds. I knew that there was a war between good and evil and I knew that I wasn't seeing the enemy clearly enough. The Lord had placed people in my path that had a very highly tuned gift of Discernment of Spirits. (I Corin 12:10)

Usually these were people that had been on drugs or in jail, been prostitutes, attempted suicide, been witches, had lived under bridges or were otherwise what one might call "unsavory" characters. It's just that now they have been redeemed by the Blood of Lamb and are joint heirs with Jesus and children of the King. But the years of experience in the belly of the beast had made them very aware of the reality of the forces of evil and tuned them in to the spiritual realms.

If there is a war between good and evil, who would you rather have on your team? Those who had looked the darkness right in eye, appreciated how far the Lord had brought them and were never, ever going back? Or the SUV-driving, sweater-wearing, suburbanites who had never missed a meal or really suffered much? Who knows the strategies of the enemy better? Who has a vendetta against the darkness for what it has stolen from them?

I prayed that God would send warriors to help me and teach me. So now most of my best friends are people with "resumes" that most of the world would frown upon. And, praise God, that's exactly who Jesus hung out with! So send me the freaks and weirdos and homeless and criminals that now have a big cup of Jesus and have nothing left to lose and are NEVER going back! I want to march with those guys!

Anyway, some of these folks had a gift of discernment that allowed them to see the demons on people. Sometimes just hot spots or just a sense of what was messing with a person. Some of them could "see" in the spirit very clearly – like things snarling at them and writhing around. Some even could smell and taste and feel the badness. Some of them couldn't shut it off (which you have to be wired special to handle or you end up sleeping under bridges trying to drown it with booze or crack) and could walk through the Mall or the grocery store pointing out the oppressions on people. In a ministry situation, this was VERY effective and very accurate. Telling a stranger what it is that they are doing that God is mad about is a very effective way of proving that God is still here and still talks to people! (But they may punch you in the nose.) Believe me or not, I don't really care, I know what I know and nobody can talk me out of it. I've seen this proven too many times to be swayed about whether it's real or not – and there are too many people that were delivered that will vouch for me and they have NO desire to go back to the way things were!

So I decided that if there was a war between good and evil, if our battle is not against flesh and blood but against powers and principalities and rulers of darkness in high places, then I probably ought to see them better. You have two choices when you go to war, you can carpet bomb everything and hope you hit a target or you can get a laser site and send one guided missile to take out a target. The pragmatic businessman in me wants to identify targets and surgically take them out without collateral damage. But you can't do that unless you can see the enemy really well.

I've seen people do deliverance by just reading a really long warfare prayer that lists all the different kinds of things that could be oppressing someone and rebukes them ALL in the name of Jesus. That's like carpet bombing or just throwing flack up into the sky and hoping you hit an enemy warplane. It might or might not be effective. Some of those oppressions have been given permission to be there and aren't going to just hop off without some effort. Jesus said, some only come out with prayer and fasting. Fasting in your own power is slightly effective. Fasting directed by God is very effective. The prayer of a righteous man is powerful and effective. The prayer of a slightly righteous man is marginally effective. In fact, it might be hard to even tell whose team a half-way righteous man is even on! Sometimes the demons will lay low and pretend they're gone for awhile and then manifest later and bring even more fear and confusion and self-doubt.

I didn't want to take the time to just carpet bomb everything and hope I hit something – and not see it well enough to know whether I got it or not. So I started begging God to give me more discernment of spirits and more wisdom to use it. Somebody would come with a strong gifting and I would ask them to pray for me so that I might have what they have. Or I would ask the Lord what it was going to take to see better and He would have me study or fast or go through some trial or test to see if I was really serious. If you want to see demons, you have to be willing to take on all that that means. Often, as in a war, direct contact with the enemy will force you to be creative and to be really hungry for new weapons and intelligence systems.

We dealt with all kinds of demonic oppressions on people, around people, on buildings, on cities, on animals – I wouldn't even know where to start to document it all. I've fought gross personal stuff like cannibalism and pedophilia and sado-masochism, as well as principalities over whole towns and countries. I didn't keep a journal because things were moving too fast. For the purposes of this writing, let me just say that the Lord used each of the people on our team (which was constantly in flux) and lots of other people to teach us lessons about how really pervasive and invasive and well-hidden the forces of darkness really are. He forced us to walk in the Spirit nearly every day and learn to hear His voice really well because the stakes were VERY high.

It was like a sort of laboratory safe-room where we could walk through the curriculum the Lord had planned and we could experiment and learn on all different kinds of demons, principalities, generational curses, filters, and other obstructions. I learned about their strategies, about their attack patterns, about weapons to stop them, about using angels, about why God allows oppressions at all, about how to make them jump screaming off of someone without a big fight. This passage motivated me substantially:

> **Acts 19:13** – *Some Jews who went around driving out evil spirits tried to invoke the name of the Lord Jesus over those who were demon-possessed. They would say, "In the name of Jesus, whom Paul preaches, I command you to come out." 14 Seven sons of Sceva, a Jewish chief priest, were doing this. 15 (One day) the evil spirit answered them, "Jesus I know, and I know about Paul, but who are you?" 16 Then the man who had the evil spirit jumped on them and overpowered them all. He gave them such a beating that they ran out of the house naked and bleeding.*

So which one do you want to be – Paul or the sons of Sceva?! They were using the right Name, so how come it didn't work? Because they weren't really disciples, they weren't bondservants of Jesus. Notice they didn't call Jesus "Lord". That's important. He was NOT their Lord. They just threw the name around, but they didn't acknowledge Him for who He truly is – Messiah, Christ, Son of God and ruler of their life. They could see some success at this on the little ones in the name of Jesus, but the really big, bad nasty stuff is going to kick their rear around the block! I didn't want to be like the sons of Sceva! I wanted to be like Paul. Even the demons had heard of Paul and feared him. They NEVER tried this kind of stuff with Paul! Why? Because Paul was 100% under the headship of Christ. He understood what a bondservant is. He obeyed all the time in every way.

I determined that I wanted the badness to know my name. People think that's nutty to try to taunt the enemy like that and make yourself a target, but I figure you can't start putting a dent in the enemy without them knowing who you are. Besides, what would happen if 10,000 Christians all started competing to see who could be the most dangerous to satan? You don't think they encourage competition like that in Top Gun school or Seal training or boot camp? Guess again, the level of skill increases across the board when people have a drive to be the best. And if God put that competitive, killer instinct and drive in me, then I might as well use it for something that furthers His kingdom!

In March of 2005 (as I recall), on a Tuesday night on the main drag in the retail district of a quiet little town in the Heartland of America, we had a prayer meeting at God's little furniture store and went out to find that someone had ritually sacrificed a cat in front of the store. One of the ladies there had come out of witchcraft and knew exactly what it was. This wasn't an animal hit by a car, this was a pet that was snatched and had it's throat slit. She came back in to tell me and I did a little jig and let out a big "WOOO HOOO!!!"

They looked at me strangely and I said, "Don't you get it?! I've been in churches all my life and NOBODY ever sacrificed a cat in front of any of them! If there is a war between good and evil and NOBODY is shooting at you, then YOU AREN'T DANGEROUS!" I was just as pleased as I could be that some principality told some familiar of some poor witch or satanist to skip doing their homework and watching American Idol and go out on a Tuesday night and find a cat to kill in front of a furniture store! Do you see? Every bullet that is aimed at me is one less bullet for somebody else. So if a giant cloud of badness follows me around trying to kill me, all the better. My God is bigger than all of them. I want to be at the top of Hell's Most Wanted list.

How do you get to be on the top of the Most Wanted list? You understand the enemy and you crush them like a bug. You know their secrets, you know where they hide, you know their most covert, most subtle strategies that fool the most people.   And then you tell EVERYBODY as loudly as you can.

Remember, the enemy is a liar and deceiver. He is sneaky and likes to hide and mask himself as something else. It's all about camouflage because nobody would fall for a full frontal assault by a scary guy in red with a pitchfork, horns and a long tail. It would drive them to their knees begging for Jesus right away. When you don't have superior firepower, a quiet, gentle invasion from the inside is always best. Misinformation and propaganda and misdirection and deceit and sabotage and guerrilla warfare are your only hope. If you can get the assets of the enemy to actually work against them and they don't even know they're doing it, that's ideal!

Who is more dangerous to you? The guy in the enemy tank on the front lines or the double agent in the Pentagon with access to all your battle plans? The captain of an enemy submarine that is somewhere out there looking for you or the saboteur on your own submarine? Since our enemy is a liar and a cheat and deceiver, you need to figure that the weapons that he most favors and is best at wielding aren't the blunt force, frontal attack kind, but the subtle, behind-the-scenes, viral kind.

ABOUT THE WOMAN NAMED JEZEBEL

The Jezebel spirit is not the actual spirit of the woman Jezebel who was the wife of King Ahab. I don't know who started calling it that, but it's just that she is a really good representation of what this spirit does. She surely had this spirit and let it have free reign in and through her. More later about the characteristics of it and why she was a good example of it. (In actuality, it's the spirit of anti-christ.)

According to Strong's Concordance, the name Jezebel means "Baal exalts" or "Baal is husband to" or "unchaste". That can't be good. Right away she's got a big strike against her. Being "married" to a false God, especially that one, is a bad thing. She shows up in the Bible in these passages (I Kings 16:31; I Kings 18-21 and 2 Kings 9).

I'm not a linguist or a historian, so I'm not going to lecture about all the nuances of the Biblical Jezebel. The point is that she was the queen, but bossed the king around and pretty much got whatever she wanted. She was a usurper. She didn't have legitimate authority but she took it from the one who was the real head and used it for her own purposes. She was in a position of weakness, but was in actuality the one running the kingdom. She was also very mean and nasty and selfish. She set out to exterminate God's prophets, she tore down the altars to God and replaced them with a weak imitation. She was able to scare Elijah into running and hiding in a cave and begging to die – even <u>after</u> God just showed up in a BIG way, 850 false prophets were killed, Elijah outran a chariot and it rained on command after 3 ½ years! (I Kings 18-19) She was a liar and cheat and a deceiver. She did whatever she had to do from a secondary position to try to be fully in charge. She was just like satan.

He is in a weak, secondary position, but tries to intercept and mangle the messages from the true Head and turn them around to a weak imitation so that God isn't the focus. It doesn't really matter whether we worship satan directly or not, so long as we're not worshiping God then the enemy has won. He engineers every situation and manipulates all the variables so that he can come out on top. He is the master of intrigue and politics and flattery and lies and jockeying for control.

In I Kings 21 we see Jezebel signing a death warrant on a subject of the kingdom just to get his land. And she does it in the name of Ahab. She orders the elders of the town to falsely accuse the man and stone him, then she victoriously presents the land to Ahab. When Ahab goes out to survey the land, God sends Elijah to him to tell him that God is going to punish him severely for his wicked deed. But it wasn't even Ahab! There's no indication that he even knew how he had gotten the land! Jezebel did it. But the head let the body usurp his authority, so he's going to get punished for it. (AND Jezebel will be eaten by dogs.) There's no question that Ahab was a bad dude, but Jezebel made it a lot worse for him.

SEARCHING FOR THE JEZEBEL SPIRIT

What I began to see is that there HAD to be some controlling influence on a person that pulled all the strings. The fear and lust and guilty and self-condemnation were very well organized and cycling in increasing spirals to ruin a persons life. They would start feeling badly about themselves, so they would eat a dozen donuts. Then they would feel guilty about eating the dozen donuts and feel worse and worse, so they would eat donuts to make themselves feel better. Then they would begin to believe and fear that people were looking at them funny because they had put on weight, which made them feel worse, so they would eat more donuts. Then they would start to worry about their heart because they didn't feel quite right. Then they would go to the doctor and get fed more fear and self-condemnation and guilt. Then they would eat a dozen donuts to make themselves feel better because they couldn't get any affection because they were fat and had a really poor self-image. And they never even realized that demons were talking to them and had succeeded in killing, stealing and destroying their peace, joy, victory and quality of life. Another Christian warrior had been immobilized and neutralized by some DONUTS and a lot of self-talk that wasn't really self-talk at all, but the forces of darkness whispering in their ear!

That's what happens when you don't take every thought captive and bring it into obedience with Christ. If you think all the voices in your head are your own, you're not going to guard the gates. That's the enemy's best hope – that you wouldn't even believe he exists at all! Then you won't even put up your defenses. Why put on the armor of God at all when the battle is won and the enemy is defeated? Why take every thought captive when we are children of the King and satan is under our feet? Ok, then why are we addicted and bitter and angry and oppressed on every side? Why are our congregations filled with sick and hurting people? If you look at them in the spirit, you will see that most congregations look like a war zone hospital triage rooms – but nobody is getting treated! They just sit there and bleed on the floor and try to convince themselves that this is the fullness of Christ.

Another common example is that people have what I call a "Dad Filter" – sort of a lens through which they look at God. Usually it's shaped like their Earth Dad and they impose it on their Heavenly Dad. Like if their father was never home and never cared for them, then they think God is distant and disinterested. Or if Earth Dad screams and yells and disciplines harshly, then God is an angry, vindictive God just waiting to catch you when you mess up. Or worse, if Earth Dad sexually abused you, you are so angry at God that you rebel against everything He says and want to punish Him for allowing it to happen.

The enemy uses this to keep our eyes off of the real Heavenly Dad by keeping Him in a box. The enemy doesn't want us to have intimacy and relationship with God, so he keeps us focused on that tiny snapshot of God and reinforces everything that agrees with it and downplays everything that is outside of our box. Then we can never really walk in the fullness of God and experience the entire kaleidescope of His presence. We can't have an Abba, Daddy who will pull us up onto His lap and kiss our boo-boo's and stroke our head and tell us He loves us and everything will be OK. We can't because it's absolutely foreign to our experiences with dads – or maybe even any man. We don't think we're worthy, we don't think He's capable, we don't think we've earned it, or we don't think it even exists. Whatever it is, it's the enemy that wants to maintain us at arms length from the Father.

I would often see this "Dad Filter" being manipulated and played and reinforced by the fear, anger, lust, guilt, self-condemnation and others all cycling and playing off of each other to keep the poor person in a constant state of anxiety. God is peace and love. He doesn't hurry. He rests. But the enemy seeks to keep us in a constant frenzy so that we can't slow down and hear God's still small voice.

Over and over and over I would see coordinated attacks where these spirits would play off of each other. Even when I pulled one or all of them off a person, often they were back in short order – sometimes much worse. And they continued to have a sort of coordination and multi-tasking that was suspicious to me. Individually they are specialists and they don't have that kind of ability to interconnect and coordinate on their own. They are very focused on the one thing that they are supposed to be doing.

My special gift is to see systems, to see connections and networks. I look at things differently than other people. My (earth) Dad said that if you had a big rock out in a field and took a hundred people and told them to describe the rock, some would take tape measures and GPS coordinates, some would draw or paint it, some would sculpt a likeness of it – but I would be the one to dig under it to see what everybody else was missing. One of my favorite pastimes as a kid was taking appliances apart to see their guts and see how the pieces all worked together. I was very good at fixing complex things. I've always been able to stand back and assess a business or a group of people and very quickly see who was in charge and who wasn't and how the "flow" of things worked. It probably comes from going to twelve schools in twelve years as a missionary kid and having to adjust to constantly changing situations and integrate quickly.

As I began to see the spirits better, when the Lord allowed, I could see a snarling black fear on top of people's heads. I could see a control/witchcraft biting on the back of their neck and self-condemnation on their right shoulder, lust over their heart and sloth/lethargy in their back. I could/can see love of money, guilt, pride and many others that are messing with them. I always see them lodged on a person in the same place. I always see a witchcraft on the back of their neck (controlling their head) and I've never seen more than one witchcraft on a person. They may be different sizes or of different nastiness levels, but there's never really more than one of anything.

It's like a computer where you have a serial port, a USB port, a video port, a network port, etc. Each is for a specific purpose and they're not interchangeable. A lust is always in the port right over the heart. Why? Because the lust is all about self and desire – not just sexual, but anything that involves self-gratification and makes an idol of something – food, cigarettes, drugs, Precious Moments collections, affection, power, etc. (All of these are adultery against God. When Jesus tells you not to eat a dozen donuts, but you do anyway, you're making Him <u>watch</u> you deny Him and commit adultery with something else. If you love Him, you'll obey Him.)

I dealt with so many spirits of fear and guilt and lust that I knew how they worked and what they did and how they thought. And I knew they weren't smart enough to coordinate a system-wide attack. And I'm standing back and looking at this and thinking, "Somebody has <u>got</u> to be pulling the strings here! This assault is too methodical, too coordinated, timed too well and too subtle and well directed to be the result of the brain power of a fear or guilt or lust. They're just not designed to direct each other like that. There MUST be a central command and control structure!

Consider it again as a warfare scenario. You have divisions or battalions of tanks and infantry and paratroopers and scouts and snipers and helicopters and airplanes all attacking on a common front. They work together seamlessly and take turns hitting soft targets and advancing. If the infantry can't get through a line, the tanks try, if the tanks can't get through they call in an air strike. Which of these specialists is capable of directing the actions of the total force? None of them. None of them are command and control. If there is not a Commander directing their actions and seeing the big picture, then they will end up defeated and maybe even a lot of friendly fire accidents. You'll have supply chain problems, you won't be able to call reinforcements, you won't know where the enemy is vulnerable because you won't be able to synthesize updated intelligence about enemy movements and communicate to all the multiple specialties.

Are you with me? There HAS to be something pulling all the strings and coordinating the assault. There just HAS to be. Our side works the same – we have our emotions, our knowledge, our intuition, our past experience, our outside voices and influences from others and more – but if we have the Holy Spirit fully in charge and directing all of those things toward maximum success we can be lethal. Without God sitting on the command throne, we are double-minded and torn between all the conflicting voices and influences on us. We end up leaning on our own understanding and directing our own paths. (Prov. 3:5-6) Or letting some Man tell us what God wants us to do. That never goes well for me! How about you? Without ONE central command and control voice, we are tossed like the wind.

I began to suspect that it was the Jezebel. Whatever it was, it had to be REALLY smart, really sneaky and really well hidden. You don't put the General that is the true brains of the operation in a tank on the front lines and put a big gold star on it. You hide him in a little bunker somewhere and give him a radio. But you don't expose the brains of the operation because you know how critical he is. Now, he may be totally harmless in a knife fight – he may be old and fat and toothless – but that's not what he's for. He's there because he's a strategist and a coordinator, because he's smart and he knows the enemy. He's not a danger one-on-one – but he is the MOST dangerous person on the battlefield because he has ALL the resources at his disposal.

I'm sure that Elijah could have pinned Queen Jezebel in an arm wrestling match. I'm sure in a knife fight he could have taken her. But even though powerless one-on-one, she had the entire resources of the kingdom at her disposal and THAT made her dangerous. She was sneaky and underhanded and knew how to coordinate it all to get what she wanted. She wasn't even the true power, but she could usurp it any time she wanted. That is what scared Elijah. She was "Command and Control" even though she wasn't the king.

It became more and more clear to me that the Jezebel would be the way satan would work best. He is a master of Judo. Using the enemy's own weight and momentum against them. He'll allow forward progress in a ministry, in fact he'll sometimes try to speed it up so it's going so fast people don't have time to pray, then they shoot past the Narrow Path and overcompensate and by the time they notice that they stopped praying, they're in jail or in a hotel room with a stripper. That's Judo – applying the minimum necessary force and their own momentum to throw an enemy off balance. Our enemy is operating from a losing position. He is outnumbered and outgunned. The only hope he has is misdirection, usurpation and sabotage. If he can co-opt our own efforts and use them against us, then he can gain territory. But he has to stay hidden to do it, otherwise we'd guard the gates and kick him out. If the double agent inside the Pentagon is found out and the alarm is sounded, then it will be harder to get another one in there in the future. The enemy thrives on secrecy and camouflage.

Are you with me? Whatever is coordinating these attacks has to be very well hidden because for all the people that talk about the Jezebel spirit, I'm not aware of anyone that has ever really SEEN one. There are lots of people out there that see demons, but I've never heard of anyone really getting a gun sight trained on an actual Jezebel. And I've heard so many stories about congregations being ripped apart by a mad witch-hunt trying to figure out WHO in the place has the spirit of Jezebel on them and then kicking them out. What fun! The enemy just ties us up in knots and has us accuse each other and divide and in-fight while we search for something that we can see the effects of, but can't quite find! That's Judo.

I knew it was out there. I knew there was a command and control influence on each person and I knew it was the Jezebel. The Lord allowed one of our own team to be used to really graphically illustrate it and made me desperate for a solution. I wanted her free and I wanted the influence out of our midst.

But I never expected to find what I found!

FINDING THE JEZEBEL

During that time, we were on a radical obedience walk and fellowshipping together and praying nearly every night. We were having amazing "church" time in the furniture store three or four times a day – all arranged by God. People were getting saved and healed and filled with the Holy Spirit. We had a food pantry and free used furniture and clothes and toys for anyone that had a need. Donated stuff was pouring into a For-Profit business! God was showing up every day and running things in miraculous ways.

One night I was feeling a little frisky and wanted to squash some serious bad guys. I had really been seeking Him and seeking understanding. Not for my glory or to build a big ministry or anything – I just wanted to pray whatever prayer would be most dangerous to the enemy. So I asked Him what I could ask for that would do the most damage to satan. And He said, "Pray to see and understand the Jezebel." So I did, I prayed, "Lord, I want to know where this thing is ported up and how to deal with it. Please show me, Lord." I'm sure that was what He wanted me to pray and I've seen the fruit of it since then.

The next day I'm alone in my office praying and I ask the Lord to show me where it is. Instantly I hear, "In the Pituitary." Well I don't really have much of a background in biology so I didn't really even know what it was or where it was. Later that day and in days following I began to research about the pituitary gland. This is what I found.

It is a pea-sized gland just about dead center in your head.

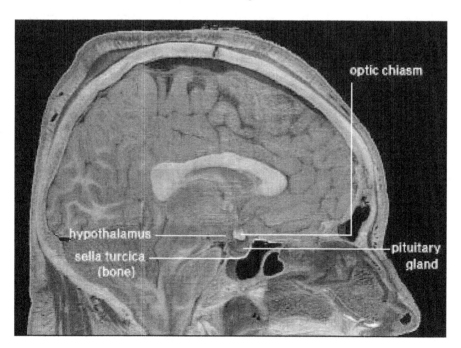

http://www.vivo.colostate.edu/hbooks/pathphys/endocrine/hypopit/anatomy.html

http://en.wikipedia.org/wiki/Pituitary_gland

Endocrine system

The **endocrine system** is under the direct supervision of the nervous system, using the negative feedback principal of homeostasis, to create hormones which act as chemical instant messengers. The hypothalamus connects directly to the pituitary gland, both through the circulatory system and by direct connection of neurons. Also, within the cranium, the pineal gland, which attaches to the thalamus, controls the body's 24 hour rhythms circadian rhythm through the release of melatonin. Endocrine indicates that the secretion is used within the body. Endocrine glands are termed as **ductless** and release their secretions directly into the blood.

The **pituitary gland** is also called hypophysis, or **master gland**. It secretes hormones that directly impact the body as well as hormones that indirectly control body functions because they activate other endocrine glands, such as the adrenal cortex (ACTH) and the thyroid gland (TSH). These two glands when stimulated by pituitary hormones then release their own hormones. The pituitary gland has two lobes, the anterior lobe and the posterior lobe. The anterior lobe secretes: growth hormone (GH), Luteinizing hormone (LH), Follicle stimulating hormone (FSH), Adrenocorticotropic hormone (ACTH), Thyroid-stimulating hormone (TSH), Prolactin (PRL), and the posterior lobe secretes: Antidieuretic hormone (ADH), and Oxytocin (OT). There is an intermediate lobe, in adult humans it is just a thin layer of cells between the anterior and posterior pituitary, nearly indistinguishable from the anterior lobe. The intermediate lobe produces melanocyte-stimulating hormone (MSH).

http://www.pituitary.org/faq/

Which hormones are secreted by the anterior pituitary?

- **Thyroid Stimulating Hormone** (TSH) causes the thyroid gland to produce and release thyroid hormones. Thyroid hormone controls the basal metabolic rate and plays an important role in growth and maturation. Thyroid hormones affect almost every organ in the body.

- **Growth Hormone** (GH) regulates growth and metabolism.
- **Adrenocorticotropic Hormone** (ACTH) triggers the adrenals to release the hormone cortisol, which regulates carbohydrate, fat, and protein metabolism and blood pressure. The adrenal glands sit above the kidneys and are also responsible for the body's fight or flight response.
- **Luteinizing Hormone** (LH) and **Follicle Stimulating Hormone** (FSH) control the production of sex hormones (estrogen and testosterone) and sperm and egg maturation and release.
- **Melanocyte-Stimulating Hormone** (MSH) regulates the production of melanin, a dark pigment, by melanocytes in the skin. Increased melanin production produces pigmentation or tanning of the skin; in certain conditions excessive production of melanocyte-stimulating hormone can cause darkening of the skin.
- **Prolactin** (PRL) stimulates production of breast milk and is necessary for normal milk production during breast feeding.

Which hormones are produced and/or controlled by the posterior pituitary or hypothalamus?

- **Oxytocin** stimulates contractions of the uterus during labor and the ejection of milk during breast-feeding.
- **Antidiuretic Hormone** (ADH) increases reabsorption of water into the blood by the kidneys and therefore decreases urine production. Also referred to as Vasopressin.

What happens if the pituitary produces either too much or too little of these hormones?

An imbalance occurs, leading to more than a dozen disorders of the endocrine system. Deficiency of thyroid hormone, adrenal cortical hormone (cortisol) or antidiuretic hormone (vasopressin) is rapidly life-threatening. In patients with abnormalities of the other hormones, quality of life is significantly compromised.

What causes the pituitary to malfunction?

Tumors (overwhelmingly benign), inflammation, infections and injury can cause the gland to malfunction, as well as metastasis or spread of other tumors to the pituitary (rare). Radiation therapy to the brain can also cause normal pituitary cells to malfunction.

PITUITARY-RELATED DISORDERS
http://www.pituitary.org

Acromegaly

Acromegaly is a hormonal disorder that most commonly occurs in middle-aged men and women. The prevalence of acromegaly is approximately 4,676 cases per million population, and the incidence is 116.9 new cases per million per year. The name "acromegaly" comes from the Greek words for "extremities" (acro) and "great" (megaly), because one of the most common symptoms of this condition is abnormal growth of the hands and feet.

Adrenal Insufficiency

Addisons disease is a rare endocrine, or hormonal disorder that affects about 1 in 100,000 people. It occurs in all age groups and afflicts men and women equally. The disease is characterized by weight loss, muscle weakness, fatigue, low blood pressure, and sometimes darkening of the skin in both exposed and non-exposed parts of the body.

The symptoms of adrenal insufficiency usually begin gradually. Chronic, worsening fatigue and muscle weakness, loss of appetite, and weight loss are characteristic of the disease. Nausea, vomiting, and diarrhea occur in about 50 percent of cases. Blood pressure is low and falls further when standing, causing dizziness or fainting. Skin changes also are common in Addisons disease, with areas of hyperpigmentation, or dark tanning, covering exposed and nonexposed parts of the body. This darkening of the skin is most visible on scars; skin folds; pressure points such as the elbows, knees, knuckles, and toes; lips; and mucous membranes.

Addisons disease can cause irritability and depression. Because of salt loss, craving of salty foods also is common. Hypoglycemia, or low blood sugar, is more severe in children than in adults. In women, menstrual periods may become irregular or stop.

Because the symptoms progress slowly, they are usually ignored until a stressful event like an illness or an accident causes them to become worse. This is called an addisonian crisis, or acute adrenal insufficiency. In most patients, symptoms are severe enough to seek medical treatment before a crisis occurs. However, in about 25 percent of patients, symptoms first appear during an addisonian crisis.

Symptoms of an addisonian crisis include sudden penetrating pain in the lower back, abdomen, or legs; severe vomiting and diarrhea, followed by dehydration; low blood pressure; and loss of consciousness. Left untreated, an addisonian crisis can be fatal.

Craniopharyngiomas

The symptoms produced by a craniopharyngioma vary depending upon the tumors location. If it compresses the pituitary stalk or involves the area of the pituitary gland itself, the tumor can cause partial or complete pituitary hormone deficiency. This frequently results in one or more of the following: growth failure, delayed puberty, loss of normal menstrual function or sexual desire, increased sensitivity to cold, fatigue, constipation, dry skin, nausea, low blood pressure, and depression.

Pituitary stalk compression can also cause diabetes insipidus and may increase prolactin levels causing a milky discharge from the breast (galactorrhea). If the craniopharyngioma involves the optic tracts, chiasm, or nerves, then visual disturbances can result. Involvement of the hypothalamus, an area at the base of the brain, may result in obesity, increased drowsiness, temperature regulation abnormalities, and diabetes insipidus (DI). Other common symptoms include personality changes, headache, confusion, and vomiting.

Cushing's Syndrome

Symptoms and signs of Cushings syndrome and disease may include:

- Change in body habitus: weight gain in face (moon face), above the collar bone (supraclavicular) and on back of neck (buffalo hump)
- Skin changes with easy bruising, purplish stretch marks (stria) and red cheeks (plethora)
- Excess hair growth (hirsutism) on face, neck, chest, abdomen, and thighs
- Generalized weakness and fatigue
- Loss of muscle
- Menstrual disorders in women (amenorrhea)
- Decreased fertility and/or sex drive (libido)
- Hypertension
- Diabetes mellitus
- Depression with wide mood swings

Empty Sella Syndrome

Symptoms

- unusual facial features
- increased bone density
- headaches
- vision problems

FSH & LH Tumors

FSH- and LH-secreting tumors very rarely present with clinical symptoms of hormone over-secretion. Hence, the presentation of these tumors is almost always identical to non-functional (or endocrine inactive) adenomas.These symptoms include:

- Headaches
- Visual disturbances
- Hypogonadism

GH Deficiency

As the name implies, GH is the pituitary hormone that stimulates body growth and development during childhood. Although GH has been used to successfully treat children whom have a deficiency of this hormone (a condition termed dwarfism) since the 1960's, adult GH deficiency was largely ignored until the early 1990's. The observation that virtually every tissue in the body contains receptors for GH coupled with the finding that GH deficiency in adults is associated with higher mortality, suggested that GH may have equally important actions during adulthood.

Adult GH deficiency is now a well-recognized clinical syndrome that includes symptoms of increased body fat, decreased muscle and bone mass with reduced strength and endurance, impaired psychological well-being, reduced vitality, and poor quality of life.

Adult GH deficiency most commonly results from damage to the pituitary gland either from a pituitary tumor or as a result of interventions (i.e., surgery or radiotherapy) used to treat a pituitary tumor. GH appears to be one of the first hormones to be lost in patients with pituitary tumors and nearly all patients with two or more pituitary deficiencies also lack GH.

Hypogonadism

Hypogonadism can occur for a number of reasons. Certain men have hypogonadism since birth while others may develop this condition later in life. Two types of hypogonadism are:

Primary hypogonadism (testicular failure) - Low serum testosterone levels and gonadotropins (FSH, LH) above the normal range.

Hypogonadotropic hypogonadism - Idiopathic gonadotropin or LHRH deficiency or pituitary - hypothalamic injury from tumors, trauma, or radiation.

In Men:
Characterized by low serum testosterone levels, but with gonadotropins in the normal or low range. Men develop testicular

suppression with decreased libido, impotence, decreased ejaculate volume, loss of body and facial hair, weakness, fatigue and often anemia. On testing, blood levels of testosterone are low and should be replaced.

Symptoms
- ·Impotence
- ·Decreased sexual desire
- ·Fatigue and loss of energy
- ·Mood depression
- ·Regression of secondary sexual characteristics (growth and maturation of prostate, seminal vesicles, penis, and scrotum; the development of male hair distribution, including facial, pubic, chest, axillary hair; laryngeal enlargement; vocal chord thickening; alterations in body musculature; fat distribution)
- ·Osteoporosis

In Women:
Women develop ovarian suppression with irregular periods or absence of periods (amenorrhea), infertility, decreased libido, decreased vaginal secretions, breast atrophy, and osteoporosis. Blood levels of estradiol are low.

Hypopituitarism

Hypopituitarism is a general term that refers to any under function of the pituitary gland. This is a clinical definition used by endocrinologists and is interpreted to mean that one or more functions of the pituitary are deficient. The term may refer to both anterior and posterior pituitary gland failure.

Causes of hypopituitarism
Deficient pituitary gland function can result from damage to either the pituitary or the area just above the pituitary, the hypothalamus. The hypothalamus contains releasing and inhibitory hormones which control the pituitary. Since these hormones are necessary for normal pituitary function, damage to the hypothalamus can also result in deficient pituitary gland function. Injury to the pituitary can occur from a variety of insults, including damage from an enlarging

pituitary tumor, irradiation to the pituitary, pituitary apoplexy, trauma and abnormal iron storage (hemochromatosis). The progression from most vulnerable to least vulnerable is usually as follows: first is growth hormone (GH), next the gonadotropins (LH and FSH which control sexual/reproductive function), followed by TSH (which control thyroid hormone release) and finally the last to be lost is typically ACTH (which controls adrenal function).

Sheehan's Syndrome

Sheehan's syndrome is a condition that may occur in a woman who has a severe uterine hemorrhage during childbirth. The resulting severe blood loss causes tissue death in her pituitary gland and leads to hypopituitarism following the birth.

Deficiency of ACTH and cortisol

Deficiency of ACTH resulting in cortisol deficiency is the most dangerous and life threatening of the hormonal deficiency syndromes. With gradual onset of deficiency over days or weeks, symptoms are often vague and may include weight loss, fatigue, weakness, depression, apathy, nausea, vomiting, anorexia and hyperpigmentation. As the deficiency becomes more serious or has a more rapid onset, (Addisonian crisis) symptoms may include confusion, stupor, psychosis, abnormal electrolytes (low serum sodium, elevated serum potassium), and vascular collapse (low blood pressure and shock) which can be fatal.

Deficiency of TSH and thyroid hormone

Deficiency of thyroid hormone causes a syndrome consisting of decreased energy, increased need to sleep, intolerance of cold (inability to stay warm), dry skin, constipation, muscle aching and decreased mental functions. This constellation of symptoms is very uncomfortable and is often the symptom complex that drives patients with pituitary disease to seek medical attention.

Deficiency of LH and FSH (Hypogonadotropic Hypogonadism)

Women develop ovarian suppression with irregular periods or absence of periods (amenorrhea), infertility, decreased libido, decreased vaginal secretions, breast atrophy, and osteoporosis. Blood levels of estradiol are low.

Men develop testicular suppression with decreased libido, impotence, decreased ejaculate volume, loss of body and facial hair, weakness, fatigue and often anemia. On testing, blood levels of testosterone are low and should be replaced.

Growth Hormone Deficiency
Growth hormone is necessary in children for growth, but also appears necessary in adults to maintain normal body composition (muscle and bone mass). It may also be helpful for maintaining an adequate energy level, optimal cardiovascular status and some mental functions. Symptoms of GH deficiency in adults include fatigue, poor exercise performance and symptoms of social isolation. GH is only available in injectable form and must be given 6-7 times per week.

Antidiuretic Hormone deficiency causing diabetes insipidus
This problem arises from damage to the pituitary stalk or the posterior pituitary gland. It may occur transiently after transsphenoidal surgery but is rarely permanent. Patients with diabetes insipidus have increased thirst and urination. Replacement of antidiuretic hormone resolves these symptoms. Antidiuretic hormone (ADH) is currently replaced by administration of DDAVP (also called Desmopressin) a synthetic type of ADH. DDAVP can be given by subcutaneous injection, intranasal spray, or by tablet, usually once or twice a day.

Hypothyroidism - Thyroid Hormone Deficiency
Deficiency of thyroid hormone causes a syndrome of decreased energy, weight gain, cold intolerance, dry skin, constipation, mood changes and decreased cognitive capability.

Other symptoms may include:

· Hair loss

· Menstrual irregularities

· Erectile dysfunction

· Infertility.

Non-Functioning Tumors

As their name indicates, these relatively common pituitary adenomas do not result in excess hormone production. Instead they typically cause symptoms because of increasing size and pressure effect on the normal pituitary gland and on structures near the pituitary such as the optic nerves and chiasm. The major symptoms of patients with endocrine-inactive tumors are those of pituitary failure (hypopituitarism), visual loss and headache. Hypopituitarism may manifest itself as nausea, vomiting, weakness, decreased mental function, loss of sexual drive, infertility and in women, irregular or absent periods (amenorrhea). The vast majority of these tumors are benign. Most are macroadenomas (over 1 cm in size) when finally diagnosed. Occasionally, they grow quite large and into the cavernous sinus causing nerve compression and double vision. Some patients with large tumors may have acute hemorrhage into the tumor (pituitary apoplexy) causing relatively sudden onset of headache, visual loss, double vision, and/or pituitary failure. Endocrine-inactive adenomas may also be discovered incidentally during an evaluation for another problem, such as a head injury. Almost half of endocrine-inactive adenomas secrete part of a hormone called the alpha-subunit, which is not hormonally active but can be measured in the blood.

Symptoms of hypopituitarism may include:
·Nausea and vomiting
·Loss of appetite
·Weight loss
·Fatigue, decreased energy
·Decreased mental function
·Dizziness
·Joint pains
·Women: infertility, irregular or nonexistent menses
·Men: infertility, impotence in men, loss of body and facial hair
·Loss of sexual drive
Symptoms of pressure or "mass" effect
·Headache
·Loss of vision - loss of peripheral vision or decreased acuity in one or both eyes

·Double vision
Prolactinomas

These pituitary tumors (also called adenomas) secrete excessive amounts of prolactin and are the most common type of pituitary tumor seen clinically. Prolactin is the hormone that stimulates milk production by the breasts. Prolactin-producing tumors exist "silently" in up to 5-10% of the adult population. Prolactinomas generally have very different presentations in women and in men. In women, relatively small elevations in prolactin cause irregular menstrual periods or complete loss of menses (amenorrhea), ability to ovulate (remain fertile) and may cause milky discharge from the breasts (galactorrhea). In addition, women may have a reduction in their sex drive. The normal prolactin level is < 20 ng/ml. In most women the tumors are detected when they are small (microadenomas) and the prolactin level is only moderately elevated (30 - 300 ng/ml). In contrast, in men prolactinomas are usually not detected until they are large (macroadenomas), most have prolactin levels over 500 ng/ml. Most men diagnosed with a prolactinoma have some degree of loss of sex hormone production. They may also have visual loss (from compression of the optic nerves or optic chiasm) and/or headache. A minority of patients with large tumors may have bleeding into the tumor (pituitary apoplexy) causing relatively sudden onset of headache, visual loss, double vision, and/or pituitary failure.

Rathkes Cleft Cysts

Rathkes pouch is a normal component of embryological development which eventually forms the pituitary gland. This pouch normally closes early in fetal development, but a remnant often persists as a cleft that lies within the pituitary gland. Occasionally, this remnant gives rise to a large cyst, called Rathkes cleft cyst (RCC), that causes symptoms. Symptomatic RCCs are relatively uncommon lesions, accounting for less than 1% of all primary masses within the brain.

RCCs can be seen at any age, although most are identified in adults. RCCs are usually asymptomatic and are found incidentally at autopsy or MR imaging. RCCs may also present with visual disturbances, symptoms of pituitary dysfunction, and headaches.

TSH Secreting Tumors

These tumors represent only about 1-2% of all pituitary adenomas that are surgically removed. They typically cause excessive thyroid hormone production (hyperthyroidism). Because many patients first have thyroid treatment of some sort, these pituitary tumors are often aggressive and invasive in their growth pattern.

{ME AGAIN}

Do you see it?! This is the place of <u>maximum</u> impact with <u>minimum</u> effort!! This tiny, pea-sized gland actually filters and control <u>everything</u> going through it from the Hypothalamus and the brain. A tiny tumor, even a handful of cells large, can completely wreck a person's quality of life. If there was ever a place for satan to plant a demon that was a command and control thing and had influence across the whole body with minimum effort, **this** would be the place. It's not just what the Pituitary can do itself, it secretes hormones that directly impact the body as well as hormones that indirectly control body functions because they activate other endocrine glands, such as the **<u>adrenal cortex</u>** (ACTH) and the **<u>thyroid gland</u>** (TSH). These two glands when stimulated by pituitary hormones then release their own hormones.

The Adrenal Cortex:

<u>http://en.wikipedia.org/wiki/Adrenal_cortex</u>

Situated along the perimeter of the adrenal gland, the **adrenal cortex** mediates the stress response through the production of <u>mineralocorticoids</u> and <u>glucocorticoids</u>, including <u>aldosterone</u> and <u>cortisol</u> respectively. It is also a secondary site of <u>androgen</u> synthesis.

Androgen:

Androgen is the generic term for any natural or synthetic compound, usually a steroid hormone, that stimulates or controls the development and maintenance of masculine characteristics in vertebrates by binding to androgen receptors. This includes the activity of the accessory male sex organs and development of male secondary sex characteristics. Androgens, which were first discovered in 1936, are also called androgenic hormones or testoids. Androgens are also the original anabolic steroids. They are also the precursor of all estrogens, the female sex hormones. The primary and most well-known androgen is testosterone.

Glucocorticoid:

Glucocorticoids are a class of steroid hormones characterised by an ability to bind with the cortisol receptor and trigger similar effects. Glucocorticoids are distinguished from mineralocorticoids and sex steroids by the specific receptors, target cells, and effects. Technically, the term *corticosteroid* refers to both glucocorticoids and mineralocorticoids, but is often used as a synonym for *glucocorticoid*.

Cortisol (or hydrocortisone) is the most important human glucocorticoid. It is essential for life and regulates or supports a variety of important cardiovascular, metabolic, immunologic, and homeostatic functions. Glucocorticoid receptors are found in the cells of almost all vertebrate tissues.

Cortisol:

Cortisol is a corticosteroid hormone produced by the adrenal cortex that is involved in the response to stress; it increases blood pressure, blood sugar levels, may cause infertility in women, and suppresses the immune system. Synthetic cortisol, also known as hydrocortisone, is used as a drug mainly to fight allergies and inflammation.

The Thyroid Gland:

The **thyroid** (from the Greek word for "shield", after its shape) is one of the larger endocrine glands in the body. It is a double-lobed structure located in the neck and produces hormones, principally thyroxine (T_4) and triiodothyronine (T_3), that regulate the rate of metabolism and affect the growth and rate of function of many other systems in the body. The hormone calcitonin is also produced and controls calcium blood levels. Iodine is necessary for the production of both hormones. Hyperthyroidism (overactive thyroid) and hypothyroidism (underactive thyroid) are the most common problems of the thyroid gland.

Diseases of the thyroid gland

Hyper- and hypofunction (affects about 2% of the population):

- Hypothyroidism (underactivity)
  - Hashimoto's thyroiditis / thyroiditis
  - Ord's thyroiditis
  - Postoperative hypothyroidism
  - Postpartum thyroiditis
  - Silent thyroiditis
  - Acute thyroiditis
  - Iatrogenic hypothyroidism
- Hyperthyroidism (overactivity)
  - Thyroid storm
  - Graves-Basedow disease
  - Toxic thyroid nodule
  - Toxic nodular struma (Plummer's disease)
  - Hashitoxicosis
  - Iatrogenic hyperthyroidism
  - De Quervain thyroiditis (inflammation starting as hyperthyroidism, can end as hypothyroidism)

Anatomical problems:

- Goitre
  - Endemic goitre
  - Diffuse goitre
  - Multinodular goitre
- Lingual thyroid
- Thryoglossal duct cyst

Tumors:

- Thyroid adenoma
- Thyroid cancer
  - Papillary

- Follicular
- Medullary
- Anaplastic
- <u>Lymphomas</u> and <u>metastasis</u> from elsewhere (rare)

Deficiencies:
- <u>Cretinism</u>

{ME AGAIN}

It would be difficult to even make a comprehensive list of all the things that the pituitary can do to you. Here's a short list:

- Blurred or no vision

- Hyperactive or underactive sexual response, erectile dysfunction, impotence, infertility

- Androgen deficiencies that result in lack of testosterone and effeminate men, homosexual tendencies

- Hyperactive or underactive andrenaline/fear response

- Sluggishness or hyperactivity, heart rate, blood pressure, blood sugar, suppressed immune system

- Tumors and cancers of all sorts, unusual hair growth

- Headaches, Nausea, Muscle Pain, Skin coloration, Osteoporosis, Allergic responses

- Depression, Mood swings, Anger, Fear, Flight responses, Bipolar and other brain chemical effects – in extreme cases, suicidal thoughts

- Eating disorders: Anorexia, Obesity, Bulimia, Weight Gain

- Loss of memory, loss of sleep, lethargy, weakness in limbs

- Controls growth of limbs, features or whole body – That means extreme attractiveness that will wreck your life or extreme disfigurement that will wreck your life.

- Controls development of mental function – Either extreme intelligence that wrecks your life or cretinism that wrecks your life

- Affects absorption of food and minerals to fuel body

- Menstrual functions and pregnancy functions suppressed or increased or irregular. Can abort babies.

- *And probably lots of other things that aren't even commonly diagnosed as a problem, like overactive sexual response. Who's going to get treated for that, unless it's an extreme health risk? But it's still a serious danger to the effective walk of a Christian! The website says one in FIVE people have a pituitary tumor. And that's just the ones that are diagnosable!*

Now, wouldn't you say that that about covers all the bases? If the enemy could gain control of **that** thing and it only took a FEW CELLS in the wrong place to whack it out, you could do some real damage to a person. Think of it like this. If your body were a nuclear power plant, that is the control center. They don't call it the "Master Gland" for nothing. From that point, every part of the body can be influenced and there are

MASSIVE impacts on self-esteem and all kinds of potential spiritual affects!

If a demon could get access to that, it would have to be really smart, but it could really wreck havoc on a person, that's for sure! Since we see Christians all over the place suffering from the things on the list above, we need to come to the conclusion that either disease is just a natural part of life or it has a spiritual demonic component that can be addressed as well. America has to be the most Pituitarily oppressed country on the planet. I don't know the stats, but we've got all of that stuff on the list RAMPANT here! Why? Maybe this book will help explain it.

Not only is it a physical hub, but this is practically dead center in the middle of your skull. Right behind the optic nerve, under the brain. Essentially, this is the "Holy of Holies" of your head! All of Israel was affected by what happened in that tiny little inner room in the Temple. If the High Priest was sacrificing wrong (or not at all), the whole nation went sour. That tiny little room was the filter through which commands came from God to the whole nation. If the high priest mangled it or acted as a "dirty filter" and put his own spin on it, the whole nation could be affected.

Ahab was the brain and the Hypothalamus, but Jezebel could coopt or mangle any messages that came from him, or send out some of her own under his authority. Jezebel was that little filter through which messages came from the king. She wasn't supposed to have any authority of her own, but she stepped into the flow and redirected it any way she wanted to. In our bodies this tiny little gland is the filter through which chemical messages come from the brain and hypothalamus and go out to the whole body. If this little gland wants to be difficult it can totally wreck a person's life!

The Bible says that the life is in the blood and the "Endocrine glands release their secretions directly into the blood."

> **Leviticus 17:11** – *For the life of a creature is in the blood, and I have given it to you to make atonement for yourselves on the altar; it is the blood that makes atonement for one's life.* (See also, Leviticus 17:14 and Deuteronomy 12:23)

Wouldn't you think that **that** would be a great place for satan to attack? It affects everything!

Are you getting this? If a Christian is on fire and doing great, just a tiny tweak to the Pituitary and they'll get high blood pressure or lethargy or headaches or anger or decreased (or hyperactivated) sexual response. Go back and look at all the great warriors of God that were taken out of the game, either by death or by falling, and I'll bet you can trace LOTS of them back to the Pituitary problems in one way or another.

If we don't actively guard this gate and the enemy gets a foothold, this one little pea-sized piece of flesh can wreck your whole life. A lot of the diseases whose symptoms we are treating are really Pituitary problems!

Ok, so the Lord said that the Jezebel was "ported" up on the Pituitary. I'm certainly seeing why it would be a great place to be. Did you ever see the movie "Men in Black"? Remember when they caught that one alien and his head popped open and the real "Prince of the Universe" they were after was a teeny, tiny, little helpless thing sitting at a control station operating the levers of the outer robot body? That's a great picture of the Jezebel.

Now if you're still reading this, you're either getting ammunition to lock me in the loony farm or you actually do believe that God talks to people and that some people can see demons. Either way, I'm just going to let it all hang out and trust God to sort it out. If you're planning to do something to try to slow me down, I would strongly recommend you read Acts 5:38-39 first. If I'm right, my Dad is really big and He's not going to like you taking potshots at His kids. If I'm wrong, He's perfectly capable of disciplining His kids without your help. I would suggest you be VERY careful.

Once I knew where to look, I began to very carefully "scan" people that were showing all the signs and to look very carefully and very specifically at that little spot in the middle of their head. At first I didn't see anything. The demons I usually see (on their head or shoulder or heart, etc.) are at least as big as baseballs (and sometimes like grizzly bears!). The Lord said, "Zoom in." So I sort of dialed in tighter on the target more and more until I could finally see a tiny, little black squiggle right in the center of their head in the Pituitary. (Now, just so we're clear, by "see" I mean seeing in the <u>spirit</u>, not in the natural. Some people see demons with their eyes in the "natural," but to date I haven't.)

It is just a tiny little worm, practically microscopic! It doesn't have an odor, it doesn't make a sound, it doesn't move around much. Unless you went looking for it and saw in the spirit <u>really</u> well AND knew where to look, I doubt anybody would ever see it. No teeth or defenses of any kind. It's just a tiny little brain, but no brawn. So small you can't even really reach in and get ahold of it (with the hand of the spirit). But it's REALLY nasty and really sneaky and really smart. It's main job is to take whatever signal is coming from the brain and turn it to the left or right, sometimes a little, sometimes a lot. Whatever it takes to cause maximum loss of peace and joy and victory, but hopefully not enough for anyone to even notice that it's there. I think it's only in the last couple of decades that the medical field is even paying much attention to the Pituitary at all! It's been pretty much hidden until this time. And I think it's been spiritually hidden until this time. But now I see it and the Lord taught me all about it and how to get rid of it.

So now its time is running out. Praise God!!

WHERE DID THE JEZEBEL COME FROM AND WHO HAS ONE?

At first I just began to see all of the reasons why this made perfect sense. That is the perfect place for it to hide and the most dangerous warriors are not the big, obvious, brawny ones, but the tiny, smart, hidden ones. Then I began to ask the Lord, "So what is this thing? Where did it come from?" That's when I started to get some really surprising answers that make PERFECT sense to me. We'll see if they make sense to you or not.

In response to my question, the Lord replied, "It's the seed of the snake."

"Ok, well, what snake? "

"The snake in the Garden of Eden."

"OH! Ok, so it's like snake-sperm. That makes sense. So how did it get there?" I said.

"When Eve listened to and received from the snake, he implanted it. He said, "Well, God really didn't meant THAT exactly." And she bought it. When the Bible is mangled and turned a little to the left or right and it's received, it makes room for the snake to leave his seed. Then Eve spread it to Adam and he received it. And everyone since then has had one."

"Whoa there!! Everybody has one?! I've got one?"

"Yep. You were born with one, but it didn't get active until you hit the age of accountability. It is that thing in you that always wants to twist and turn the messages from the head and make them more palateable or self-serving."

"OK, so how do I get it out! I don't want that thing in there messing with me! I don't want it! Can I just reach in and grab it and cast it out?"

"Nope. You can't grab it, it's too small. What do you do with a tiny irritant? You make a pearl. Just pray the Blood of Jesus around it until you make a pearl, then grab ahold of it, pull it out and call up an angel to take it to the Abyss. Don't cast it into dry places – it will just come right back. And don't throw it at the Abyss – it will boomerang. That port is magnetically charged and will try to suck it back. You have to hand it to an angel and they will take it to the Abyss. Then flood the whole area with the Blood of Jesus and make sure your cup is full."

If you've already decided that I'm wrong and full of it, then stop reading and keep on doing whatever you're doing now in your walk with God. I hope it's working for you. I love you no matter what.

If you've decided that I might actually be onto something, then keep reading and just know that your gifts will operate in proportion to your faith. If you believe, you're more likely to see results. Faith like a child is best of all.

Well, so here's the thing. In order to really be sure that you got this thing out of somebody, you need to be able to see in the spirit really well AND you need to hear God's voice really well AND you need to have authority to call up angels to help (and preferably see them, too) AND you need to have spiritual authority to cast demons straight to the Abyss. Pretty much everybody I've ever met doesn't have all of those. Some people don't even believe in some of those. That makes it pretty darn difficult to find somebody to actually help you get a Jezebel out (unless God shows you some other way to do it, which I would love to hear about). And keeping it out is even harder.

If you believe that God can impart spiritual gifts through others, then consider that physical proximity doesn't make any difference in the spiritual realms and ask the Lord if He's ready for you to receive this:

> **Lord, I offer up everything you've ever given me toward the upbuilding and equipping of Your Body. Those who are reading this who believe in faith and can receive and are ready, please give them whatever you gave me. Whatever I have, they are welcome to drink in, even if I don't get it back. I trust You, Lord. Give them Discernment of Spirits, give them Wisdom, give them authority over the demons that confront them and give them Fear of the Lord. In proportion to their faith and Your willingness and perfect will. Let them see the bad guys real clearly. In the name of Jesus, Amen.**

CAN YOU GET IT OUT?

Yes and no.

It's not just a matter of removing it. When the Lord first showed us how to handle it and get it out, I was thrilled. I understood how nasty this thing was and really believed that if you could pull out the nerve center, the "command and control" structure, you could get the upper hand on all of it. While I still had things that the Lord was crucifying in me, at the time I thought I was demon-free until the Lord showed me the Jezebel. *(Then a year later showed us the Psyphon!)*

We had a handful of folks in our fellowship that were walking in obedience (to the best of their knowledge) and had great big cups of Jesus and we pulled the Jezebel out of them. (It's pretty much worthless to try to pull one out of someone that isn't really, REALLY trying to let God direct all their paths.) For some of them it wasn't particularly outwardly noticeable that much changed. They had already put up defenses and contained its influence pretty well. For some of them it made a dramatic difference nearly instantly. It did result in an amazing clarity of communication with God and a very interference-free walk.

But ... within a few hours it was back! Not the same demon that had been cast to the Abyss, but another Jezebel nonetheless. You see, if there is a void in that port, even if it's covered with the Blood of Jesus, we can still invite it back in the same way Eve did. The first time that God says to do something and we do it 99% right, we've mangled the message from the Head and gone our own way – and made room for the Jezebel again! It was getting really frustrating. For people VERY sensitive to the spiritual realms and who see the enemy in all their various forms and are constantly checking each other so each can stay "clean" before God, it's a pretty distressing thing to have this little worm keep coming back all the time and mangling up what God is trying to do through you.

Eventually we learned to just immobilize it by binding it up and putting a pearl around it and maintaining it. You could actually go longer by doing that, than by constantly pulling it out. That gets pretty frustrating but was the way the Lord did it with us so that I would get really hot to find a permanent solution. One evening we were having a prayer meeting and one of the prophets present heard very clearly from the Lord that we had an open heaven and could each ask for anything and He would answer. I know God is not a "wishing well" and He would never offer unless He knew we were going to pray His will anyway, but it was still a really big deal. At the time there were lots of things pressing in on me. I could have prayed for restoration of my family, my business, solutions to money problems or any of several other things that were pretty severe, heavy issues at that moment. I believe that if I had prayed for a billion dollars, He would have done it somehow. But my goal is always to have maximum impact on the kingdom in eternal ways and this Jezebel thing was killing me. So I asked that the Lord would show me a permanent solution to the Jezebel problem.

Later that night the Lord began showing me the theory behind the Jezebel and the need for a replacement in that port of something that would reverse the polarity of all the ports and would block it so the Jezebel couldn't come back. Simultaneously, across town, brother Chris who wasn't at the meeting and had no idea what had happened or what I had prayed, was getting revelation from God about the mechanics of how exactly to go about the Jezebel replacement! The next morning we came together at the furniture store as usual and he had to tell me right away what the Lord had shown him – and that the Lord said I would have the missing pieces. When we compared notes, it all fit together perfectly. It was a double-check and verification that it was God speaking and it was an equipping of the two of us who were then prepared to try it out on each other. (I don't think you can self-deliver permanently of the Jezebel. At least I haven't seen it so far.)

Basically, it works like this. Imagine if you had a negatively charged brain (CPU) in a computer and so all the ports were negatively charged. (I know it doesn't really work like that, just play along.) You could put a cover over each of the ports and defend it against negative things "porting up" there, but it will be a constant battle. In order to really deal with it long-term, you have to replace the negatively charged CPU with a positively charged one. Then all the ports will put out a positive charge and attract the right kind of things to them – and repel the wrong ones.

A sister that knows absolutely nothing about computers was totally baffled when I used that analogy, so she gave me a simpler one. She said, "So it's like if you have a black light bulb that attracts bad bugs, you just unscrew it and replace it with a white light bulb that doesn't attract them." Yep. That's pretty much it. You need to replace the darkness with light.

OK, but what do we use to replace it and where do we get it? The revelation I was given that night was that we need to do a permanent replacement to keep the port plugged once and for all and that the Jezebel is the seed of the snake in the Garden of Eden – the worm from the apple of the Tree of the Knowledge of Good and Evil, if you will. It constantly wants us to do something – anything – other than fully and completely obey God all the way. This seed from the Tree of the Knowledge of Good and Evil has to be replaced with a seed from the Tree of Life.

While the Lord was telling me all of that, across town He was explaining to Chris how to actually do it. The Lord amplified on the previous instruction about how to remove the Jezebel. In this case, you would call up two angels and one would come with the necessary tool to grab and remove the Jezebel after you had covered it in the Blood of Jesus and made a pearl, then that angel would take it directly the Abyss. The second angel would come with a tiny pinpoint of light. A little pulsing nugget of pure brightness. This is a sliver of the Morning Star, a seed from the Tree of Life, a chunk of pure Love, a tear of Jesus. However you want to think of it, it's a really good thing! Then you would insert it into the port where the Jezebel was, cover it in the Blood and "reboot" the system. Basically, just dial them up really bright until you could see the light coming out of all their "ports". Preferably, you would have already cleaned them off before doing this, but if you hadn't, the light would blast everything off anyway and incinerate it.

Then it's just a matter of them keeping their light dialed up bright and keeping their cup full of Jesus.

But there's just one thing. You can't do this without permission from the Lord – it's God doing it anyway, not you – and He seems to only allow it on someone who has a REALLY, REALLY big cup of Jesus and a lid and a seal. That is, someone who is already very refined and purified and mature and sacrificially seeking Him. They better be REALLY serious.

Part of the reason for this is that, after the Jezebel replacement, if you turn your back and walk away, after having tasted that Light, things are going to go VERY badly for you. I think that is what Paul talked about when he said that those who have tasted the fullness of the Holy Spirit and turned away there is no sacrifice remaining for them. (Hebrews 6:4) I know it's possible to turn your Light off because the Lord had a sister here do it (showed her a big "Off" button), but it resulted in her being nearly **immediately** swarmed with every imaginable demon and pretty much no way to fight them off. Had she not been able to get help quickly, it would have gone very badly. We had to deliver her of things I had never even seen before! (Which was kind of part of the plan, because right after that we needed to have seen them to free someone else and know what to look for.) I believe that without intervention she would have been hallucinating and suicidal and totally freaked out in short order. As it was, she was only able to get by because she has faced a lot of badness in the past and could take every thought captive until she could get help. But we were on the outer fringes of her capacity to deal with it much longer. Please make a mental note: **DO NOT HIT THE OFF BUTTON!**

I don't know how to separate this out from all the other stuff He showed us about the "cups" and getting a bigger cup and crucifying the YOU in your cup so that more Jesus will fit. Basically, the Lord has raised up people here that can see how big your cup is and what's in it. When your cup reaches a certain size then you get a lid and get sealed, God will not allow the Jezebel replacement until then. (Maybe He'll allow it other times, maybe we're not seeing all the possibilities. I'm perfectly willing to admit that. He is in constant flux in the teaching He is doing in me and, since He makes the rules, He can decide on the exceptions.) I think some of it has to do with needing a "containment system" that can keep the "singularity" in.

There was a period of time where I knew the Jezebel was there, I could feel it messing with me, but we hadn't been told how to do a permanent replacement. During that time, I was constantly self-delivering of the Jezebel, but it didn't seem to last more than a few hours. So I just gave up and started binding the Jezebel and wrapping it in a "pearl" of the Blood of Jesus and that would buy me six to eight hours of clarity without any interference. I could tell when it had "eaten" through the pearl pretty immediately.

I really feel like I have to write this, but I know that it doesn't sound good. I'm not sure what advice to offer except that you get as big a cup of Jesus, as fast as you possibly can. And I doubt you understand the scale on which God works. You don't need twice as big a cup – God works in scales of hundreds of decimal places! Lay down everything and drink in Jesus in as big a measure as you can. Hold nothing back and seek Him only. Give sacrificially and pour yourself out and your cup will grow really fast. He will show you how to resist the Jezebel or bind it and when the time is right, He'll send somebody to remove it (or do it Himself). When your cup hits maximum size, He'll slap a lid on it, crimp it down and put His seal on you (like on the rock on the tomb of Jesus). Read Deuteronomy 19 and ask the Lord to explain it to you. (Basically this whole planet is a tent full of dead bodies and He needs somebody that's going to stay clean, even if they're in the tent. You can't get the other people clean if you're unclean all the time.)

At this point, there are VERY few people on the planet that have had the Jezebel removed (as a percentage of the population). I know it's happening elsewhere or by some other means, because I've met some that already had a white light bulb and I didn't do it. I can tell you that my walk with Christ changed dramatically from that moment and I heard Him a lot better and with less interference and it's been a lot easier to keep the badness from interfering. I think it's a requirement for anybody that wants to be fully equipped or to lead, but it's not something that can be done haphazardly. I know that we can equip people to see the Jezebels and deal with them – because I've seen people raised up from scratch for that by impartation of the gift of discernment of spirits that God has given us. But it also requires authority and wisdom and knowledge and faith – and not everybody is ready to have the replacement done. Only those who have been stretched to the maximum and have very little of them left in their cup are ready. How exactly you explain that to somebody, I'm still working on. Up to this point it's just been easier to not talk about it at all. (I know how crazy this sounds, but I don't have a choice to hold it in anymore evidently.)

I explained the cups and the lid and the seal and the Jezebel and the white light bulb and all this to a Nazarene pastor friend of mine and he totally got it. In fact, he said, "That's the purest description of Wesleyan holiness I've ever heard!" All I know is what God taught me. I've never read anything of John Wesley's, but I'm aware of the holiness teaching. What I've come to understand is that what I'm talking about with the lids and the seals and the white light bulb is the Baptism of Fire and sanctification. It's the same thing, but I'm seeing the mechanisms behind the scenes instead of just the outward effects. (Which is typical because I want to dig under the rock and see what's going on, not just see what everybody else sees.) And I'm seeing the fruit of it because we got folks around here that are RADICALLY different and walking in holiness because of this process and the Jezebel replacement. They have all the indications of having got the Baptism of Fire that some of the old-school churches preached (and Jesus promises).

When you are stretched enough and cleaned out enough and enough of you is dead and you have a big enough cup of Jesus, He will put a lid on you that will help you keep your cup very cleaned out from then on. That's what they called Sanctification. Now I know that it's not necessarily permanent. The enemy can crack it or jam wedges under the lid or you can let things in. (I'm not saying you'll never sin again.) But it's a LOT easier to walk in holiness and stay clean before the Lord. But you still have to contend with your own fallen nature – and that's the Jezebel. When the fire of God comes in the form of that "Lovebug" – that seed from the Tree of Life, that singularity of pure white flame of Love, that sliver of the Morning Star, that tear of Jesus, whatever you want to call it – and replaces and burns out the Jezebel port and fills you with His fire, then everything about your walk changes! The enemy loses command and control and the Holy Spirit takes over. From then on, it's an obedience walk and a matter of daily hearing Him and keeping your light burning bright. Everything starts to make more sense and your sacrificial love for the Brethren takes on a freakish dimension that's beyond human nature. I really believe that the Lord has shown me the mechanics of how to operationally and procedurally help people get to and through the Baptism of Fire that we were promised. (Matt. 3:11, Luke 3:16) You'd think that would be important, wouldn't you?

I know I left a lot of questions unanswered. The whole issue intersects with the "Cup Model" and an understanding of their maximum cup size and their preparedness for the Jezebel replacement. I haven't been allowed to fully write about that yet, so you'll just have to work it out with God. Ask Him what you have to do to be ready for the replacement. If I can help, let me know.

(fotm@fellowshipofthemartyrs.com)

It's really better to work it out with Him anyway, because I don't want you leaning on MY understanding! And the LAST thing I want is to direct anyone's paths. That's His job - and I'm glad of it!

But I can say this that I believe will be helpful. I have repeatedly been in congregations or small groups where I really felt like the speaker had a word from the Lord and was preaching important stuff, but I could see the spirits on the people keep them from hearing and acting on the message given. In nearly all occasions, when a person fails to make a decision for Christ, it's because of the Jezebel and the Fear. Those two work together to lie to them, to twist the truth ("You already prayed that. You can do it at home. You don't need that." etc.) and to make them afraid to go up ("You'll look weird. God might call you to Africa. Your friends will laugh at you." etc). Any leader of the Body would do really well to have their spiritual warriors and intercessors actively binding the Fear and the Jezebel in the whole audience. I have seen the same group of people sit like bumps on a log and do nothing – and then be all on their knees or their faces after binding up all the Jezebels and the Fears in the room. There are certainly others, like Pride, that will mess with a person, but those two are the most likely culprit when someone can't repent or make a decision for Christ.

Father, please grease this down with the Holy Spirit and let it settle into people's hearts as You intend for it. If there is anything here that wasn't You, please scrub it out of our memories and don't let it bring division into the Body. I accept responsibility for anything that wasn't pure. Please, Abba, please just teach each person to watch for this demon and show them how to combat it in themselves and in others. Please just help us all get free of this monster. Whatever it takes. We love You, Lord. We trust You. Please help us to understand what You're saying through all of this. Help us to walk in Your ways so that we aren't susceptible to this stuff anymore. Please be God in whatever way You want to. In the mighty Name of Jesus, Amen.

More about the Cups -

www.FellowshipOfTheMartyrs.com/pdf/rain.pdf

2 Kings 9:36-37 – *They went back and told Jehu, who said, "This is the word of the Lord that he spoke through his servant Elijah the Tishbite: On the plot of ground at Jezreel dogs will devour Jezebel's flesh. Jezebel's body will be like refuse on the ground in the plot at Jezreel, so that no one will be able to say, "This is Jezebel."*

Lord, make it so – and soon. I want to see this nasty thing destroyed for good! Amen.

APPENDIX D

Links and Resources

Paul Norcross
Books and Seminars and Resources on Curses, Hearing God,
Kingdom Living, and others
http://www.kingdomfaith.org

Spiritual Tuneup
http://www.fellowshipofthemartyrs.com/spritual_tuneup.htm

Hear God
http://fellowshipofthemartyrs.com/hear_the_voice_of_god.htm

The Apology to the World
http://fellowshipofthemartyrs.com/apology_to_the_world.htm

The Red Dragon Book
http://www.fellowshipofthemartyrs.com/red_dragon.htm

Rain Down NOW, Lord!
http://www.fellowshipofthemartyrs.com/rain_down_now.htm

Do It Yourself City Church Restoration
http://www.fellowshipofthemartyrs.com/pdf/diycitychurch.pdf

Who Neutered the Holy Spirit?!
http://www.fellowshipofthemartyrs.com/neutered.htm

The Church of Liberty –
the first Pre-Denominational Church in America
http://www.TheChurchOfLiberty.com

To reach Fellowship of the Martyrs

Mail: FOTM, c/o Doug Perry
118 N. Conistor, #B251,
Liberty, MO 64068

www.FellowshipOfTheMartyrs.com
fotm@fellowshipofthemartyrs.com

To donate mail to the address above or PayPal to
fotm@fellowshipofthemartyrs.com

Below is the link to a massive website with lots of info.
We're not endorsing or not endorsing them.
It's just a place with LOTS of specifics that you may find helpful.
I know they've got Jesus in them, so they're part of the Body and
we love them, even if we disagree with them on something.
(Which I'm sure I do on something.)
www.DemonBuster.com

WHAT'S IN YOUR CUP?

 Got No Jesus? Then you had better get Him soon!

 Got Lots of Sin? He really doesn't like being in there with it. Better turn.

 Got A Little Sin? That's still not victory, is it?

 **Got No Rest?** Life can shake you up. Prayer can sort it out.

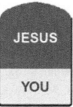 **Got Lots of Jesus?** Only walking in HOLINESS means peace and joy and victory!.

 **Got Less of You?** He must increase and YOU must decrease.

Got a BIG Cup of Jesus?

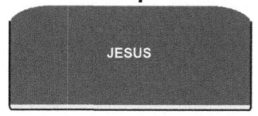

Better keep it full EVERY DAY or the red stuff will come crush you! It's a DAILY walk! Never forget that.

If you already are one of these, then what are you doing for the Kingdom and how can I help? The prayer of a righteous man is powerful and effective.

Which One ARE You Today?
Which One Do You WANT To Be?

(Which one's prayers do think God answers the best?)

www.Fellowship Of The Martyrs.com

APPENDIX F

Verses about Witchcraft, Sorcery, Divination, Curses, Abyss, Demon, Unclean Spirit, Evil Spirit, etc.

These are just the references, please go look them up in context. Not comprehensive, but sufficient.

Genesis 3:14 - And the LORD God said unto the serpent, Because thou hast done this, thou art **cursed** above all cattle, and above every beast of the field; upon thy belly shalt thou go, and dust shalt thou eat all the days of thy life:

Exodus 7:22 (NIV) - But the Egyptian magicians did the same things by their **secret arts**, and Pharaoh's heart became hard; he would not listen to Moses and Aaron, just as the Lord had said.

Exodus 8:7 (NIV) - But the magicians [Jannes and Jambres] did the same things by their **secret arts**; they also made frogs come up on the land of Egypt.

Exodus 8:18 (NIV) But when the magicians tried to produce gnats by their **secret arts**, they could not. And the gnats were on men and animals.

Exodus 22:18 - Thou shalt not suffer a **witch** to live.

Leviticus 17:7 - And they shall no more offer their sacrifices unto **devils**, after whom they have gone a whoring. This shall be a statute for ever unto them throughout their generations.

Leviticus 19:26 (NIV) ... "Do not practice **divination** or **sorcery**."

Leviticus 19:31 - Regard not them that have **familiar** spirits, neither seek after wizards, to be defiled by them: I am the LORD your God.
Leviticus 20:6 - And the soul that turneth after such as have **familiar** spirits, and after wizards, to go a whoring after them, I will even set my face against that soul, and will cut him off from among his people.

Leviticus 20:9 - For every one that curseth his father or his mother shall be surely put to death: he hath **cursed** his father or his mother; his blood shall be upon him.

Leviticus 20:27 - A man also or woman that hath a **familiar** spirit, or that is a wizard, shall surely be put to death: they shall stone them with stones: their blood shall be upon them.

Leviticus 24:11 - And the Israelitish woman's son blasphemed the name of the Lord, and **cursed**. And they brought him unto Moses: (and his mother's name was Shelomith, the daughter of Dibri, of the tribe of Dan:)

Leviticus 24:14 - Bring forth him that hath **cursed** without the camp; and let all that heard him lay their hands upon his head, and let all the congregation stone him.

Leviticus 24:23 - And Moses spake to the children of Israel, that they should bring forth him that had **cursed** out of the camp, and stone him with stones. And the children of Israel did as the LORD commanded Moses.

Numbers 22:6 - Come now therefore, I pray thee, **curse** me this people; for they are too mighty for me: peradventure I shall prevail, that we may smite them, and that I may drive them out of the land: for I wot that he whom thou blessest is blessed, and he whom thou cursest is **cursed**.

Numbers 22:7 - And the elders of Moab and the elders of Midian departed with the rewards of **divination** in their hand; and they came unto Balaam, and spake unto him the words of Balak.

Numbers 23:8 - How shall I **curse**, whom God hath not **cursed**? or how shall I defy, whom the LORD hath not defied?

Numbers 23:23 - Surely there is no enchantment against Jacob, neither is there any **divination** against Israel: according to this time it shall be said of Jacob and of Israel, What hath God wrought!

Deuteronomy 32:17 - They sacrificed unto **devils**, not to God; to gods whom they knew not, to new gods that came newly up, whom your fathers feared not.

Deuteronomy 7:26 - Neither shalt thou bring an **abomination** into thine house, lest thou be a **cursed** thing like it: but thou shalt utterly detest it, and thou shalt utterly abhor it; for it is a **cursed** thing.

Deuteronomy 13:17 - And there shall cleave nought of the **cursed** thing to thine hand: that the LORD may turn from the fierceness of his anger, and shew thee mercy, and have compassion upon thee, and multiply thee, as he hath sworn unto thy fathers;

Deuteronomy 18:10 - There shall not be found among you any one that maketh his son or his daughter to **pass through the fire** *{ritual or human sacrifice}*, or that useth **divination**, or an **observer of times** *{astrologer}*, or an **enchanter**, or a **witch**.

Deuteronomy 18:11 - Or a **charmer**, or a **consulter with familiar spirits**, or a **wizard**, or a **necromancer**.

Deuteronomy 21:23 - His body shall not remain all night upon the tree, but thou shalt in any wise bury him that day; (for he that is hanged is **accursed** of God;) that thy land be not defiled, which the LORD thy God giveth thee for an inheritance.

Deuteronomy 27:15 - **Cursed** be the man that maketh any graven or molten image, an **abomination** unto the LORD, the work of the hands of the craftsman, and putteth it in a secret place. And all the people shall answer and say, Amen.

Deuteronomy 27:17 - **Cursed** be he that removeth his neighbour's landmark. And all the people shall say, Amen.

Deuteronomy 27:18 - **Cursed** be he that maketh the blind to wander out of the way. And all the people shall say, Amen.

Deuteronomy 27:19 - **Cursed** be he that perverteth the judgment of the stranger, fatherless, and widow. And all the people shall say, Amen.

Deuteronomy 27:20 - **Cursed** be he that lieth with his father's wife; because he uncovereth his father's skirt. And all the people shall say, Amen.

Deuteronomy 27:21 - **Cursed** be he that lieth with any manner of beast. And all the people shall say, Amen.

Deuteronomy 27:22 - **Cursed** be he that lieth with his sister, the daughter of his father, or the daughter of his mother. And all the people shall say, Amen.

Deuteronomy 27:23 - **Cursed** be he that lieth with his mother in law. And all the people shall say, Amen.

Deuteronomy 27:24 - **Cursed** be he that smiteth his neighbour secretly. And all the people shall say, Amen.

Deuteronomy 27:25 - **Cursed** be he that taketh reward to slay an innocent person. And all the people shall say, Amen.

Deuteronomy 27:26 - **Cursed** be he that confirmeth not all the words of this law to do them. And all the people shall say, Amen.

{If you don't carefully obey the Lord your God in times of prosperity, then:}

Deuteronomy 28:16 - **Cursed** shalt thou be in the city, and **cursed** shalt thou be in the field.

Deuteronomy 28:17 - **Cursed** shall be thy basket and thy store.

Deuteronomy 28:18 - **Cursed** shall be the fruit of thy body, and the fruit of thy land, the increase of thy kine, and the flocks of thy sheep.

Deuteronomy 28:19 - **Cursed** shalt thou be when thou comest in, and **cursed** shalt thou be when thou goest out.

Joshua 6:18 - And ye, in any wise keep yourselves from the **accursed** thing, lest ye make yourselves **accursed**, when ye take of the **accursed** thing, and make the camp of Israel a **curse**, and trouble it.

Joshua 6:26 - And Joshua adjured them at that time, saying, **Cursed** be the man before the LORD, that riseth up and buildeth this city Jericho: he shall lay the foundation thereof in his firstborn, and in his youngest son shall he set up the gates of it. {And it worked just like that.}

Joshua 7:1 - But the children of Israel committed a trespass in the **accursed** thing: for Achan, the son of Carmi, the son of Zabdi, the son of Zerah, of the tribe of Judah, took of the **accursed** thing: and the anger of the LORD was kindled against the children of Israel.

Joshua 7:11 - Israel hath sinned, and they have also transgressed my covenant which I commanded them: for they have even taken of the **accursed** thing, and have also stolen, and dissembled also, and they have put it even among their own stuff.

Joshua 7:12 - Therefore the children of Israel could not stand before their enemies, but turned their backs before their enemies, because they were **accursed**: neither will I be with you any more, except ye destroy the **accursed** from among you.

Joshua 7:13 - Up, sanctify the people, and say, Sanctify yourselves against to morrow: for thus saith the LORD God of Israel, There is an **accursed** thing in the midst of thee, O Israel: thou canst not stand before thine enemies, until ye take away the **accursed** thing from among you.

Joshua 7:15 - And it shall be, that he that is taken with the **accursed** thing shall be burnt with fire, he and all that he hath: because he hath transgressed the covenant of the LORD, and because he hath wrought folly in Israel.

Joshua 13:22 (NIV) In addition to those slain in battle, the Israelites had put to the sword Balaam son of Beor, who practiced divination.

Joshua 22:20 - Did not Achan the son of Zerah commit a trespass in the **accursed** thing, and wrath fell on all the congregation of Israel? and that man perished not alone in his iniquity.

Judges 9:23 - Then God sent an **evil spirit** between Abimelech and the men of Shechem; and the men of Shechem dealt treacherously with Abimelech:

1 Samuel 15:23 - For rebellion is as the sin of **witchcraft**, and stubbornness is as iniquity and **idolatry**. Because thou hast rejected the word of the LORD, he hath also rejected thee from being king.

1 Samuel 16:14 - But the Spirit of the LORD departed from Saul, and an **evil spirit** from the LORD troubled him.

1 Samuel 16:15 - And Saul's servants said unto him, Behold now, an **evil spirit** from God troubleth thee.

1 Samuel 16:16 - Let our lord now command thy servants, which are before thee, to seek out a man, who is a cunning player on an harp: and it shall come to pass, when the **evil spirit** from God is upon thee, that he shall play with his hand, and thou shalt be well.

1 Samuel 16:23 - And it came to pass, when the **evil spirit** from God was upon Saul, that David took an harp, and played with his hand: so Saul was refreshed, and was well, and the **evil spirit** departed from him.
1 Samuel 18:10 - And it came to pass on the morrow, that the **evil spirit** from God came upon Saul, and he prophesied in the midst of the house: and David played with his hand, as at other times: and there was a javelin in Saul's hand.

1 Samuel 19:9 - And the **evil spirit** from the LORD was upon Saul, as he sat in his house with his javelin in his hand: and David played with his hand.

1 Samuel 28:3 - Now Samuel was dead, and all Israel had lamented him, and buried him in Ramah, even in his own city. And Saul had put away those that had **familiar** spirits, and the wizards, out of the land.

1 Samuel 28:7 - Then said Saul unto his servants, Seek me a woman that hath a **familiar** spirit, that I may go to her, and enquire of her. And his servants said to him, Behold, there is a woman that hath a **familiar** spirit at Endor.

1 Samuel 28:8 - And Saul disguised himself, and put on other raiment, and he went, and two men with him, and they came to the woman by night: and he said, I pray thee, divine unto me by the **familiar** spirit, and bring me him up, whom I shall name unto thee.

1 Samuel 28:9 - And the woman said unto him, Behold, thou knowest what Saul hath done, how he hath cut off those that have **familiar** spirits, and the wizards, out of the land: wherefore then layest thou a snare for my life, to cause me to die?

2 Kings 9:22 - And it came to pass, when Joram saw Jehu, that he said, Is it peace, Jehu? And he answered, What peace, so long as the whoredoms of thy mother Jezebel and her **witchcrafts** are so many?

2 Kings 17:17 - And they caused their sons and their daughters to **pass through the fire**, and used **divination** and **enchantments**, and **sold themselves to do evil** in the sight of the LORD, to provoke him to anger.

2 Kings 21:6 - And he made his son **pass through the fire**, and **observed times**, and **used enchantments**, and dealt with **familiar spirits** and **wizards**: he wrought much wickedness in the sight of the LORD, to provoke him to anger.

2 Kings 23:24 - Moreover the workers with **familiar spirits**, and the **wizards**, and the **images**, and the **idols**, and all the **abominations** that were spied in the land of Judah and in Jerusalem, did Josiah put away, that he might perform the words of the law which were written in the book that Hilkiah the priest found in the house of the LORD.

1 Chronicles 2:7 - And the sons of Carmi; Achar, the troubler of Israel, who transgressed in the thing **accursed**.

1 Chronicles 10:13 - So Saul died for his transgression which he committed against the LORD, even against the word of the LORD, which he kept not, and also for asking counsel of one that had a **familiar spirit**, to enquire of it;

2 Chronicles 11:15 - And he ordained him priests for the high places, and for the **devils**, and for the calves which he had made.

2 Chronicles 33:6 - And he caused his children to **pass through the fire** in the valley of the son of Hinnom: also he **observed times**, and **used enchantments**, and used **witchcraft**, and **dealt with a familiar spirit**, and with **wizards**: he wrought much evil in the sight of the LORD, to provoke him to anger.

Job 1:5 - And it was so, when the days of their feasting were gone about, that Job sent and sanctified them, and rose up early in the morning, and offered burnt offerings according to the number of them all: for Job said, It may be that my sons have sinned, and **cursed** God in their hearts. Thus did Job continually.

Psalm 106:37 - Yea, they sacrificed their sons and their daughters unto **devils**,

Psalm 119:21 - Thou hast rebuked the proud that are **cursed**, which do err from thy commandments.

Isaiah 8:19 - And when they shall say unto you, Seek unto them that have **familiar spirits**, and unto **wizards** that peep, and that mutter: should not a people seek unto their God? for the living to the dead?

Isaiah 19:3 - And the spirit of Egypt shall fail in the midst thereof; and I will destroy the counsel thereof: and they shall seek to the **idols**, and to the **charmers**, and to them that have **familiar spirits**, and to the **wizards**.

Isaiah 29:4 - And thou shalt be brought down, and shalt speak out of the ground, and thy speech shall be low out of the dust, and thy voice shall be, as of one that hath a **familiar spirit**, out of the ground, and thy speech shall whisper out of the dust.

Isaiah 47:9 (NIV) Both of these will overtake you in a moment, on a single day: loss of children and widowhood. They will come upon you in full measure, in spite of your many **sorceries** and all your **potent spells**.

Isaiah 47:12 (NIV) "Keep on, then, with your **magic spells** and with your many **sorceries**, which you have labored at since childhood. Perhaps you will succeed, perhaps you will cause terror."

Isaiah 57:1-5 (NIV) "The righteous perish, and no one ponders it in his heart; devout men are taken away, and no one understands that the righteous are taken away to be spared from evil. Those who walk uprightly enter into peace; they find rest as they lie in death. But you--come here, you sons of a **sorceress**, you offspring of adulterers and prostitutes! Whom are you mocking? At whom do you sneer and stick out your tongue? Are you not a brood of *rebels,* the offspring of *liars?* You burn with lust among the oaks and under every spreading tree..."

Isaiah 57:7-8 (NIV) "You have made your bed on a high and lofty hill; there you went up to offer your sacrifices. Behind your doors and your doorposts you have put your **pagan symbols**. Forsaking me, you uncovered your bed, you climbed into it and opened it wide; you made a pact with those whose beds you love, and you looked on their nakedness."

Isaiah 57:10-12 (NIV) "You were wearied by all your *ways,* but you would not say, 'It is hopeless.' You found renewal of your strength, and so you did not faint. Whom have you so dreaded and feared that you have been false to me, and have neither remembered me nor pondered this in your hearts? Is it not because I have long been silent that you do not fear me? I will expose your righteousness and your works, and they will not benefit you."

Jeremiah 3:13 (NIV) "Only acknowledge your guilt--you have *rebelled* against the Lord your God, you have scattered your favors to foreign gods under every spreading tree, and have not obeyed me," declares the Lord.

Jeremiah 11:3 - And say thou unto them, Thus saith the LORD God of Israel; **Cursed** be the man that obeyeth not the words of this covenant,

Jeremiah 14:14 - Then the LORD said unto me, The prophets prophesy lies in my name: I sent them not, neither have I commanded them, neither spake unto them: they prophesy unto you a false vision and **divination**, and a thing of nought, and the deceit of their heart.

Jeremiah 17:5 - Thus saith the LORD; **Cursed** be the man that trusteth in man, and maketh flesh his arm, and whose heart departeth from the LORD.

Jeremiah 27:9-10 (NIV) "So do not listen to your prophets, your **diviners**, your **interpreters of dreams**, your **mediums** or your **sorcerers**... Do not let the prophets and diviners among you deceive you. Do not listen to the dreams **you** encourage them to have."

Jeremiah 48:10 - **Cursed** be he that doeth the work of the LORD deceitfully, and **cursed** be he that keepeth back his sword from blood.

Ezekiel 12:24 - For there shall be no more any vain vision nor flattering **divination** within the house of Israel.

Ezekiel 13:6 - They have seen vanity and lying **divination**, saying, The LORD saith: and the LORD hath not sent them: and they have made others to hope that they would confirm the word.

Ezekiel 13:7 - Have ye not seen a vain vision, and have ye not spoken a lying **divination**, whereas ye say, The LORD saith it; albeit I have not spoken?

Ezekiel 13:23 - Therefore ye shall see no more vanity, nor divine **divination**s: for I will deliver my people out of your hand: and ye shall know that I am the LORD.

Ezekiel 21:21 - For the king of Babylon stood at the parting of the way, at the head of the two ways, to use **divination**: he made his arrows bright, he consulted with images, he looked in the liver.

Ezekiel 21:22 - At his right hand was the **divination** for Jerusalem, to appoint captains, to open the mouth in the slaughter, to lift up the voice with shouting, to appoint battering rams against the gates, to cast a mount, and to build a fort.

Ezekiel 21:23 - And it shall be unto them as a false **divination** in their sight, to them that have sworn oaths: but he will call to remembrance the iniquity, that they may be taken.

Micah 5:12 - And I will cut off **witchcrafts** out of thine hand; and thou shalt have no more **soothsayers**:

Nahum 3:4 - Because of the multitude of the whoredoms of the wellfavoured harlot, the mistress of **witchcrafts**, that selleth nations through her whoredoms, and families through her **witchcrafts**.

Zechariah 13:2 - And it shall come to pass in that day, saith the LORD of hosts, that I will cut off the names of the idols out of the land, and they shall no more be remembered: and also I will cause the prophets and the **unclean spirit** to pass out of the land.

Malachi 2:2 - If ye will not hear, and if ye will not lay it to heart, to give glory unto my name, saith the LORD of hosts, I will even send a **curse** upon you, and I will **curse** your blessings: yea, I have **cursed** them already, because ye do not lay it to heart.

Malachi 3:5 (NIV) "So I will come near to you for judgment. I will be quick to testify against **sorcerers**, adulterers and perjurers..." says the Lord Almighty.

Malachi 3:9 - Ye are **cursed** with a curse: for ye have robbed me, even this whole nation.

Matthew 4:24 - And his fame went throughout all Syria: and they brought unto him all sick people that were taken with divers diseases and torments, and those which were possessed with **devils**, and those which were lunatick, and those that had the palsy; and he healed them.

Matthew 7:22 - Many will say to me in that day, Lord, Lord, have we not prophesied in thy name? and in thy name have cast out **devils**? and in thy name done many wonderful works?

Matthew 8:16 - When the even was come, they brought unto him many that were possessed with **devils**: and he cast out the spirits with his word, and healed all that were sick:

Matthew 8:28 - And when he was come to the other side into the country of the Gergesenes, there met him two possessed with **devils**, coming out of the tombs, exceeding fierce, so that no man might pass by that way.

Matthew 8:31 - So the **devils** besought him, saying, If thou cast us out, suffer us to go away into the herd of swine.

Matthew 8:33 - And they that kept them fled, and went their ways into the city, and told every thing, and what was befallen to the possessed of the **devils**.

Matthew 9:34 - But the Pharisees said, He casteth out **devils** through the prince of the **devils**.

Matthew 10:8 - Heal the sick, cleanse the lepers, raise the dead, cast out **devils**: freely ye have received, freely give.

Matthew 12:24 - But when the Pharisees heard it, they said, This fellow doth not cast out **devils**, but by Beelzebub the prince of the **devils**.

Matthew 12:27 - And if I by Beelzebub cast out **devils**, by whom do your children cast them out? therefore they shall be your judges.

Matthew 12:28 - But if I cast out **devils** by the Spirit of God, then the kingdom of God is come unto you.

Matthew 12:43 - When the **unclean spirit** is gone out of a man, he walketh through dry places, seeking rest, and findeth none.

Matthew 25:41 - Then shall he say also unto them on the left hand, Depart from me, ye **cursed**, into everlasting fire, prepared for the devil and his angels:

Mark 1:23 - And there was in their synagogue a man with an **unclean spirit**; and he cried out,

Mark 1:26 - And when the **unclean spirit** had torn him, and cried with a loud voice, he came out of him.

Mark 1:32 - And at even, when the sun did set, they brought unto him all that were diseased, and them that were possessed with **devils**.

Mark 1:34 - And he healed many that were sick of divers diseases, and cast out many **devils**; and suffered not the **devils** to speak, because they knew him.

Mark 1:39 - And he preached in their synagogues throughout all Galilee, and cast out **devils**.

Mark 3:15 - And to have power to heal sicknesses, and to cast out **devils**:

Mark 3:22 - And the scribes which came down from Jerusalem said, He hath Beelzebub, and by the prince of the **devils** casteth he out **devils**.

Mark 3:30 - Because they said, He hath an **unclean spirit**.

Mark 5:2 - And when he was come out of the ship, immediately there met him out of the tombs a man with an **unclean spirit**,

Mark 5:8 - For he said unto him, Come out of the man, thou **unclean spirit**.

Mark 5:12 - And all the **devils** besought him, saying, Send us into the swine, that we may enter into them.

Mark 6:13 - And they cast out many **devils**, and anointed with oil many that were sick, and healed them.

Mark 7:25 - For a certain woman, whose young daughter had an **unclean spirit**, heard of him, and came and fell at his feet:

Mark 9:38 - And John answered him, saying, Master, we saw one casting out **devils** in thy name, and he followeth not us: and we forbad him, because he followeth not us.

Mark 16:9 - Now when Jesus was risen early the first day of the week, he appeared first to Mary Magdalene, out of whom he had cast seven **devils**.

Mark 16:17 - And these signs shall follow them that believe; In my name shall they cast out **devils**; they shall speak with new tongues;

Luke 4:41 - And **devils** also came out of many, crying out, and saying, Thou art Christ the Son of God. And he rebuking them suffered them not to speak: for they knew that he was Christ.

Luke 8:2 - And certain women, which had been healed of evil spirits and infirmities, Mary called Magdalene, out of whom went seven **devils**,

Luke 8:27 - And when he went forth to land, there met him out of the city a certain man, which had **devils** long time, and ware no clothes, neither abode in any house, but in the tombs.

Luke 8:29 - (For he had commanded the **unclean spirit** to come out of the man. For oftentimes it had caught him: and he was kept bound with chains and in fetters; and he brake the bands, and was driven of the devil into the wilderness.)

Luke 8:30 - And Jesus asked him, saying, What is thy name? And he said, Legion: because many **devils** were entered into him.

Luke 8:31 - "Legion," he replied, because many demons had gone into him. And they begged him repeatedly not to order them to go into the **Abyss**.

Luke 8:33 - Then went the **devils** out of the man, and entered into the swine: and the herd ran violently down a steep place into the lake, and were choked.

Luke 8:35 - Then they went out to see what was done; and came to Jesus, and found the man, out of whom the **devils** were departed, sitting at the feet of Jesus, clothed, and in his right mind: and they were afraid.

Luke 8:36 - They also which saw it told them by what means he that was possessed of the **devils** was healed.

Luke 8:38 - Now the man out of whom the **devils** were departed besought him that he might be with him: but Jesus sent him away, saying,

Luke 9:1 - Then he called his twelve disciples together, and gave them power and authority over all **devils**, and to cure diseases.

Luke 9:42 - And as he was yet a coming, the devil threw him down, and tare him. And Jesus rebuked the **unclean spirit**, and healed the child, and delivered him again to his father.

Luke 9:49 - And John answered and said, Master, we saw one casting out **devils** in thy name; and we forbad him, because he followeth not with us.

Luke 10:17 - And the seventy returned again with joy, saying, Lord, even the **devils** are subject unto us through thy name.

Luke 11:15 - But some of them said, He casteth out **devils** through Beelzebub the chief of the **devils**.

Luke 11:18 - If Satan also be divided against himself, how shall his kingdom stand? because ye say that I cast out **devils** through Beelzebub.

Luke 11:19 - And if I by Beelzebub cast out **devils**, by whom do your sons cast them out? therefore shall they be your judges.

Luke 11:20 - But if I with the finger of God cast out **devils**, no doubt the kingdom of God is come upon you.

Luke 11:24 - When the **unclean spirit** is gone out of a man, he walketh through dry places, seeking rest; and finding none, he saith, I will return unto my house whence I came out.

Luke 13:32 - And he said unto them, Go ye, and tell that fox, Behold, I cast out **devils**, and I do cures to day and to morrow, and the third day I shall be perfected.

Acts 8:9 - But there was a certain man, called Simon, which beforetime in the same city used **sorcery**, and bewitched the people of Samaria, giving out that himself was some great one:

Acts 8:11 - And to him they had regard, because that of long time he had bewitched them with **sorceries**.

Acts 13:6 - And when they had gone through the isle unto Paphos, they found a certain **sorcerer**, a false prophet, a Jew, whose name was Barjesus:

Acts 13:8 - But Elymas the **sorcerer** (for so is his name by interpretation) withstood them, seeking to turn away the deputy from the faith.

Acts 16:16 - And it came to pass, as we went to prayer, a certain damsel possessed with a spirit of **divination** met us, which brought her masters much gain by soothsaying:

Acts 19:15 - And the **evil spirit** answered and said, Jesus I know, and Paul I know; but who are ye?

Acts 19:16 - And the man in whom the **evil spirit** was leaped on them, and overcame them, and prevailed against them, so that they fled out of that house naked and wounded.

Acts 19:19 (Jer) Some believers, too, came forward to admit in detail how they had used spells and a number of them who had practiced **magic** collected their books and made a bonfire of them in public. The value of these was calculated to be fifty thousand silver pieces.

1 Corinthians 10:20 - But I say, that the things which the Gentiles sacrifice, they sacrifice to **devils**, and not to God: and I would not that ye should have fellowship with **devils**.

1 Corinthians 10:21 - Ye cannot drink the cup of the Lord, and the cup of **devils**: ye cannot be partakers of the Lord's table, and of the table of **devils**.

1 Corinthians 12:3 - Wherefore I give you to understand, that no man speaking by the Spirit of God calleth Jesus **accursed**: and that no man can say that Jesus is the Lord, but by the Holy Ghost.

Galatians 1:8 - But though we, or an angel from heaven, preach any other gospel unto you than that which we have preached unto you, let him be **accursed**.

Galatians 1:9 - As we said before, so say I now again, if any man preach any other gospel unto you than that ye have received, let him be **accursed**.

Galatians 3:13 - Christ hath redeemed us from the curse of the law, being made a curse for us: for it is written, **Cursed** is every one that hangeth on a tree:

Galatians 5:20 - **Idolatry, witchcraft**, hatred, variance, emulations, wrath, strife, seditions, heresies, *{those who do these things will not inherit the kingdom of God}*

1 Timothy 4:1 - Now the Spirit speaketh expressly, that in the latter times some shall depart from the faith, giving heed to seducing spirits, and doctrines of **devils**;

James 2:19 - Thou believest that there is one God; thou doest well: the **devils** also believe, and tremble.

Revelation 9:1 - The fifth angel sounded his trumpet, and I saw a star that had fallen from the sky to the earth. The star was given the key to the shaft of the **Abyss**.

Revelation 9:2 - When he opened the **Abyss**, smoke rose from it like the smoke from a gigantic furnace. The sun and sky were darkened by the smoke from the **Abyss**.

Revelation 9:11 - They had as king over them the angel of the **Abyss**, whose name in Hebrew is Abaddon, and in Greek, Apollyon.

Revelation 9:20 - And the rest of the men which were not killed by these plagues yet repented not of the works of their hands, that they should not worship **devils**, and idols of gold, and silver, and brass, and stone, and of wood: which neither can see, nor hear, nor walk:

Revelation 9:21 - Neither repented they of their murders, nor of their **sorceries**, nor of their fornication, nor of their thefts.

Revelation 11:7 - Now when they have finished their testimony, the beast that comes up from the **Abyss** will attack them, and overpower and kill them.

Revelation 16:14 - For they are the spirits of **devils**, working miracles, which go forth unto the kings of the earth and of the whole world, to gather them to the battle of that great day of God Almighty.

Revelation 17:8 - The beast, which you saw, once was, now is not, and will come up out of the **Abyss** and go to his destruction. The inhabitants of the earth whose names have not been written in the book of life from the creation of the world will be astonished when they see the beast, because he once was, now is not, and yet will come.

Revelation 18:2 - And he cried mightily with a strong voice, saying, Babylon the great is fallen, is fallen, and is become the habitation of **devils**, and the hold of every foul spirit, and a cage of every unclean and hateful bird.

Revelation 18:23 - And the light of a candle shall shine no more at all in thee; and the voice of the bridegroom and of the bride shall be heard no more at all in thee: for thy merchants were the great men of the earth; for by thy **sorceries** were all nations deceived.

Revelation 20:1 - [*The Thousand Years*] And I saw an angel coming down out of heaven, having the key to the **Abyss** and holding in his hand a great chain.

Revelation 20:3 - He threw him into the **Abyss**, and locked and sealed it over him, to keep him from deceiving the nations anymore until the thousand years were ended. After that, he must be set free for a short time.

Revelation 21:8 - But the fearful, and unbelieving, and the abominable, and murderers, and whoremongers, and **sorcerers**, and **idolaters**, and all liars, shall have their part in the lake which burneth with fire and brimstone: which is the second death.

Revelation 22:15 - For without are dogs, and **sorcerers**, and whoremongers, and murderers, and idolaters, and whosoever loveth and maketh a lie.

Hosea 14:9

Who is wise? He will realize these things.
Who is discerning? He will understand them.
The ways of the Lord are right;
the righteous walk in them,
but the rebellious stumble in them.

VERSES ABOUT SATAN, BEELZEBUB OR LUCIFER

He is a <u>REAL</u> entity,

not a philosophical construct to personify evil!!

Church Researcher George Barna says that only 27% of church members in America believe satan is real!

http://www.barna.org/FlexPage.aspx?
Page=BarnaUpdate&BarnaUpdateID=92

Who benefits most from a theology that says satan isn't real?!

If Osama Bin Ladin convinced us he was just a "theoretical construct" to scare little children into behaving, wouldn't that be a really good thing for him?

OLD TESTAMENT

1 Chronicles 21:1 - And **Satan** stood up against Israel, and provoked David to number Israel.

Job 1:6 - Now there was a day when the sons of God came to present themselves before the LORD, and **Satan** came also among them.

Job 1:7 - And the LORD said unto **Satan**, Whence comest thou? Then **Satan** answered the LORD, and said, From going to and fro in the earth, and from walking up and down in it.

Job 1:8 - And the LORD said unto **Satan**, Hast thou considered my servant Job, that there is none like him in the earth, a perfect and an upright man, one that feareth God, and escheweth evil?

Job 1:9 - Then **Satan** answered the LORD, and said, Doth Job fear God for nought?

Job 1:12 - And the LORD said unto **Satan**, Behold, all that he hath is in thy power; only upon himself put not forth thine hand. So **Satan** went forth from the presence of the LORD.

Job 2:1 - Again there was a day when the sons of God came to present themselves before the LORD, and **Satan** came also among them to present himself before the LORD.

Job 2:2 - And the LORD said unto **Satan**, From whence comest thou? And **Satan** answered the LORD, and said, From going to and fro in the earth, and from walking up and down in it.

Job 2:3 - And the LORD said unto **Satan**, Hast thou considered my servant Job, that there is none like him in the earth, a perfect and an upright man, one that feareth God, and escheweth evil? and still he holdeth fast his integrity, although thou movedst me against him, to destroy him without cause.

Job 2:4 - And **Satan** answered the LORD, and said, Skin for skin, yea, all that a man hath will he give for his life.

Job 2:6 - And the LORD said unto **Satan**, Behold, he is in thine hand; but save his life.

Job 2:7 - So went **Satan** forth from the presence of the LORD, and smote Job with sore boils from the sole of his foot unto his crown.

Psalm 109:6 - Set thou a wicked man over him: and let **Satan** stand at his right hand.

Isaiah 14:12 - How art thou fallen from heaven, O **Lucifer**, son of the morning! how art thou cut down to the ground, which didst weaken the nations!

Zechariah 3:1 - And he shewed me Joshua the high priest standing before the angel of the LORD, and **Satan** standing at his right hand to resist him.

Zechariah 3:2 - And the LORD said unto **Satan**, The LORD rebuke thee, O **Satan**; even the LORD that hath chosen Jerusalem rebuke thee: is not this a brand plucked out of the fire?

NEW TESTAMENT

Matthew 4:10 - Then saith Jesus unto him, Get thee hence, **Satan**: for it is written, Thou shalt worship the Lord thy God, and him only shalt thou serve.

Matthew 10:25 - It is enough for the disciple that he be as his master, and the servant as his lord. If they have called the master of the house **Beelzebub**, how much more shall they call them of his household?

Matthew 12:26 - And if **Satan** cast out **Satan**, he is divided against himself; how shall then his kingdom stand?

Matthew 12:24 - But when the Pharisees heard it, they said, This fellow doth not cast out devils, but by **Beelzebub** the prince of the devils.

Matthew 12:27 - And if I by **Beelzebub** cast out devils, by whom do your children cast them out? therefore they shall be your judges.

Matthew 16:23 - But he turned, and said unto Peter, Get thee behind me, **Satan**: thou art an offence unto me: for thou savourest not the things that be of God, but those that be of men.

Mark 1:13 - And he was there in the wilderness forty days, tempted of **Satan**; and was with the wild beasts; and the angels ministered unto him.

Mark 3:22 - And the scribes which came down from Jerusalem said, He hath **Beelzebub**, and by the prince of the devils casteth he out devils.

Mark 3:23 - And he called them unto him, and said unto them in parables, How can **Satan** cast out **Satan**?

Mark 3:26 - And if **Satan** rise up against himself, and be divided, he cannot stand, but hath an end.

Mark 4:15 - And these are they by the way side, where the word is sown; but when they have heard, **Satan** cometh immediately, and taketh away the word that was sown in their hearts.

Mark 8:33 - But when he had turned about and looked on his disciples, he rebuked Peter, saying, Get thee behind me, **Satan**: for thou savourest not the things that be of God, but the things that be of men.

Luke 4:8 - And Jesus answered and said unto him, Get thee behind me, **Satan**: for it is written, Thou shalt worship the Lord thy God, and him only shalt thou serve.

Luke 10:18 - And he said unto them, I beheld **Satan** as lightning fall from heaven.

Luke 11:15 - But some of them said, He casteth out devils through **Beelzebub** the chief of the devils.

Luke 11:18 - If **Satan** also be divided against himself, how shall his kingdom stand? because ye say that I cast out devils through **Beelzebub**.

Luke 11:19 - And if I by **Beelzebub** cast out devils, by whom do your sons cast them out? therefore shall they be your judges.

Luke 13:16 - And ought not this woman, being a daughter of Abraham, whom **Satan** hath bound, lo, these eighteen years, be loosed from this bond on the sabbath day?

Luke 22:3 - Then entered **Satan** into Judas surnamed Iscariot, being of the number of the twelve.

Luke 22:31 - And the Lord said, Simon, Simon, behold, **Satan** hath desired to have you, that he may sift you as wheat:

John 13:27 - And after the sop **Satan** entered into him. Then said Jesus unto him, That thou doest, do quickly.

Acts 5:3 - But Peter said, Ananias, why hath **Satan** filled thine heart to lie to the Holy Ghost, and to keep back part of the price of the land?

Acts 26:18 - To open their eyes, and to turn them from darkness to light, and from the power of **Satan** unto God, that they may receive forgiveness of sins, and inheritance among them which are sanctified by faith that is in me.

Romans 16:20 - And the God of peace shall bruise **Satan** under your feet shortly. The grace of our Lord Jesus Christ be with you. Amen.

1 Corinthians 5:5 - To deliver such an one unto **Satan** for the destruction of the flesh, that the spirit may be saved in the day of the Lord Jesus.

1 Corinthians 7:5 - Defraud ye not one the other, except it be with consent for a time, that ye may give yourselves to fasting and prayer; and come together again, that **Satan** tempt you not for your incontinency.

2 Corinthians 2:11 - Lest **Satan** should get an advantage of us: for we are not ignorant of his devices.

2 Corinthians 11:14 - And no marvel; for **Satan** himself is transformed into an angel of light.

2 Corinthians 12:7 - And lest I should be exalted above measure through the abundance of the revelations, there was given to me a thorn in the flesh, the messenger of **Satan** to buffet me, lest I should be exalted above measure.

1 Thessalonians 2:18 - Wherefore we would have come unto you, even I Paul, once and again; but **Satan** hindered us.

2 Thessalonians 2:9 - Even him, whose coming is after the working of **Satan** with all power and signs and lying wonders,

1 Timothy 1:20 - Of whom is Hymenaeus and Alexander; whom I have delivered unto **Satan**, that they may learn not to blaspheme.

1 Timothy 5:15 - For some are already turned aside after **Satan**.

Revelation 2:9 - I know thy works, and tribulation, and poverty, (but thou art rich) and I know the blasphemy of them which say they are Jews, and are not, but are the synagogue of **Satan**.

Revelation 2:13 - I know thy works, and where thou dwellest, even where **Satan**'s seat is: and thou holdest fast my name, and hast not denied my faith, even in those days wherein Antipas was my faithful martyr, who was slain among you, where **Satan** dwelleth.

Revelation 2:24 - But unto you I say, and unto the rest in Thyatira, as many as have not this doctrine, and which have not known the depths of **Satan**, as they speak; I will put upon you none other burden.

Revelation 3:9 - Behold, I will make them of the synagogue of **Satan**, which say they are Jews, and are not, but do lie; behold, I will make them to come and worship before thy feet, and to know that I have loved thee.

Revelation 12:9 - And the great dragon was cast out, that old serpent, called the Devil, and **Satan**, which deceiveth the whole world: he was cast out into the earth, and his angels were cast out with him.

Revelation 20:2 - And he laid hold on the dragon, that old serpent, which is the Devil, and **Satan**, and bound him a thousand years,

Revelation 20:7 - And when the thousand years are expired, **Satan** shall be loosed out of his prison,

Satan is REAL! He's BAD!

And you're <u>toast</u> without Jesus!

Better get full of Jesus and stay on the Narrow Path.

APPENDIX G

Open Letter of Apology to The World

Please bear with me, this is long overdue and there's lots of ground to cover. I want to make sure that I get it all out. Not just for me, but because I think you need to hear it. Maybe there are other Christians out there as well that need to make apologies and will find courage here. I appreciate your time, I know it's valuable.

Dear Members of the World,

I'm just a guy, nobody really. Son of a preacher and missionary. Years and years of Vacation Bible Schools, summer camps, youth ski trips, puppet shows, revivals, choir trips - you name it. Even went to a Christian college and got a degree in religion. I ended up in the business world, but I spent two decades tithing, sitting on committees, teaching Sunday School, going to seminars and conferences, etc. I even met my wife in the single's class at church. I'm not a bad guy, I've been mostly behaving myself and everybody seems to like me. I do some good stuff here and there.

But lately I've been trying to understand Jesus more and stuff I never noticed before has really started to bug me. I've been taking a look around and I'm having a hard time making sense of what it is we've built here. So, it just seemed like, whether anybody else says it or not, I need to take responsibility for the part I played and say what I have to say.

Here we go ...

I know you think that Christians are a big bunch of hypocrites. We say we're more "religious" and we're going to heaven and you're not, and then we drive our big shiny cars with little fishies on the trunk and cut you off in traffic as we race by the homeless guy on the corner. We average just 2% of our money to church and charity, despite that we say the Bible is the word of God and **it** says we're supposed to give **everything**. On average, we buy just as many big screen TVs and bass boats and fur coats and makeup and baseball cards and online porn as anybody else. Maybe more. You've seen leader after leader end up in jail or court or a sex scandal of one sort or another.

Well ... you're right. We're guilty of all of it. We've done it all. And, I'm really sorry.

You see our cheesy TV shows and slick guys begging for money and you get that there's something seriously sneaky and wrong here. A high-pressure call for money so they can stay on the air? Were we supposed to use Jesus as just another form of entertainment? Who do we think we're kidding? Where's Jesus in all this? Aren't we supposed to rely on him? Isn't He going to meet our needs if we're inside His will? What happened to sacrifice and suffering and helping the poor? I'm just sick about this. I mean, the church leaders, they're not all bad guys, there are lots and lots of really hard-working well-meaning folks who love and care and are meeting real needs in the community. Some of them understand and love Jesus - but I'm just real sure those pastors don't drive Bentley's, have multi-million dollar homes and their own lear jets! I mean, what "god" are we worshipping? Money? Ego? Power?

You see our massive shiny new buildings all over the place. Heck, maybe we even kicked you out of your house so we could expand our parking lots. You can't figure out why we need four different Christian churches on four corners of the same intersection. We've got playgrounds and bowling alleys and basketball leagues. We've got Starbucks coffee in the sanctuary. We've got orchestras and giant chandeliers and fountains out front. We've got bookstores full of "jesus junk" with every imaginable style and flavor of religious knick-knack. But where's Jesus? Is this what HE wanted?

Oh, sure, there are good folks all over and not every church is such a mess, but Christians are the ones that say we're supposed to be "One Body." So even the good ones are guilty of not putting a stop to it sooner. We were supposed to keep each other in line and not tolerate factions and dissensions and greed and idolatry and all this other bad stuff. Man, we really blew it! We've got 33,000 denominations and most of them won't talk to the other ones. We lose over $5 million a day to fraud from "trusted" people inside the church! We spend 95% of all our money on our own comforts and programs and happy family fun time shows and we let 250 MILLION Christians in other countries live on the very edge of starvation. Not to mention the billion or so that have never even once heard of Jesus - or the homeless guy downtown we almost ran over when we cut you off.

We're as guilty as we can be. All of us. Nobody is exempt. We should have put a stop to it a lot sooner. But I can't apologize on behalf of anyone else. This is about me.

I know that you might have gone to church as a kid and stopped going as soon as you could. I know that you might even have been abused by somebody in the church! Maybe we got you all fired up and then just let you drift off like we didn't really care. Maybe you just don't fit our "profile." You might have piercings and purple hair or tattoos or been in jail -- and somewhere inside you just know that even if you wanted to go to church one Sunday, it would not go well. I'm sorry for that. Jesus loves you. He always hung out with the most unexpected people. He had the biggest heart for the folks everybody else tried to ignore. What have we done? We've told you to put on a sweater and some loafers or you can't go to heaven. I just want to throw up.

Look, I know you're mad. And you have a right to be. We've done you wrong for a LONG time now. There's some things about Jesus that people need to hear, but we've buried a beautiful masterpiece under hundreds of layers of soft pink latex paint. If you have a Bible handy, look up Matthew 23. (If you don't, you can look it up here - www.BibleGateway.com .)

Find it? Read it carefully, the Pharisees were the "religious" people of the day, the leaders of the faith. In this chapter Jesus SEVEN times says how pitiful and wretched and cursed they are for what they're doing to the people they're supposed to be leading. He even calls them "white washed tombs of dead mens bones" and a "brood of vipers"! I don't have time here, but read it and see if we're not doing EVERY single one of those things. Jesus can't possibly be happy about what we've done to you.

Sure, we like to kid ourselves and pretend everything is OK - but it's not. We're hated. Now, please understand, Jesus was hated, too. But that was because he said hard things and sometimes people don't like hearing the Truth. And he promised we would be hated if we were like him. But that's not why we're hated at the moment. We're hated right now because we're a giant pack of lying hypocrites that say one thing and do something else altogether. If we were hated because we were like Jesus, that would be one thing, but that's not it at all. You see right through our happy music and fluffy services and you can tell there's something desperately wrong here. We're no different than anybody else - except that we say we're better than you.

It was never supposed to be like this. Jesus asked us to care for the widows and orphans, to feed the hungry, care for the sick, visit those in prison, reach the lost. He wanted us to love our enemies and pray for them. He cared about human justice and suffering, the lost and lonely. But I don't think He would have marched on a picket line - He had His mind on much bigger problems. He wanted us to focus on the eternal things, not the everyday. He never once said to go into all the world and build big buildings and divide up into factions and buy Bentleys. Just the opposite! I get that you're mad at us and I think you have a right to be, but please understand, you're mad at what we've made under our own power, you're mad at "Churchianity." That's different than Christ and what he wanted. Don't be mad at Jesus! This mess wasn't His idea!

Look, I'm really sorry. I accept responsibility for my part in having hurt you. But I'm committing to you all, dear Members of the World, that I'm not going to do it any more. Not a single penny more. I'm not going to put my faith in "Churchianity" or any leader or program or TV show -- but in Christ Jesus and His salvation. That's when I was set free and began to see that God wants and expects more of us than this. And I'm not helping anybody that's not fully committed to the same thing.

It took centuries to build this monster, so it's not like it's going to just turn around overnight. But the times are changing and we're way overdue for something new. Big bad things are happening - like the tsunami in Asia - and I think more are coming. I don't want any more time to go by without having said this. I'm sorry for all the time and money I've wasted. But Jesus saves. Really. The church itself isn't even the point. Jesus is the real deal. He lived and He died for my sins and He rose again. He is who He said He was and He cares about me - and you. He's our only hope. We need places you can go that will only teach Jesus and will not be swayed or tempted or distracted by anything else. God willing, that's coming.

Please don't think all Christians are just posers. Some of them really mean it when they say they belong to

Christ. The problem is mostly in the West where we're all comfy and complacent and seem to like it that way. The Christians in China and other places are deadly serious. There's no room for anything but Jesus when you're on the run from the government. They are dying every day for their faith and doing crazy hard things because they're absolutely committed to Christ. These are martyrs. People willing to crucify little pieces of themselves every day to be more like Christ. People willing to set aside everything they want, to do what Christ wants. People willing to rot in prison or take a beating or die if that's what it's going to take. People that act in pure love and never back down. I'm not worthy to tie their shoes. And there are some like that here, too, and I hope we can get a lot more people to start living that way. It's way overdue.

If you're talking to someone and they tell you they're a Christian, ask them if they're the kind of Christian that really means it all the time or the kind that just means it on Sunday. The Bible says we'll know them by their "fruits" - by the faith and purity and love in their deeds and words. When you find one that proves Christ is in them by how much they love you, ask them to tell you all about Jesus. If you know one of those fearless martyrs that speaks nothing but pure, clean, hard Truth - ask lots of questions. Truth is a lot more rare than you would think. But don't settle for soft, fluffy and comfortable anymore - that's not in the Bible.

As for me and my house, we're really sorry. From now on, we're going to serve the Lord, not "Churchianity." We're going to try to call together as many of those martyrs as we can and start doing what Christ wanted. If I run into you someday, please give me a chance to shake your hand and apologize in person. I'm going to try harder from now on, I promise. I think there are lots of others feeling the same way, so don't be surprised if you start hearing stuff like this more often.

Thanks for your time. I hope it helps.

Doug Perry – from the Church in Liberty, Missouri, USA
fotm@fellowshipofthemartyrs.com

ABOUT THE AUTHOR

Doug Perry has been going 200 miles an hour with his hair on fire since November 23, 2004 when God showed him an open vision of how much God loves His children, how angry God is for how we're killing His children, and how much we have to hurry. It's safe to say that praying to see through the eyes of Jesus and be dangerous to satan wrecked his life. He had a nice home, a wife, two kids, two dogs, a foreign car with a sunroof, and a multimillion dollar, award-winning business that was named the #4 fastest growing company in Kansas City in 2006. Shoot, he was even teaching Sunday School.

Then he realized what he was, what we've built, and how it looks in the light of holiness. He realized he was a friend of the world – and an enemy of God. (James 4:4) So he sold all he had and gave it to the poor – or it was stripped from him one way or another.

And it was all worth it.

Now he's the author of seven books, nearly a thousand videos, music, poetry, and founder of a homeless shelter and a food pantry that feeds 5,000+ people every month. He has cried on the sidewalk in public for days. He's been arrested on false charges. He's spent weeks at a time in prayer, fasting and weeping for the sad state of things.

And he's been spit on, lied about, abandoned, forsaken by friends, banned by pastors, ejected from sanctuaries – and looks more like Jesus all the time. He's even had people try to physically kill him! Just for speaking the hard truth nobody wants to hear. But Jesus said it would be like that. Praise God! Bring it on.
If nobody is shooting at you, then you're not dangerous.

OTHER TITLES FROM
FELLOWSHIP OF THE MARTYRS PUBLISHING

***Rain Right <u>NOW</u>, Lord!* - from Doug Perry**
What is it going to take for God to pour His Spirit out on all flesh? Or is He waiting for us? Are spiritual gifts real and for today – and how do you get more of them?

***The Apology to the World* – from Doug Perry**
The "Apology to the World" letter has influenced thousands and been all over the world. This book spawned from responses to that letter and collected writings about the need for change.

***Left-Handed Warriors* – from Linda Carriger**
A suspenseful tale of the supernatural vs. the natural. What was it like for kids growing up in the book of Acts? Linda paints a picture of what it's like to be radically sold out to Christ – and still a kid.

***Missionaries are Human, Too* – from Nancy Perry**
A sweet, candid look at what it's like to be a missionary family learning to trust God in a foreign country. Written in 1976.

***Dialogues With God* – from Doug Perry**
Some discussions between Doug and the Almighty, along with a trouble-shooting guide to help you get unclogged, get your cup full and hear God better.

***DEMONS?! You're kidding, right?* - from Doug Perry**
A very detailed guide to spiritual warfare – how the bad guys act, what they look like, where they hide and much more. For experts only. Not for sissies. Seriously. We're not kidding.

***Do It Yourself City Church Restoration* – from Doug Perry**
What was 'church' supposed to be like all along? Are we doing it right? What's it going to take to fix it? If Jesus Christ wrote a letter to the Body of Christ in your city, could you bear to read it? What would happen if you were One Body in your town?

Who Neutered the Holy Spirit?! - from Doug Perry
Why do people say that the Holy Spirit stopped doing all the cool stuff that used to happen? This details the scriptural evidence of the work of the Spirit in the Old Testament, in the New Testament, after Pentecost, and in the church today. Along with help to get you unclogged so you can walk in the fullness of what God has for you.

The Red Dragon: the horrifying truth about why the 'church' cannot seem to change – from Doug Perry
How bad are things? How did they get this bad? In fact, they're SO bad, they have to be considered supernaturally bad! In fact, it's a curse from God. A delusion sent on those that went their own way. Weep. No really, weep! That's your only hope.

Expelling Xavier – from Dorothy Haile
A love story between a girl possessed by something dark and a boy just learning who he is in Christ – and their Savior. A very different kind of Christian novel, gritty, rough and fiercely transparent about the realities of life under the control of the darkness.

The Big Picture Book – from Doug Perry
Coming soon. Answers to some of the DEEP questions.

Fellowship Of The Martyrs Volume 1 – from Doug Perry
One mega book combining:
> The Apology to the World
> The Red Dragon
> Dialogues with God
> Rain Right NOW, Lord!
> Do It Yourself City Church Restoration

A compete course; from what's wrong with the church, how to fix YOU first, how to get your cup full and get big and strong and then how to bring real revival and restore the manifestation of "church" in your town as it was always meant to be.

And LOTS more titles coming soon!!
And in SPANISH!

Made in the USA
Monee, IL
11 July 2020